The Justice Dilemma

A VOLUME IN THE SERIES

Cornell Studies in Security Affairs

Edited by Robert J. Art, Robert Jervis, and Stephen M. Walt

A list of titles in this series is available at cornellpress.cornell.edu.

The Justice Dilemma

Leaders and Exile in an Era of Accountability

Daniel Krcmaric

Cornell University Press

Ithaca and London

Cornell University Press gratefully acknowledges receipt of a grant from the Kaplan Institute for the Humanities, Northwestern University, which aided in the publication of this book.

First published 2020 by Cornell University Press

Printed in the United States of America

Library of Congress Cataloging-in-Publication Data

Names: Krcmaric, Daniel, 1986– author.
Title: The justice dilemma : leaders and exile in an era of accountability / Daniel Krcmaric.
Description: Ithaca [New York] : Cornell University Press, 2020. | Series: Cornell studies in security affairs | Includes bibliographical references and index.
Identifiers: LCCN 2020001955 (print) | LCCN 2020001956 (ebook) | ISBN 9781501750212 (hardcover) | ISBN 9781501750236 (pdf) | ISBN 9781501750229 (epub)
Subjects: LCSH: International criminal law. | Criminal justice, Administration of—International cooperation. | Heads of state—Legal status, laws, etc. | Exile (Punishment). | International crimes—Prevention. | Political atrocities—Prevention. | Civil war.
Classification: LCC KZ7235 .K73 2020 (print) | LCC KZ7235 (ebook) | DDC 341.6/9—dc23
LC record available at https://lccn.loc.gov/2020001955
LC ebook record available at https://lccn.loc.gov/2020001956

Contents

Figures and Tables

Figures

Tables

Acknowledgments

People often say writing a book is like running a marathon. Having only done one of the two, I cannot quite confirm the analogy. But it has certainly been a long run, and I am excited to have the opportunity to thank everyone who helped along the way.

This book's origins go back to Duke University. My greatest intellectual debt is to Alex Downes. Ever since I started as his lowly research assistant in 2009, Alex has been a fantastic mentor and friend as he taught me how to navigate the strange world of academia. My time at Duke also brought the good fortune of meeting several other advisers who helped get this project off the ground. Erik Wibbels is always the smartest person in the room, and I hope at least a tiny bit of his intellect rubbed off on me. Laia Balcells joined our department halfway through my time at Duke, and it took all of my self-control to give her a few days on campus before I started asking her for advice. Peter Feaver pushed me to think seriously about the policy implications of academic work and consistently found pockets of research money for which I will always be grateful.

I completed this book as a faculty member at Northwestern University. I have been lucky to benefit from the insights of all my colleagues in Scott Hall, but a few deserve special recognition for generously taking the time to offer detailed feedback on my book. I hope Hendrik Spruyt, Karen Alter, Steve Nelson, Will Reno, Marina Henke, Ana Arjona, Jay Seawright, Andrew Roberts, and Robert Braun will notice their fingerprints scattered across these pages. Al Tillery has been a tireless advocate since I arrived in Evanston. The J+ happy hour group gets credit for helping maintain my sanity. Thanks also to the smart students at Northwestern (especially

Alex Deckler, my former undergraduate research assistant for this book) who make my job so fun and fulfilling.

My book manuscript underwent the equivalent of major surgery during a workshop in April 2017. I thank Hein Goemans, Paul Staniland, and Alex Downes (yet again) for traveling to Evanston to participate in the all-day workshop. For someone whose work crosses the boundaries of international security, civil war, and political leadership, this trio was as good as the 1992 Dream Team. I am sure they can see the difference they made in the final version of the book.

I have racked up a slew of thank-yous owed to other colleagues over the past several years. Keeping track of them all has been a challenge, but I want to express my gratitude for helpful comments and insightful conversations to Ben Barber, Kyle Beardsley, Andy Bell, Andy Bennett, Stephen Chaudoin, Jeff Colgan, Mark Crescenzi, Sarah Croco, Chris DeSante, Cassy Dorff, Abel Escribà-Folch, Max Gallop, Chris Gelpi, Stephen Gent, Thomas Gift, Charlie Glaser, Emilie Hafner-Burton, Larry Helfer, Courtney Hillebrecht, Florian Hollenbach, Mike Horowitz, Hyeran Jo, Michael Joseph, Judith Kelley, Ashley Leeds, Bahar Leventoglu, Jack Levy, Yon Lupu, Jacqueline McAllister, Sara Mitchell, Monika Nalepa, Andy Owsiak, Andy Reiter, Elizabeth Saunders, Greg Schoeber, Anna Schultz, Kathryn Sikkink, Richard Steinberg, Ben Valentino, Erik Voeten, Michael Weintraub, and Simon Weschle. My sincere apologies to anyone I have forgotten. My coauthors from a pair of previous projects—Thomas Gift and Abel Escribà-Folch—deserve a special shout-out for their advice and friendship.

Several institutions provided fellowships and financial support that allowed me to conduct the research for this book. For their generosity, I thank the National Science Foundation, the Harry Frank Guggenheim Foundation, the Bradley Foundation, the Graduate School at Duke University, the Elliott School of International Affairs at George Washington University, and the program on Equality Development and Globalization Studies at Northwestern University.

At Cornell University Press, I had the pleasure of working with Roger Haydon, whose legendary reputation in the field is well deserved. During the review process, I was lucky to receive a set of extraordinarily thoughtful anonymous comments (whoever you are, thank you). I also thank the editors of the Cornell Studies in Security Affairs series for including my book among such distinguished company.

Some portions of this book, most notably the statistical analysis presented in chapter 3, are loosely derived from my article "Should I Stay or Should I Go? Leaders, Exile, and the Dilemmas of International Justice," published in *American Journal of Political Science* 62, no. 2 (April 2018): 486–98.

On a more personal note, I thank my family. My parents, Mark and Laurie, offered much-appreciated enthusiasm as I embarked on a somewhat unexpected career path. Little did they know that all those trips to the South Bend Public Library would eventually result in my decision to write a book. My siblings, Kathleen and Tommy, deserve credit for keeping it real by teasing me about some of my "professorial" tendencies. Last but certainly not least, I thank my wife, Laura. More than anyone else, she guided me through the highs and lows of wrestling with this project for nearly a decade. Not only has she read several drafts of this book (except for this paragraph!) but her love and support also helped me get through the days when I thought about giving up. I dedicate this book to her. And just days before submitting the final draft of this manuscript, our son, Theodore, entered the world. The next one is for him.

Abbreviations

AU	African Union
CAT	Convention against Torture
CDP	Congress for Democracy and Progress in Burkina Faso
EAC	Extraordinary African Chambers
ECCC	Extraordinary Chambers in the Courts of Cambodia
ECOMOG	military unit deployed by ECOWAS
ECOWAS	Economic Community of West African States
ETA	Euskadi Ta Askatasuna, Basque nationalist and separatist organization
ETT	East Timor Tribunal
EWP	Early Warning Project, a statistical risk assessment project affiliated with the US Holocaust Museum
FARC	Revolutionary Armed Forces of Colombia
FROLINAT	Chad National Liberation Front
ICC	International Criminal Court
ICCPR	International Covenant on Civil and Political Rights
ICTR	International Criminal Tribunal for Rwanda
ICTY	International Criminal Tribunal for the former Yugoslavia
INPFL	Independent National Patriotic Front of Liberia
LIFG	Libyan Islamic Fighting Group
LRA	Lord's Resistance Army
LURD	Liberians United for Reconciliation and Democracy

MODEL	Movement for Democracy in Liberia
NPFL	National Patriotic Front of Liberia
NTC	National Transitional Council in Libya
RAM	Reform the Army Movement in the Philippines
RSP	Burkina Faso security forces
RUF	Revolutionary United Front
SCSL	Special Court for Sierra Leone

The Justice Dilemma

CHAPTER 1

Justice Goes Global

By 1979, the Ugandan dictator Idi Amin had presided over the killing of some three hundred thousand people, pillaged his country's economy, and started a war with neighboring Tanzania. After eight tumultuous years in power, Amin's regime was on the verge of collapse. Ugandan rebels and their Tanzanian allies, both determined to take down Amin, were rapidly closing in on the capital city of Kampala. Despite his long-standing claim to be the indispensable "Big Daddy" of Uganda, Amin opted *not* to make a last stand against his adversaries. He had a better option: exile. Before Kampala fell, Amin and his family boarded a plane that delivered them to safety. After a brief stop in Libya, Amin settled into a long-term retirement in a beautiful villa in Jeddah, Saudi Arabia. According to a journalist who caught up with Amin during his exile, the former leader liked to spend much of his time frequenting Jeddah's finer hotels. Indeed, Amin "had spent the previous years taking a morning swim in the pool of the local Hilton, having his back massaged by an Egyptian masseur at the Intercontinental, and finally having lunch at a third hotel."[1]

As shocking as the Amin example may seem, there is a long history of abusive rulers finding safe havens abroad once they were no longer welcome at home. In 1986, for instance, the Philippines' Ferdinand Marcos retired to Hawaii when the People Power Revolution toppled him following a fraudulent election. That same year, as protests raged throughout Haiti, Jean-Claude Duvalier took a similar exit option by fleeing to the French Riviera. In short, exile was once the default option for dictators in distress.

Today, however, embattled leaders seem to think twice about exile. Consider the tale of Libya's Muammar Gaddafi. In 2011, as the Arab Spring spread throughout the region, Gaddafi faced growing unrest within Libya.

1. Riccardo Orizio, "Idi Amin's Exile Dream," *New York Times*, August 21, 2003.

Peaceful protests morphed into a full-blown civil war, and the Libyan rebels eventually gained the upper hand in the conflict. As the rebels marched on Tripoli, Gaddafi faced a predicament eerily similar to the one Idi Amin had encountered several decades earlier. Should Gaddafi stay in Libya to battle it out or flee to a foreign safe haven? Guided by a desire to avoid further bloodshed in Libya, speculation among the punditocracy ran rampant about possible exile destinations for Gaddafi.[2] But unlike Amin, Gaddafi opted to fight rather than take flight, a move that ultimately cost him his life.

Gaddafi is not the only leader digging in his heels instead of retiring abroad these days. After Laurent Gbagbo refused to recognize that he had lost the Ivory Coast's 2010 presidential election, opposition fighters advanced toward Abidjan. As he hunkered down in the presidential palace, it must have been a moment of soul searching for the former strongman. Just a couple of months earlier, a delegation of West African diplomats had visited Gbagbo and pressed him to stop the violence and go into exile.[3] But Gbagbo refused to go quietly into the night and instead clung to power until opposition forces captured him. Similarly, when Syrian rebels pushed toward Damascus in December 2012, many thought that Bashar Assad would try to save himself by fleeing abroad.[4] Assad himself appeared open to this possibility if the circumstances were right and reportedly was "looking for a way out."[5] Yet, in the end, Assad decided to keep fighting in Syria rather than seek a retirement home abroad.

What explains the divergent behavior of these leaders? Why have recent leaders like Gaddafi, Gbagbo, and Assad desperately clung to power whereas past leaders such as Amin, Marcos, and Duvalier were willing to spend their days in exile? The answer, I argue in this book, is that something new is happening in the world of international justice. For a long time, advocates of global accountability had little to celebrate. Despite employing lofty rhetoric about ending impunity for the world's worst war criminals, tangible successes were elusive. In fact, proponents of international justice—relying on the idea that some crimes are so heinous that the perpetrator should be punished regardless of national borders—were

2. Among others, see William J. Dobson, "Dictator Seeks Second Home? A Guide to Gaddafi's Exile Options," *Washington Post*, March 29, 2011; and David Smith, "Where Could Colonel Muammar Gaddafi Go If He Were Exiled?," *Guardian*, February 21, 2011.

3. On Gbagbo's finals days, see Colum Lynch and William Branigin, "Ivory Coast Strongman Arrested after French Forces Intervene," *Washington Post*, April 11, 2011.

4. Andrew E. Kramer, "In Russia, Exile in Comfort for Leaders Like Assad," *New York Times*, December 28, 2012.

5. Anne Barnard and Hwaida Sadd, "No Easy Route If Assad Opts to Go, or to Stay, in Syria," *New York Times*, December 24, 2012.

frequently mocked as out-of-touch idealists.[6] Accordingly, the prospects for international accountability were once bleak: oppressive leaders simply went into exile in posh locales where they could retire without fear of prosecution.

But the world is now a smaller place for tyrants. Consider the leaders just described: Gaddafi faced an International Criminal Court (ICC) arrest warrant at the time of his death, Gbagbo was extradited to the ICC and charged with crimes against humanity, and Assad was widely condemned as a war criminal.[7] In a world of globalized justice, fleeing abroad to a quiet exile no longer guarantees that a violent ruler can escape the long arm of the law.

A variety of international criminal tribunals have proliferated since the 1990s. To address mass atrocities, the United Nations (UN) created ad hoc international tribunals for the former Yugoslavia and Rwanda, and hybrid tribunals popped up to judge war criminals in places such as Sierra Leone, East Timor, Cambodia, and Chad, among others. Foreign courts also joined the fray by invoking universal jurisdiction to initiate prosecutions for crimes committed on the other side of the globe. The tribunal-building process culminated with the Rome Statute in 1998, the treaty establishing the ICC, the first permanent international court with broad jurisdiction over mass atrocities. Equally important, many of the world's most powerful states—especially Western democracies—started to provide the muscle to make tribunals work by apprehending and transferring indicted war criminals. The results have been impressive. In the world of international legal proceedings, few scenes are as striking as watching once-untouchable tyrants face justice for their misdeeds. Though the march toward global accountability has been uneven and undoubtedly remains a work in progress, it is hard to disagree with human rights activist Paul van Zyl's claim that "the international justice genie is out of the bottle."[8]

This book is about the effects of this dramatic change in world politics, sometimes called the "justice cascade" (Sikkink 2011) or the "revolution in accountability" (Sriram 2005). More precisely, I examine one specific part of this justice cascade: the new trend toward international prosecutions of heads of state.[9] I focus on prosecutions that (1) are international/foreign in

6. Consider the tribulations of Raphael Lemkin—widely regarded as the father of the Genocide Convention—as he attempted to outlaw the "crime without a name" (Power 2003).

7. After spending seven years behind bars, Gbagbo was acquitted in 2019. But the Gbagbo saga likely is not over. The ICC released him to Belgium following the surprise acquittal. While Gbagbo technically is free, Belgium forced him to surrender his passport and will keep him under surveillance. Belgium also promised to send Gbagbo back to the ICC if the court's prosecution team appeals the case.

8. Christina Lamb, "Trapped in the Palace," *Spectator*, May 28, 2011.

9. Hence, when I colloquially mention the effects of the justice cascade throughout the book, I am referring to international or foreign prosecutions of heads of state. Many other

nature and (2) target political leaders because this sort of prosecution raises unique implications for the exile dynamics that are at the core of the book.[10] While other aspects of the justice cascade (e.g., domestic trials of unpopular rulers or international prosecutions of the rank and file) are important in their own right, the pursuit of globalized accountability for those at the very top is a qualitatively different phenomenon. As I explain later, heads of state have historically been a protected class of individuals who were essentially immune to arrest on foreign soil no matter how badly they behaved. Only in the past couple of decades has the special status of political leaders in international law been challenged.

I primarily take a positive perspective rather than a normative one. From a normative or moral standpoint, things seem relatively straightforward. Few would dispute that it is appropriate to hold leaders legally accountable for committing atrocity crimes. Moreover, most would agree that fewer oppressive rulers escaping to comfortable, if not luxurious, foreign retirements is a welcome change. But from a perspective that investigates the political effects of international prosecutions, things are far more complicated. As I will show, pursuing global justice for abusive leaders produces difficult and inescapable trade-offs. Simply put, there is a justice dilemma.

The Argument in Brief

My argument starts with a simple observation: exile can be a pragmatic political solution. Specifically, exile provides a mechanism for leaders, especially those facing domestic unrest, to give up power in a manner that is relatively costless. Leaders who might refuse to step down because they fear domestic punishment upon retirement can instead go into exile and find a safe haven abroad. Thus, exile offers a "golden parachute" exit strategy that facilitates leadership transitions. Though they give up power, leaders will likely view exile abroad—and the secure retirement it typically affords—as the best option available when the risk of domestic punishment

scholars, including Kathryn Sikkink in her seminal book, *The Justice Cascade* (2011), use the term to refer to a wider range of human rights prosecutions (i.e., domestic and international, leaders and foot soldiers, etc.). As outlined later, my more specific focus is justified because of this book's emphasis on exiled leaders. However, in the concluding chapter, I speculate about how my argument might apply to other actors (rebel leaders, military officers, titans of industry, etc.).

10. For ease of exposition, I use the terms head of state, leader, and ruler interchangeably. There are, however, some technical differences among these terms. Note also that I use masculine pronouns for leaders for the sake of clarity and consistency. Though not all exiled leaders are men, the vast majority are (the only female leader to go into exile during the time period examined in the analysis in chapter 3 is Bolivia's Lidia Gueiler Tejada).

is high. For this reason, there has been an extensive history of rulers fleeing abroad once they were no longer safe in their home countries.

The justice cascade, however, complicates the exile option for some leaders. The globalization of accountability means that leader culpability (whether leaders have previously presided over atrocity crimes) now influences the search for a safe haven. Today's culpable leaders have to worry that fleeing into exile will ultimately land them in the jail cell of an international tribunal, which creates incentives to entrench in power rather than retire abroad. But nonculpable leaders—those who refrain from committing mass atrocities against civilians—can still safely go into exile because they do not need to fear international arrest. In more concrete terms, exile remains a viable exit strategy for "merely" unpopular or corrupt leaders such as Bolivia's Evo Morales and Burkina Faso's Blaise Compaoré, but a similar retirement for culpable mass killers like Muammar Gaddafi, Laurent Gbagbo, and Bashar Assad is increasingly problematic.[11]

By making the availability of a safe post-tenure exile conditional on a leader's behavior while still in power (i.e., the leader's culpability), the justice cascade generates two effects that pull in opposite directions. On the negative side, the justice cascade exacerbates conflict. By undermining the possibility of a secure exile for culpable leaders, international justice incentivizes such leaders to double down on the battlefield and keep fighting during civil wars when they otherwise would have retired abroad. On the positive side, the justice cascade deters atrocities. Precisely because leaders now know that committing abuses will decrease their future exit options, international justice effectively increases the costs of brutality. Taken together, these predictions form the justice dilemma: deterring atrocities and prolonging conflicts are two sides of the same coin.

To test the argument, I exploit stark over-time variation in the threat international justice poses to leaders. In the past, punishment expectations were low because realpolitik strategies consistently trumped concerns about international justice. Moreover, prevailing ideas about international legal order, based on respect for sovereignty and head-of-state immunity, protected leaders from arrest while in foreign countries. As a result, all leaders—even notoriously brutal ones—historically had little to fear from international justice. In recent years, however, the landscape for pursuing justice across borders has changed dramatically: a slew of oppressive leaders have been arrested and transferred to foreign or international courts as part of the justice cascade. This rapid change in the likelihood of

11. Due to the growth of international anticorruption laws and the associated weakening of bank secrecy, amassing the funds required for a luxurious exile may be increasingly difficult as well. On the international campaign against grand corruption, see Sharman 2017. For a normative political theorist's take on recovering the wealth of exiled leaders, see Nili 2019.

international punishment provides a unique empirical opportunity, perhaps even "some kind of natural experiment" (Kim and Sikkink 2010, 944).

Building on this insight, I argue that the push for international justice reached a tipping point in the late 1990s. Specifically, I suggest that two key events in 1998 marked a critical juncture. First, the signing of the Rome Statute of the International Criminal Court institutionalized the previously ad hoc legal regime and signaled to leaders that the international community was interested in pursuing justice globally on a permanent basis. Second, the arrest of former Chilean leader Augusto Pinochet in the United Kingdom—the first time a leader was actually arrested in a foreign state for international crimes—provided a powerful demonstration effect that shattered the expectation of impunity leaders had once enjoyed. While these are certainly not the only two factors that mattered, the landmark events of 1998 constitute the watershed moment in a shift from an era of impunity to an era of accountability.

Much of my book is devoted to evaluating how this shift from global impunity toward accountability has shaped patterns of exile, civil war duration, and mass atrocity onset using both quantitative and qualitative methods. While neither method of inquiry is without potential pitfalls, a multimethod research design allows the strengths of each approach to help compensate for the weaknesses of the other.

The statistical tests, by establishing correlations between independent and dependent variables across a wide variety of contexts, demonstrate the generalizability of the theory. The quantitative approach also prevents cherry-picking only the cases that are consistent with my theoretical expectations. Three main statistical findings bolster my argument. First, leader culpability had no effect on the likelihood of exile during the impunity era, but today's culpable leaders are nearly six times less likely to go into exile. Second, because they lack good exit options, today's culpable leaders tend to fight longer civil wars. During the accountability era, the likelihood of a war ending is cut in half if a culpable leader is in power. Third, this dark side of justice also produces a benefit: deterrence. Today's leaders are over six times less likely to initiate mass killings than their peers were during the impunity era.

While the quantitative tests provide data on general trends, qualitative case studies are generally better at illustrating causal processes. If my theory is correct, we should not only observe the predicted correlation between variables, but we should also see leaders reasoning and behaving in a manner consistent with my argument's expectations. By turning to creative sources of qualitative data such as the testimonies of arrested leaders, the accounts of the diplomatic contacts who helped arrange leaders' escapes into exile, and the perspectives of killed leaders' surviving deputies, I work to reconstruct the decision-making processes of embattled leaders. Specifically, I offer case studies of Charles Taylor, Muammar Gaddafi, and Blaise

Compaoré to illustrate how leaders think and act in ways that are consistent with the theory.[12] Overall, the combination of quantitative and qualitative evidence provides compelling support for the argument.

Debating Peace and Justice

Evaluating international justice is a tricky business. One challenge is that there is "a dizzying array of lofty objectives for international war crimes tribunals" (Bass 2000, 284). The absence of a clear benchmark for judging success or failure has even led some to conclude "that the performance of international criminal courts cannot be assessed reliably" (Damaska 2008, 330). There are, however, certain objectives that repeatedly show up in discussions of international justice. Some draw on the legal maxim *fiat justitia et pereat mundus* (let justice be done, even if the world were to perish) to argue that there is an ethical responsibility to pursue justice regardless of the consequences. Others highlight how international justice might play a role in building the rule of law, moderating desires for revenge, giving voice to victims, rehabilitating abusers, erasing past animosities between groups, creating a reliable historical record, and propagating new norms and values.[13]

Though these goals are doubtlessly important, this book largely focuses on the issues where lives are at stake—deterring atrocities and prolonging wars. Relative to the large normative and legal literatures, much less is known about the real-world effects of international justice on the behavior of the individuals who are targeted for punishment.[14]

Existing work on this topic is primarily a debate between optimists and pessimists. The optimist position holds that international justice can deter atrocities. Some scholars reach this conclusion by building off the logic of rationalist theories of domestic criminal punishment, which assert that crime decreases as the likelihood and/or severity of punishment increases.[15]

12. The decision to examine three African leaders in detail was intentional. As I will describe later, the international legal regime (especially the ICC) is sometimes accused of bias against African leaders. By focusing on these three leaders in the case studies, I am able to hold this potential source of cross-case variation constant. Note that exploring only African leaders in the case studies should not raise generalizability concerns since the statistical analyses use global samples.

13. For an overview of the many potential justifications for international criminal accountability, see Bass 2000; Damaska 2008; Drumbl 2007; and Shklar 1964.

14. As Kate Cronin-Furman (2013, 435) concludes in an assessment of research on international trials and deterrence: "The study of the practical impacts of international criminal law is, in general, characterized by an absence of empirical evidence."

15. Gary Becker (1968) provides the seminal rationalist model of crime and punishment. In the next chapter, I will address the debate among criminologists on whether the

Since the international legal regime is designed to increase the likelihood of punishment for the architects of atrocities (though not necessarily the severity of punishment), many argue that it will create a deterrent effect (e.g., Appel 2018; Gilligan 2006; Jo and Simmons 2016; Kim and Sikkink 2010; Olsen, Payne, and Reiter 2010; Orentlicher 1991; Sikkink 2011). Others move beyond the rationalist approach to argue that prosecutions reduce violence by stigmatizing war criminals and producing a political culture that views atrocities as unacceptable (e.g., Akhavan 1998, 2001). Regardless of the precise mechanism, however, all optimists share the conviction that international justice can prevent abuse.

Outside the academy, the optimist view enjoys widespread popularity with policymakers, international lawyers, and human rights activists. Consistent with the claim of Kenneth Roth of Human Rights Watch that "behind much of the savagery of modern history lies impunity" (Roth 2001, 150), the presumption is that the promise of legal accountability might prevent the next bloody campaign of atrocities. In the words of the ICC prosecutor Luis Moreno-Ocampo, "My mission is to end impunity for these crimes in order to contribute to the prevention of future crimes" (Moreno-Ocampo 2010). In fact, policymakers often cannot help but use triumphalist language when describing the development of international criminal law, sometimes considered one of the international community's landmark achievements in the post–Cold War era.[16]

The pessimist perspective explores a negative consequence of legal accountability.[17] If belligerents are vulnerable to criminal prosecution, they may decide to keep fighting when they otherwise would lay down their arms.[18] For example, Jack Snyder and Leslie Vinjamuri (2003) critique the view that justice—whether domestic or international—should be applied to all cases of atrocities. Instead, they argue that neutralizing potential spoiler groups (typically the losing side in a civil war) should take precedence over retroactive judicial punishment.[19] Overall, the pessimistic view implies that

likelihood or the severity of punishment has a greater effect on the decision-making of potential criminals.

16. For instance, David Wippman (1999, 473) describes how many internationalists see international criminal law as "the last, best hope for stemming the tidal wave of atrocities that all too frequently have marked both international and internal armed conflicts."

17. Beyond the assertion that international justice might exacerbate conflict, others critique it for being too expensive (Cobban 2006) and for imposing universalist norms on local communities (Hopgood 2013).

18. This argument echoes claims first made in a related literature on transitional justice and democratization, particularly Samuel Huntington's (1991) classic work on the dilemmas of punishing outgoing autocrats in the "third wave" of democratization. For more recent work on this topic, see Escribà-Folch and Wright 2015b; and Nalepa and Powell 2016.

19. According to Geoff Dancy and Eric Wiebelhaus-Brahm (2018), it might matter which side is targeted with prosecutions. They find that rebel trials tend to shorten civil wars, whereas trials of state officials often lengthen them.

international justice will create perverse incentives that could exacerbate conflict and ultimately increase civilian victimization (e.g., Goldsmith and Krasner 2003; Prorok 2017; Snyder and Vinjamuri 2003). Jack Goldsmith and Stephen Krasner (2003, 51) even warn that "a universal jurisdiction prosecution may cause more harm than the original crime it purports to address."

This view is less popular among policymakers and pundits, but it occasionally receives attention in the public sphere. Writing in the *Guardian* during Libya's civil war, Philippe Sands worried that the ICC arrest warrant for Muammar Gaddafi "made an early departure from Libya less likely" and instead gave him a reason "to dig in his heels."[20] Secretary of State Hillary Clinton also implicitly endorsed the pessimist view when discussing the humanitarian catastrophe in Syria. Clinton acknowledged that Bashar Assad was a war criminal, but she warned that initiating an international prosecution could "complicate the resolution of a difficult, complex situation because it limits options perhaps to persuade leaders to step down from power."[21]

While the existing literature offers useful insights, it suffers from shortcomings at both the theoretical and empirical levels. On the empirical side, most research is oddly ahistorical. Instead of thinking about broad trends in the international justice landscape, almost all studies zoom in on a specific tribunal or sometimes even a particular arrest warrant.[22] To give just one example, scholars have provided nuanced case studies of the Yugoslav tribunal (e.g., Hagan 2003; Subotic 2009) and conducted rigorous quantitative tests of the effects of its judgments (e.g., Meernik 2005). However, by focusing on one tree instead of the whole forest, this sort of analysis misses the opportunity to exploit remarkable over-time variation in the international legal regime. As I show in this book, stepping back to examine the historical arc of international justice offers rich new insights.[23]

On the theoretical side, optimists and pessimists alike take narrow views on the consequences of pursuing international justice. In particular, scholars tend to hypothesize exclusively "good" effects such as deterring atrocities or exclusively "bad" effects like prolonging conflicts.[24] Optimists, for example,

20. Philippe Sands, "The ICC Arrest Warrant Will Make Colonel Gaddafi Dig in His Heels," *Guardian*, May 4, 2011.

21. Richard Spencer, "Bashar al-Assad Could Be Regarded as a War Criminal, Says Clinton," *Telegraph*, February 28, 2012.

22. When referring to international tribunals, I follow the general convention of using the terms indictments and arrest warrants interchangeably. However, for some tribunals (such as the ICC), these terms technically are not equivalent.

23. I discuss several other empirical challenges in the specific chapters on exile, civil war duration, and mass killing.

24. One possible reason why many scholars hypothesize causal effects in only one direction is that the study of international justice often comes with political, legal, and moral

insist that "there are many claims about the negative effects of trials but relatively little solid evidence to support them" (Sikkink and Walling 2007, 429) and that "practically no systematic evidence has been produced to date to support such concerns" (Jo and Simmons 2016, 445). On the other side, pessimists worry that international justice is "not robust enough to act as a reliable deterrent against depredations by leaders—but it may be just enough to complicate their exits from power."[25]

The existing theoretical approaches each get part of the story right, but they both fail to see the bigger picture: the atrocity-preventing and conflict-prolonging effects of international justice are two sides of the same coin. If the threat of international punishment lacks credibility, we should see *neither effect*. An international legal regime that is not strong enough to deter atrocities is also not strong enough to incentivize leaders to keep fighting in some desperate attempt to evade justice. On the flip side, if the threat of international punishment is sufficiently credible, we should see *both effects together*. An accountability regime robust enough to convince culpable leaders to spurn the exile option and instead risk everything on the battlefield is also strong enough to deter at least some other leaders from committing atrocities in the first place.

As a result, one of the major contributions of this book is to show both theoretically and empirically that these effects—the positive and the perverse—are intimately linked. Simply put, international justice is helpful in some ways and harmful in others.

One Theory, Many Puzzles

One of the strengths of the argument presented here is that it generates a wide variety of empirical predictions using a single theoretical framework. According to Gary King, Robert Keohane, and Sidney Verba in their classic book on political methodology, "The scholar who searches for additional implications of a [theory] is pursuing one of the most important achievements of all social science: *explaining as much as possible with as little as possible*" (King, Keohane, and Verba 1994, 29, emphasis in original). I take this advice seriously by exploring several different testable implications of my argument. In fact, the theory and evidence presented in this book shed light on three puzzles in world politics. Though each of these puzzles is typically

strings attached. As Oskar Thoms, James Ron, and Roland Paris (2010, 354) point out, there is an "urgent need for . . . greater attention to fact-based rather than faith-based claims" in the study of international justice.

25. David Bosco, "How International Justice Makes It Harder for Dictators to Step Down," *Washington Post*, January 24, 2017.

treated as a separate issue, I show that they are in fact intertwined and can be explained by a single, parsimonious theory.

The first puzzle involves the risky, some would even say foolhardy, behavior of leaders. Why do some rulers choose to fight until they are killed or captured? Why not simply save oneself by going into exile? The behavior of leaders like Muammar Gaddafi and Laurent Gbagbo has been particularly puzzling because fleeing into exile, at least at first glance, appeared to be better for their physical safety and financial interests. Many journalistic accounts speculated that the refusal to retire abroad was the result of delusional or "tribal" leadership,[26] but my work suggests it was a rational, though risky, response to the changing incentives international justice creates. Thus, my theory helps explain why ousting a brutal leader occurs easily in some cases but requires the complete defeat of the old regime in others.

The second puzzle relates to the resolution of civil wars. Why do some civil conflicts last so much longer than others? In the existing literature, most accounts of civil war duration examine characteristics of either the state or the rebel group. State-centric explanations underscore variables that are thought to augment or limit state capacity such as economic development, rough terrain, and the presence of foreign patrons. Rebel-centric explanations for war duration focus on a group's capacity to resist the state by examining the rebel group's military strength, political and ethnic cohesiveness, and ability to secure funding. While these factors are certainly important, this book makes a new contribution by examining how international justice can affect the decision of a leader to keep fighting.

The third puzzle concerns deterrence. Why has state-sponsored violence against civilians fallen in recent years? While media reports may give the opposite impression, the decline of most types of violence over time has been celebrated in academia.[27] The reason for this decline, however, is unclear. Some focus on psychology (Pinker 2011) or peacekeeping (Goldstein 2011), but others maintain that scholars have "failed to provide convincing explanations for the dramatic decline in the incidence and severity of political violence that has occurred" (Valentino 2014, 91). The evidence reported here supports an alternative explanation: A credible threat of post-tenure international punishment can, under some conditions, stay the hand of would-be mass killers while they are still in power.

Broader Implications

Moving beyond the scope of the justice dilemma itself, this book raises broader implications for several key debates in international relations.

26. Robert Kaplan (2011) provides an example of this genre.
27. For counterpoints to the decline of war hypothesis, see Fazal 2014; and Braumoeller 2019.

LEADERS IN INTERNATIONAL POLITICS

To begin, the book teaches us something new about how individual leaders can shape important, big-picture outcomes in world politics. Kenneth Waltz (1959) famously offered the concept of three images to structure the study of international relations. The first image referred to leaders, the second to the state, and the third to the international system. The popularity of studying the first image, individual leaders, has waxed and waned over time. For instance, political scientists took the study of leaders seriously in the immediate post–World War II era. On some level, this was a natural response to real-world events. Decisions made by individual leaders were widely understood to be both the cause of the war's outbreak (e.g., Hitler and Chamberlain) and its eventual termination (e.g., Roosevelt and Churchill). Consequently, landmark works in international relations, such as Hans Morgenthau's *Politics among Nations* (1948) and Henry Kissinger's *A World Restored* (1957), brought leaders to the forefront of world politics.

The publication of Kenneth Waltz's seminal *Theory of International Politics* (1979), which privileged the structure of the international system over the other images, changed things. Political scientists shied away from studying leaders for several decades. For the most part, the study of heads of state was left to historians, particularly "great man" theorists, who asserted that many world-historical events could be understood by referring to just a handful of influential leaders.[28] Yet such arguments are easily attacked for invoking post hoc justifications for why some leaders proved consequential and others did not. Hence, there was room for political scientists to bring leaders back into the study of world politics in a more systematic manner.

Over the past decade, the field of international relations has come full circle by returning to the study of leaders in a striking fashion. A slew of scholars have attempted to unpack the black box of leaders by examining their personal attributes.[29] Leader characteristics such as military experience, education, age, and gender appear to shape a host of outcomes including international conflict (Colgan 2013a; Horowitz and Stam 2014; Horowitz, Stam, and Ellis 2015), foreign policy decision-making (McDermott 2007; Saunders 2011), democratization (Gift and Krcmaric 2017), nuclear proliferation (Fuhrmann and Horowitz 2015), access to international credit (Nelson 2017), and economic growth (Besley, Montalvo, and Reynal-Querol 2011). The results presented here contribute to this literature

28. The great man approach to world history is often traced back to the Victorian-era intellectual Thomas Carlyle. For more recent discussions, see Byman and Pollack 2001; and Jervis 2013.

29. For an extensive review of this research agenda, see Krcmaric, Nelson, and Roberts 2020.

by showing that leaders behave in predictable ways depending on their prior history of using violence (i.e., culpable versus nonculpable leaders) and on the international context in which they operate (i.e., impunity era versus accountability era).

A second strand of research on leaders explores how expectations of post-tenure punishment influence the behavior of leaders during their time in office. A large body of literature finds that the anticipated domestic punishment for leaders affects international conflict primarily by giving leaders incentives to "gamble for resurrection" during wars (Bueno de Mesquita et al. 2003; Chiozza and Goemans 2011; Croco 2015; Debs and Goemans 2010; G. W. Downs and Rocke 1994; Goemans 2000; Weeks 2014). To give just one example, Henk Goemans (2000) shows that the First World War lasted for so long because some leaders, such as Germany's Kaiser Wilhelm II, had good reasons to fear severe domestic punishment (including threats to their personal safety) if they ended the war on losing terms. This book makes a new contribution by examining the opposite dynamic: How do expectations of international punishment for leaders influence civil conflict?

INTERNATIONAL ACTORS AND INTERNAL VIOLENCE

Another one of the book's broader implications speaks to a pressing policy question: How does the international community shape internal violence? To continue with the "images" framework, my contribution is an example of the "second image reversed," a term Peter Gourevitch (1978) coined to describe the international sources of domestic politics. Arguments in the second image reversed tradition have illuminated a variety of different outcomes that were once studied exclusively as domestic political affairs. The study of democratization is a prime example. Rather than solely examining the internal characteristics of states such as economic development or inequality, researchers taking a second image reversed perspective stress the role of international election observers (e.g., Hyde 2011; Kelley 2012), regional organizations (e.g., Pevehouse 2005), and other transnational connections (e.g., K. S. Gleditsch and Ward 2006) in promoting democracy from above. Regardless of the specific topic examined, the key insight about the second image reversed is that domestic politics are at least in part determined by events taking place in the international realm.

Following in that tradition, this book joins an emerging literature on how international actors influence civil wars. A number of scholars have examined how international and transnational variables—such as foreign military intervention (Kuperman 2008; Kydd and Straus 2013; R. M. Wood, Kathman, and Gent 2012), peacekeeping (Doyle and Sambanis 2011; Fortna 2008), international mediation (Beardsley 2011), cross-border refugee flows (Krcmaric 2014; Lischer 2005; Salehyan and Gleditsch 2006), and transnational diasporas (Collier and Hoeffler 2004)—influence the onset, dynamics, duration, and recurrence of civil conflict. This work is important because it advances our understanding of civil war by combining insights from both international relations and comparative politics. With this book, I attempt to do the same for the study of international justice. By seeking to hold leaders accountable for massive human rights violations regardless of where the leaders currently reside or where the crimes were initially committed, the pursuit of international justice both deters atrocities and prolongs conflicts.

THE POLITICS OF MORAL OUTRAGE

My findings also touch on debates about how the actions of well-intentioned international actors can go awry. When bad things happen around the globe—whether it is gratuitous violence, extreme poverty, or the spread of horrific diseases—there often is pressure on policymakers in powerful, wealthy countries to "do something." The moral imperative for drastic action may be especially compelling in today's information environment given the potent combination of social media and celebrity activism. Not only do people around the world see almost instantaneous images of human suffering, but they can also hear their favorite celebrities advocate for specific policy responses (such as Bono on global poverty, Angelina Jolie on refugee crises, and George Clooney on war crimes in Sudan). Without a doubt, the combination of new technology and social activism has succeeded in raising the profile of certain issues and building momentum for international action.[30]

But basing policy on moral outrage, even if the outrage is unambiguously justified, risks obscuring complex dynamics in favor of simple solutions. Indeed, this book emphasizes the value of thinking seriously about the unintentional consequences of policies meant to alleviate suffering abroad. It is important to remember that new policies—especially international ones designed to shape domestic politics—interact with preexisting political circumstances featuring strategic actors who may not respond as advocates hope. For instance, foreign aid meant to alleviate poverty can instead weaken growth and help autocrats consolidate power (e.g., Easterly 2006); military interventions designed to save lives may encourage additional rebellions (e.g., Kuperman 2008); humanitarian assistance can easily fall into the hands of warlords rather than the civilians who need

30. To give just one example, the human rights activist John Prendergast was rewarded with an Oval Office meeting with President Obama after a high-profile trip to Sudan with George Clooney. Prendergast spoke candidly about the importance of celebrity activism in advancing his cause: "I wouldn't be getting a 45-minute meeting with the president if it weren't for Clooney." See Daniel Bergner, "Attention-Grabber for Sudan's Cause," *New York Times Magazine*, December 2, 2010.

help (e.g., Lischer 2005); and UN peacekeeping operations may spread diseases to the very countries the UN is trying to assist (e.g., Pillinger, Hurd, and Barnett 2016). My findings indicate that a similar effect may occur in the context of international justice. Despite the good intentions of human rights advocates, pursuing global accountability can make it harder to get rid of abusive leaders because prosecutions give them an incentive to hold on to power at all costs.

HISTORICAL CONTEXT

My book's approach stresses the importance of historical context in international relations scholarship. In most research, especially but not exclusively the quantitative variety, it is common to pool observations across long stretches of time without justifying why doing so is appropriate. Indeed, most studies have "largely set aside concern about systematic discontinuities across time periods" and therefore tend to ignore "period specific variables and effects" (Jenke and Gelpi 2017, 2263). To the extent that international relations scholars think about historical periodization, it usually involves polarity (i.e., the number of great powers in the international system). For instance, scholars have argued that the bipolarity associated with the Cold War produced relatively stable international relations (Mearsheimer 2001; Waltz 1979) and that the end of the Cold War ushered in new changes in civil conflict (Kaldor 1999; Kalyvas and Balcells 2010). But changes in polarity represent only one of many possible macrohistorical shifts of consequence. Hence, one of the book's contributions is to examine another historical change—this one related to the shift from impunity to accountability for atrocity crimes—that shapes world politics. Going forward, scholars working across a variety of different research agendas in international relations would do well to take historical context more seriously.

LAW, ORDER, AND POWER

Finally, the book sheds light on the complicated relationship between law, order, and power. Scholars have long argued about whether "right" or "might" matters most in international affairs. In other words, can (and should) legal standards of right and wrong trump political calculations about power and order? Realist thinkers have long assumed that power was the natural ordering principle of world politics. For instance, the Athenian general and historian Thucydides famously concluded that "the strong do what they can and the weak suffer what they must."[31] Yet others have

31. This famous line is part of the Melian Dialogue in Thucydides's *History of the Peloponnesian War*.

pushed back, suggesting instead that an international society bound by common laws and norms is both possible and desirable.

When it comes to dealing with atrocity crimes, these debates take on a particular level of urgency. How, if at all, should law be used to address past abuses? After atrocities occur, "societies have to struggle over how much to acknowledge, whether to punish, and how to recover. How to treat the continuing presence of perpetrators . . . after the violence has ended is a central problem" (Minow 1998, 2).[32] Consider the prosecution of surviving Nazis after World War II at the Nuremberg Trials, now celebrated as the trial of the century. At the time, however, many doubted the appropriateness of pursuing a legal remedy to address war crimes. Legal responses can seem weak—they certainly pale in comparison to genocide or crimes against humanity. Hannah Arendt captured this notion while observing the trials of Nazis, wondering whether some crimes "explode the limits of the law . . . [and] we are simply not equipped to deal on a human, political level, with a guilt that is beyond crime" (Arendt 1992, 54). Similarly, the British foreign minister Anthony Eden opposed Nuremberg on the grounds that "the guilt of such individuals is so black that they are outside and go beyond the scope of any judicial process" (Bass 2000, 13).

Others critique judicial remedies to atrocity crimes for a different reason: it may be better to focus on political expediency over legal accountability. In *The Third Wave*, as part of his advice to countries transitioning out of conflict and toward democracy, Samuel Huntington advocates for eschewing prosecutions of the old regime. While acknowledging that there is no perfect solution, Huntington concludes that transitioning countries should devote their energy to crafting politically expedient bargains that reflect the distribution of power between groups, thus producing stability. In other words, simply doing nothing about past crimes might be best. As Huntington (1991, 231) memorably puts it, "The least unsatisfactory course may well be: do not prosecute, do not punish, do not forgive, and, above all, do not forget."

The school of thought known as legalism puts forth a different viewpoint. According to one leading theorist, Judith Shklar, "Politics is regarded not only as something apart from law, but as inferior to law. . . . Law aims at justice, while politics looks only to expediency. The former is neutral and objective, the latter the uncontrolled child of competing interests and ideologies" (Shklar 1964, 110). The desire of legalists to replace the rule of power with the rule of law frequently makes its way into policy debates.[33]

32. My book focuses on abuses committed against domestic populations, but see Lind 2008 for a treatment of similar issues in the context of foreign relations.

33. For an analysis that questions some of the traditional distinctions between law and politics, see Hurd 2017.

For instance, the long process of building the ICC was not only a march toward the rule of law but was also "conceived of as a march away from something else: politics and expediency" (Bosco 2014, 3).

During the past few decades, ideas about legalism and justice have apparently gained favor at the expense of calculations of power and expediency.[34] Many people now consider it normal, even essential, to hold individuals legally accountable for atrocity crimes. In addition to the prosecutions of heads of state that form the core of this book, consider also the recent resolution of the Colombian civil war. In June 2016, the Colombian government and the main rebel group, the FARC, signed a historic peace agreement ending the fifty-two-year conflict that had killed an estimated 220,000 people. The negotiators followed Huntington's advice to avoid judicial punishments: rank-and-file FARC fighters were given a blanket amnesty and rebel leaders would have light sentences, if any.[35] There was only one hurdle before the peace deal could be implemented: the Colombian people had to approve it in a referendum. In a vote that surprised many, the majority of Colombians rejected the peace deal. Why? A *New York Times* report concluded, "To many Colombians who had endured years of kidnappings and killings by the rebels, the agreement was too lenient." One individual summed up the way much of the country felt when he explained his "no" vote by saying, "There's no justice in this accord."[36] Thus, for most Colombians in 2016, achieving peace and order was not enough—they also wanted justice and accountability.[37]

Roadmap

The rest of the book is divided into five chapters. In the next chapter, chapter 2, I develop my theory about the justice dilemma and derive testable hypotheses on how international justice shapes patterns of exile, civil war duration, and mass killing onset. The remainder of the book then empirically tests the predictions generated in this chapter. All the empirical chapters offer both quantitative and qualitative evidence to assess the theory in multiple ways.

34. On the triumph of legalist sensibilities, consider the question Gary Bass poses: "Why not just shoot them [war criminals]? If one considers such a brutal solution to be out of the question, that only a barbarian state would do such a thing, that only testifies to the extent to which legalism has permeated our political culture" (Bass 2000, 12).

35. According to the terms of the peace deal, even if FARC leaders were convicted of war crimes, they would face only minor punishments such as community service work.

36. Julia Symmes Cobb and Nicholas Casey, "Colombia Peace Deal Is Defeated, Leaving a Nation in Shock," *New York Times*, October 2, 2016.

37. Colombian voters later approved a revised peace deal.

In chapter 3, I present evidence on patterns of exile. Using a large dataset of political leaders and a newly constructed measure of leader culpability for mass atrocities, I show that the decision to flee into exile is conditional on whether leaders can expect to face post-tenure international punishment. Whereas culpable leaders were no more or less likely to flee abroad than nonculpable leaders in the impunity era, culpable leaders are about six times less likely to go into exile during today's accountability era. I pair the statistical analysis with a case study of Liberia's Charles Taylor. At first glance, Taylor—one of the very few culpable leaders to go into exile in the accountability era—might seem like an odd candidate for a case study. Upon deeper inspection, however, this case is valuable precisely because Taylor fled abroad during Liberia's civil war in 2003. The Taylor case study not only permits me to investigate why some leaders might still choose exile but it also allows me to answer a crucial question: Do culpable leaders who go into exile in the accountability era actually get punished? As I show, the quest for international justice undermined Taylor's safety during his exile in Nigeria and eventually led to his arrest and trial at the Special Court for Sierra Leone.

Chapters 4 and 5 examine the conflicting effects of the justice cascade. In chapter 4, I investigate civil war duration. Rather than flee abroad, I show that culpable leaders now respond to incentives to fight until the bitter end. While there is no evidence of a relationship between leader culpability and conflict duration during the impunity era, the quantitative analysis demonstrates that civil wars last significantly longer when culpable leaders are in power during the accountability era. After the statistical tests, I turn to a case study of Muammar Gaddafi during the 2011 Libyan revolution to illustrate how the justice cascade has altered the decision calculus of culpable leaders. Unlike his peers during the impunity era, Gaddafi was worried enough about an international prosecution to spurn the exile option. Instead, he decided to risk it all on the battlefield, a tactic that ultimately prolonged the Libyan conflict.

In chapter 5, I explore the deterrent effect of international justice. I estimate statistical models of mass killing onset to show how the same conditions that exacerbate conflict also create deterrence. Specifically, because leaders want to keep the exile escape route open in the event they need it, leaders in today's accountability era are about six times less likely to commit atrocities than their peers were during the impunity era. A case study of Blaise Compaoré during Burkina Faso's 2014 revolution complements the quantitative results. The Compaoré case highlights the connection between the decision to commit atrocities and the availability of a safe exile option. Burkina Faso in 2014 represents a case where a number of factors suggested that mass violence was possible, perhaps even likely. Yet, because Compaoré knew that a safe foreign retirement was conditional on his behavior during Burkina Faso's crisis, he had a powerful incentive to exercise restraint. As a nonculpable leader, Compaoré ultimately was able to retire abroad once it became clear that he could no longer maintain political control in Burkina Faso.

In chapter 6, the concluding chapter, I summarize the theory and the supporting empirical evidence. I also offer a discussion of the theoretical and policy implications that follow from my results. In a world where the pursuit of peace and the demands of legal accountability often conflict with each other, how should we think about international justice?

CHAPTER 2

The Justice Dilemma

This chapter presents my theory of the justice dilemma. The theory helps explain several puzzles: Why do some embattled leaders desperately cling to power while others flee abroad at the first sign of trouble? Why do some civil wars end quickly whereas others drag on for so long? Why do some regimes victimize civilians but others exercise restraint?

I present the argument in four parts. First, I explain how exile provides a mechanism for leaders, especially those facing domestic unrest, to give up power in a manner that is relatively costless. Rulers who worry about their personal safety at home can instead flee abroad to a foreign sanctuary. For this reason, there has been a long tradition of leaders going into exile as part of a golden parachute exit strategy.

Second, I describe the global justice cascade that has occurred in recent years. While the push to end impunity for oppressive leaders has a long history, it reached a tipping point in the late 1990s. In fact, two events in 1998—the signing of the ICC's Rome Statute and the arrest of former Chilean leader Augusto Pinochet under the principle of universal jurisdiction—suddenly made the threat of arrest on foreign soil appear far more realistic. Moreover, these seminal events ushered in a new period of holding other leaders accountable for atrocity crimes at the international level, destroying the expectation of impunity leaders had previously enjoyed. The watershed events of 1998, I show, represent the beginning of a shift from an era of impunity to an era of accountability.

Third, this shift in the international environment from impunity toward accountability complicates the exile option. I explain why the justice cascade has a differential effect on leaders based on their culpability for atrocity crimes. Nonculpable leaders can still safely retire abroad because they have little reason to fear international arrest. Culpable leaders, by contrast, now have incentives to entrench in power because a credible threat of international justice can undermine the possibility of a secure exile.

Fourth, by influencing the viability of exile as a retirement option, the justice cascade shapes the behavior of leaders while they are still in office. On the negative side, international justice prolongs civil wars by incentivizing culpable leaders to continue fighting when they would otherwise flee abroad. On the positive side, international justice deters atrocities because leaders now know that committing human rights abuses will decrease their exit options should they need a foreign safe haven in the future. Taken together, the theory implies that there is a justice dilemma: deterring atrocities and prolonging conflicts are two sides of the same coin.

Exile as a Golden Parachute

One of the fundamental assumptions of political science has long been that leaders choose policies to maximize the probability of staying in office (e.g., A. Downs 1957). International relations scholarship, however, has shifted the focus to the *consequences* of losing office (e.g., Chiozza and Goemans 2011; Croco 2015; Debs and Goemans 2010; G. W. Downs and Rocke 1994; Goemans 2000; Weeks 2014). If we add the uncontroversial assumption that leaders prefer a cushy post-tenure fate to punishments like death or imprisonment, leaders might not always pursue strategies that maximize their time in office. Instead, leaders' behavior may reflect a desire to avoid punishment. This focus on the consequences of losing office is crucial for understanding the justice dilemma.

I address the logic of one way in which leaders can give up power: exile. I explain how leaders must weigh the relative risks of facing domestic punishment and international punishment. Leaders are apt to flee abroad when the likelihood and costs of domestic punishment are high relative to those of international punishment. As I describe in this section, the status quo has traditionally been that the threat of domestic punishment far outstripped the threat of international punishment. Given the norm of impunity at the international level, exile was an attractive retirement option for embattled leaders regardless of how they had behaved while in office.

THE THREAT OF DOMESTIC PUNISHMENT

Life is often dangerous for political rulers. This point is vividly illustrated in "The Sword of Damocles," an Ancient Roman tale that centers on King Dionysius of Syracuse. Dionysius is a typical tyrant: powerful and wealthy but also hated by his own people for his cruelty. Over time, Dionysius comes to fear assassination so much that he begins sleeping in a special fortress protected by a moat. One day, an obsequious courtier named Damocles remarks that Dionysius is fortunate since he is a man of great power and prestige. In response, King Dionysius offers to trade places with Damocles. Damocles eagerly agrees and soon finds himself seated on the king's throne with all the trappings of power. When Damocles glances up, however, he notices that Dionysius has hung a sword from the ceiling using only a single strand of horsehair. Fearing for his safety, Damocles quickly gives the throne back to Dionysius. The anecdote's lesson, of course, is that political rulers are by definition in a precarious position. The ever-present possibility of danger casts a long shadow over everything leaders do.

Dionysius's insight is not confined to the realm of fable. History is replete with political leaders—spanning different historical eras, cultures, and regime types—who paid the ultimate price. At the onset of the French Revolution, an angry mob forced King Louis XVI out of the Tuileries Palace. Following his arrest, Louis was humiliated and then guillotined in front of a crowd at the Place de la Révolution in Paris. During the American Civil War, a Confederate sympathizer assassinated President Abraham Lincoln at a theater in Washington, DC. Near the end of World War II, Italian partisans captured and murdered the fascist leader Benito Mussolini. Mussolini's corpse was then hung upside down in the Piazzale Loreto in Milan for public viewing. At the Cold War's close, protests against the regime of Romania's Nicolae Ceausescu erupted in Bucharest. The opposition caught Ceausescu as he attempted to escape and, after a hasty show trial, Ceausescu and his wife were killed by firing squad on Christmas Day.

Leaders naturally hope to avoid such grisly fates. If threats to a ruler's personal safety loom on the horizon—such as when the leader's popularity falls, people take to the streets in protest, or civil war breaks out—the leader may try to negotiate his way out of trouble. One potential strategy is to step down from office and give the opposition what they want: political power. The problem, however, is that a domestic retirement often is not an attractive option for a beleaguered leader. Even if the opposition promises not to harm the leader after he steps down, the outgoing ruler still may be wary of a domestic retirement due to the credible commitment problem inherent to transitions of power.

A credible commitment problem refers to a situation in which two actors struggle to reach an agreement due to the issue of time inconsistency.[1]

1. This discussion draws on the theoretical framework known as the bargaining model of war. The intuition behind the bargaining model is that war is costly, and therefore the two actors in the bargaining game have an incentive to reach a mutually acceptable deal rather than fight (e.g., Fearon 1995; R. Powell 2004; Reiter 2003; Slantchev 2003; A. Smith and Stam 2004; Wagner 2000). Despite this powerful incentive to reach peaceful settlements, wars nonetheless occur. To explain the outbreak, conduct, and termination of violent conflict, rationalist explanations point to the role of private information, credible commitment problems, and issue indivisibility. Of these, commitment problems are most relevant to my argument.

Specifically, a cooperative arrangement that both sides prefer in the present can fall apart because of the changing desirability of abiding by the terms of the deal in the future. If Actor A knows that Actor B will have incentives to renege on an agreement in the future—perhaps because Actor B will be stronger and will want a better deal—Actor A will be hesitant to settle in the first place. Why make a deal if the other side cannot be expected to follow through? In other words, Actor B's inability to commit to future restraint can make it difficult for the two sides to reach a mutually beneficial agreement in the present. An example from international relations, power transitions between two states, illustrates the nature of the commitment problem. During a power transition, the rising state may try its best to assure the declining state that it has benign intentions. Regardless of any promises the rising state makes in the present, however, it cannot credibly commit to refrain from exploiting its power advantage in the future. Hence, even if both sides want to find a way to live together and thereby avoid a costly war, the declining state may decide it is better off fighting now because it fears the rising state will take advantage of it in the future. Many view the coming power transition between the United States and China as a situation that will be fraught with uncertainty and commitment problems (e.g., Mearsheimer 2010; Rosato 2015).

Returning to the context of leaders and domestic punishment, a similar credible commitment problem exists if and when a leader retires. For instance, a leader facing a rebellion could cut a deal in which he hands over the reins of the government in exchange for a promise of a safe retirement. Once again, however, there is an issue of time inconsistency. As soon as power is transferred to the former opposition, it has the ability to renege on any agreement it made with the ex-ruler.[2] Knowing this, a leader has little incentive to step down if he expects that the opposition will be tempted to retaliate over old grievances. A leader will want an "exit guarantee" (Dix 1982; Sutter 1995) that protects him from punishment even after he is out of power. Yet it is hard for the opposition to create a credible exit guarantee for the leader because, once the leader steps down, the opposition could cheat on any promise it has made.[3]

2. The literature on democratic transitions emphasizes similar dynamics (e.g., Przeworski 1991).

3. On the flip side, negotiated settlements that keep the leader in power typically require the rebel group to demobilize and disarm its members in return for some policy concession. Yet, once the rebel group demobilizes, it no longer possesses the military capability to force the regime to abide by the terms of the recently struck bargain (Walter 1997). Anticipating this, the opposition group will be reluctant to agree to lay down its arms. Overall, commitment problems can explain why civil conflicts often persist despite a long series of seemingly generous offers and counteroffers between the two sides with regard to peace terms. As Barbara Walter (2002, 5) puts it in her study of civil war resolution, the main reason why

To be clear, this does not mean negotiated transitions of power will never occur. Due to the unique circumstances of particular cases, some leaders will have reason to believe they can safely cede power and retire. Yet this is always a risky move for the leader because circumstances can change quickly after giving up power. Egypt's Hosni Mubarak offers a cautionary tale. Facing mass protests against his regime, Mubarak stepped down in 2011 after apparently receiving assurances that he would be allowed to retire to the resort town of Sharm el-Sheikh on the Egyptian coast. The incoming regime, however, had other plans and arrested Mubarak just a few months after he arrived there, marking a "breathtaking reversal for Egypt's former strongman."[4] In other cases, domestic punishment for an ex-ruler takes more time. Efrain Rios Montt took power in Guatemala in a 1982 military coup but was forced out of office less than two years later by his own defense minister. At least initially, Rios Montt's post-tenure fate was quite good. He remained active in Guatemalan politics, serving multiple terms in Congress and even running for president in 2003. However, after the army's role in politics had weakened substantially, Rios Montt was arrested and charged in 2012 with directing genocide against the country's indigenous Mayan population in 1982–83.[5] As these examples illustrate, a retired leader is at the mercy of the successor regime.

Moreover, an ex-leader can never be sure that old enemies will not resurface during a domestic retirement. In 2004, for instance, the Lebanese business magnate turned prime minister Rafik Hariri resigned his position amid a growing split with powerful pro-Syrian elements within Lebanon. After retiring, Hariri remained in Lebanon to tend to his business interests. Clearly aware that punishment at the hands of his domestic political adversaries was a possibility, Hariri "surrounded himself with bodyguards and lived in a heavily fortified compound" after giving up political power.[6] But even these precautions proved to be insufficient. Less than a year after his resignation, Hariri's motorcade was bombed as it passed through Beirut, killing the former leader.[7]

"civil war negotiations fail is because it is almost impossible for the combatants . . . to arrange credible guarantees on the terms of the settlement."

4. David D. Kirkpartrick and Liam Stack, "Prosecutors Order Mubarak and Sons Held," *New York Times*, April 13, 2011.

5. Sibylla Brodzinky and Jonathan Watts, "Former Guatemalan Dictator Convicted of Genocide and Jailed for 80 Years," *Guardian*, May 10, 2013. Rios Montt's conviction was later overturned on a technicality, and the case was in the midst of a retrial when he died in 2018.

6. Susan Sachs, "Rafik Hariri, Ex-Premier of Lebanon, Dies at 60," *New York Times*, February 15, 2005.

7. While there is still some ambiguity surrounding Hariri's murder, many suspect that Hezbollah, a militant group and political party in Lebanon with close links to Syria, orchestrated the attack.

Overall, this discussion suggests that both the costs and the likelihood of domestic punishment for leaders, particularly those threatened by domestic unrest, are typically quite high. As John Wiseman (1993, 657) aptly put it, "To be a political leader in many parts of the world is to follow an extremely hazardous and insecure occupation. . . . The element of personal danger exists in a particularly acute form." Indeed, a ruler who holds on to power for too long risks meeting an untimely and violent end. But a domestic retirement may be equally unappealing because the leader puts his fate in the hands of the successor regime—often the very people who fought to remove the leader. This dynamic puts embattled leaders in a difficult position. There is, however, another option: exile.

THE (MISSING) THREAT OF INTERNATIONAL PUNISHMENT

Exile is a valuable political tool because it can help solve the problems surrounding a leader's post-tenure fate. As the preceding discussion implies, a leader will be reluctant to cede power to the opposition when he expects them to settle old scores. Exile, however, offers a way out of this impasse. Leaders worried about punishment at home can go into exile and obtain foreign protection. When a leader is able to retire to a third-party state, he no longer needs to fear punishment since he is outside the grasp of the former opposition. In fact, physically leaving the state he once ruled is arguably the best exit guarantee a leader can have against retribution from his old adversaries. Therefore, as the threat of domestic punishment increases, rulers become more likely to view exile abroad as the best option available. Though they give up power, leaders manage to avoid punishment and can live out their years abroad.

For this reason, leaders historically have been willing to take the exile option when facing threats to their rule. When a comfortable, if not luxurious, international retirement is on the table, leaders have little incentive to run high risks in an attempt to hold on to power. Many leaders therefore have been content to find a safe haven abroad once they were no longer welcome at home. Even a relatively small chance of suffering domestic punishment has sometimes been enough to send leaders scurrying for the safety of a foreign sanctuary.

A pair of examples illustrates this point. Juan Peron's popularity declined in the mid-1950s after Argentina's economy faltered and his increasingly liberal social policies alienated the country's mostly conservative population. In 1955, Peron's political opponents joined forces with conservative Catholics in the army to launch an uprising that took control of Cordoba, Argentina's third largest city. Additionally, part of Argentina's navy joined the rebellion, and a small fleet approached the mouth of the Rio de la Plata, putting it within striking distance of Buenos Aires. Despite the turmoil, Peron likely could have put down the rebellion if he had been willing to hold out for longer in Argentina. According to one historian, "The balance of forces did not appear to favor the revolutionary cause. . . . [Peron] could have elected to stay on and fight, with good prospects of success on both the military and the civilian fronts" (Crassweller 1987, 287).[8] Peron, however, opted not to stay in Argentina and fight it out. Doing so would have risked severe punishment at the hands of his enemies, whereas fleeing abroad offered better prospects for Peron personally. One general who joined the anti-Peron movement captured this intuition about Peron and the threat of domestic punishment: "What brought Peron down . . . was a failure of nerve, not a military defeat" (Alexander 1979, 108). In other words, Peron probably could have remained in power in Argentina, but he was not willing to put his life on the line to do so.[9] Just a few days after the revolution started, Peron fled for the safety of Paraguay, where Alfredo Stroessner welcomed him with open arms (Crassweller 1987, 291).[10] In the following years, Peron spent his time gracing the finer hotels of Panama, Venezuela, the Dominican Republic, and Nicaragua, before eventually settling in Madrid.[11]

The Filipino leader Ferdinand Marcos provides another example. In 1986, Marcos lost an election to Corazon Aquino, the widow of Marcos's longtime political rival, Benigno Aquino (whose murder was widely blamed on Marcos). When Marcos refused to recognize the election results, millions of Aquino's supporters took to the streets of Manila, launching the People Power Revolution. At the same time, a coterie of military officers calling themselves the Reform the Army Movement (RAM) attempted to push Marcos out of power. When this failed, RAM joined forces with Aquino's People Power Revolution.[12] How would Marcos respond? Recognizing the

8. Several other historians agree with the assessment that Peron likely could have put down the rebellion if he had stayed in Argentina. Joseph Page (1983, 324) notes that "a military victory was certainly within reach [for Peron]." Similarly, Robert Alexander (1979, 108) points out, "Only the outlying parts of the republic were in revolt, their resources were severely limited. . . . Peron, having the bulk of the army still loyal, could have put down this insurrection."

9. Another factor potentially contributing to Peron's decision to flee rather than fight—and one that Peron liked to discuss after his ouster—was saving his beloved city of Buenos Aires from bombardment (Alexander 1979, 108; Page 1983, 324). Of course, it is debatable whether this explanation can be taken at face value, but it certainly is possible that leaders take into account factors other than their personal fate.

10. Stroessner himself would be forced into exile in 1989 after ruling Paraguay with an iron fist for thirty-five years.

11. Many members of Argentina's political class "felt that Peron had the best of both worlds—living in Madrid in comfortable circumstances but still maintaining the loyalty of a substantial part of the Argentine population" (Alexander 1979, 113). Peron remained in exile in Spain until 1973, when he triumphantly returned to Argentina and once again assumed the presidency.

12. On the 1986 anti-Marcos revolution in the Philippines, see Bonner 1987; Karnow 1989; and Thompson 1995.

election results and taking a domestic retirement in the Philippines was a nonstarter. During her campaign, Aquino had insisted she would put Marcos on trial, pledging that he would "be given [the] justice which was denied my husband."[13] Upon hearing that, Marcos had a compelling reason to refuse to put his fate in Aquino's hands. Another option for Marcos was escalating the fight with the opposition. Just three days before his ouster, a CIA assessment acknowledged that the military defections and civilian protests had weakened Marcos but concluded, "Nonetheless the balance of military power in Manila heavily favored Marcos."[14] Hence, remaining in the Philippines to put down the rebellion would have been risky—Marcos faced arrest or death if he was toppled—but he also had a decent chance of coming out victorious. Ultimately, however, Marcos decided not to take the gamble. This surprised many, including Juan Ponce Enrile, Marcos's former defense minister turned RAM leader. Looking back, Enrile acknowledged, "I never expected [Marcos] to give up that soon" (Enrile 2012, 634). But my theoretical framework provides an explanation for Marcos's early departure: Given that there was an attractive exit option which ensured his personal safety, Marcos had little reason to risk doubling down in the Philippines. On February 26, 1986, Marcos fled Manila for the safety of exile and lived out his remaining days in a villa in Hawaii.

These are not isolated examples. There is a seemingly endless list of leaders who have retired to safe havens abroad. Once the political situation at home became too dicey, exile provided an inviting escape route for rulers, making it the second most common post-tenure fate for ousted dictators in the post–World War II era (Escribà-Folch and Krcmaric 2017).

Why was exile historically such a safe retirement option for leaders? Simply put, there was no established legal mechanism to punish oppressive leaders once they were in exile. In fact, widely accepted notions of international order that prized political convenience over legal accountability explicitly *protected* exiled rulers even if they had engaged in horrendous abuses while they were in power.

Two pillars of the international order, sovereignty and head-of-state immunity, formed the basis of this protection. Sovereignty refers to the notion that all states are equal under international law and therefore each state has the right to govern itself without outside interference.[15] When it

13. Seth Mydans, "Aquino Says If She Is Elected Marcos Faces a Murder Trial," *New York Times*, December 16, 1985.

14. This CIA assessment is referenced in Secretary of State George Shultz's memoirs. Shultz himself agreed that it was "possible for Marcos to keep control through military power" (Shultz 1993, 633).

15. For a discussion of how sovereignty remains a durable norm in international politics even though it is often violated, see Krasner 1999. On the historical evolution of sovereign nation-states, see Spruyt 1996.

came to dispensing justice, sovereignty meant that each state wielded complete authority within its own territory but possessed no judicial authority beyond its borders. Any attempt by one state to prosecute crimes committed in another state, regardless of the massive scale or the heinous nature of the crimes, would violate the principle of sovereign equality. As Jeremy Rabkin (2007, 99) put it, "If sovereignty means anything, it means very sharp limits to any serious notion of international criminal justice."

Head-of-state immunity refers to the legal principle that a current or former leader cannot be arrested in another state or tried by its courts. Head-of-state immunity developed through international custom rather than any particular treaty. Considered every bit as binding as treaty law, customary international law is a branch of international law that focuses more on states' actions than on their written agreements. In the words of one legal scholar, customary international law "arises from a general and consistent practice of states followed by them from a sense of legal obligation" (Scharf 2006, 360). In simpler terms, arresting the leader of another state simply was not done in international politics—there was a lawlike prohibition that made doing so virtually unthinkable.

States consistently chose to follow this norm (at least until very recently) because head-of-state immunity is useful for the conduct of foreign policy. By allowing a nation's leader to engage in his official duties when traveling abroad without fear of arrest or detention, head-of-state immunity has long been viewed as crucial to diplomacy. For example, without head-of-state immunity it is hard to imagine some of history's great diplomatic breakthroughs that involved leaders traveling abroad to engage with their one-time rivals (e.g., the European leaders who gathered at the Congress of Berlin in 1878 or "Nixon to China" in 1972). Of course, unpopular leaders could never count on immunity when facing the wrath of their own people, as the aforementioned examples ranging from the guillotining of France's Louis XVI to the show trial and execution of Romania's Nicolae Ceausescu illustrate dramatically.[16] But at the international level, respect for the principle of head-of-state immunity ensured that leaders were inviolable.

Head-of-state immunity also meant that exile could be used to provide a secure exit option even for leaders with unsavory personal histories. This dynamic encouraged third-party states to offer asylum to embattled leaders as part of a strategy to manage violence and instability abroad. Indeed, policymakers traditionally understood exile to be a mechanism of conflict resolution rather than an egregious example of impunity for

16. The Ceausescu case is particularly illuminating because he was attempting to escape to the safety of exile—first by helicopter and then by car—when the Romanian opposition captured him. See Clyde Haberman, "Pilot of Helicopter Describes Ceausescu's Escape Attempt," *New York Times*, January 1, 1990.

abusive rulers. The international community therefore tended to support using exile as a golden parachute.

To see this conflict management strategy at play, return to the Ferdinand Marcos case. Marcos had long enjoyed unquestioned American support as a staunch anticommunist, but American policymakers eventually became "convinced that Marcos was the problem, not the solution" (Shultz 1993, 613). At the height of the 1986 crisis, Philip Habib, a diplomatic troubleshooter for the Reagan administration, returned from a special mission to Manila. Habib's conclusion was simple: "Marcos is finished, and we ought to offer him asylum in the United States" (Karnow 1989, 415). Reagan immediately signed National Security Directive 215, which reversed the US policy of supporting Marcos: "Our objectives in the Philippines are to prevent violence between the parties concerned and facilitate a peaceful transition."[17] Marcos soon accepted an offer of safe haven from the United States, who provided a plane to transport Marcos and his family to Hawaii. In America, there was nothing but praise for the Reagan administration's role in coaxing Marcos out of power, which allowed prodemocracy candidate Corazon Aquino to take office. Even the US congressman Stephen Solarz, a Reagan opponent and frequent critic of Marcos's human rights record, extolled the US policy by saying, "If the price we had to pay to avoid massive bloodshed . . . in the Philippines was to offer Mr. Marcos asylum in the United States, then it was a price worth paying."[18]

Other examples show just how common this peace-for-exile dynamic was. With violent protests raging throughout Haiti in 1986, Jean-Claude Duvalier threw one final champagne-infused party at the National Palace before heading to the airport in Port-au-Prince. He then boarded a US Air Force plane for exile in France, where he took up residence in a mansion on the Riviera. This cushy post-tenure landing for the Haitian dictator was no accident—it was the result of extensive coordination between French and American policymakers who hoped to ease Duvalier out of power with as little bloodshed as possible (Shultz 1993, 622).[19] For their parts, the United Kingdom and Russia both have extensive histories of providing safe haven to troubled rulers within their respective spheres of influence

17. National Security Decision Directive 215, February 23, 1986, available in the National Archives Catalog at https://catalog.archives.gov/id/6879803.

18. David K. Shipler, "Does Marcos Deserve U.S. Asylum?," *New York Times*, March 4, 1986. Solarz was not the only one pleased with US policy and Marcos's early retirement to Hawaii. In his diary entry for February 26, President Reagan happily summed up the events in the Philippines by noting, "So—no civil war and we've proceeded to recognize the new Philippine government" (Reagan 2009, 394).

19. From the US perspective, Duvalier's foreign retirement was conflict resolution on the cheap. One American official even quipped: "Duvalier and his wife wanted to go to France, so the only price we paid was giving him a plane ride." See Bernard Gwertzman, "Challenge to Marcos: Asylum," *New York Times*, February 25, 1986.

(Escribà-Folch and Krcmaric 2017). Furthermore, even in cases where powerful states have not hosted fleeing rulers themselves, they have been profoundly involved in finding sanctuaries for outgoing leaders. When Chadian rebels marched on the capital city of N'Djamena, Hissène Habré fled the country for Senegal in an exile allegedly arranged by French intelligence (Bronner 2014). During the Ethiopian civil war, Mengistu Haile Mariam fled to Zimbabwe, an escape supported by American officials looking for a way to end the civil war.[20] In each case, the availability of a safe exile destination made the ruler's exit smoother—and less violent—than it otherwise might have been.

A strong head-of-state immunity doctrine, of course, severely limits any attempt to pursue international justice. It is hard to end impunity for the world's worst criminals when brutal leaders can rely on a widely accepted legal doctrine that shields them from prosecution while in exile. As one human rights activist vividly put it, the norm traditionally was: "If you kill one person, you go to jail; if you kill 20, you go to an institution for the insane; if you kill 20,000, you get political asylum."[21] Robert Jackson, the chief justice at the Nuremberg Trials, similarly complained that "this idea [head-of-state immunity] is a relic of the doctrine of the divine right of kings" and bitterly noted "the paradox that legal responsibility is the least where power is the greatest" (Cassese 2008, 245). Overall, then, concerns about sovereignty and head-of-state immunity ensured that impunity was the norm for exiled leaders.

To be sure, exile has never quite offered a perfect "bullet-proof" guarantee that ousted leaders would avoid all forms of punishment. Once in exile, ex-rulers are forced to rely on a host state for protection. Though this has rarely been problematic, a handful of exceptions exist. As Albania's King Zog discovered, an exiled leader may find that he is no longer welcome if the host state experiences a regime change itself. Zog was initially forced into exile during the political turmoil surrounding the outbreak of World War II and bounced around various European capitals before settling into a long-term retirement in Egypt as a guest of King Farouk. After Farouk was overthrown, the successor regime made it clear it had little desire to continue hosting Zog. Yet the Egyptians made no attempt to punish Zog—as a former head of state, he was close to untouchable—and he simply relocated to France (Tomes 2003). Another potential concern for exiled leaders is assassination. Security provided by the host state and/or private bodyguards are typically sufficient for protection, but there is at

20. Given the United States' poor relationship with both Mengistu and Zimbabwe's Robert Mugabe, this case illustrates the extent to which major powers previously relied on exile as a tool for conflict resolution.

21. The quote is from Human Rights Watch's Reed Brody. See Ethan Bronner, "The Obscenely Easy Exile of Idi Amin," *New York Times*, August 19, 2003.

least one exception in the modern era.[22] In 1979, Nicaragua's Anastasio Somoza Debayle fled into exile as the Sandinista revolution toppled his regime. Somoza retired to a stately ranch in Paraguay, but a Sandinista commando team tracked him down, ambushed his car as it returned to the ranch, and assassinated him in a barrage of machine-gun fire.[23] These rare exceptions, however, only serve to highlight the general rule: exile historically has come close to offering the ideal exit guarantee for troubled leaders.

To recap, this section has shown two things. First, the threat of domestic punishment for unpopular or embattled leaders has always been high. Second, the threat of international punishment has traditionally been extremely low. As several of the previous examples illustrated, leaders tended to view a foreign retirement as the best available option when the risk of punishment at home became sufficiently large. Despite giving up political power, they could safely live out their remaining days abroad. In this way, exile offered a golden parachute that leaders—even notoriously brutal ones—often preferred to the alternative of risking death or imprisonment in their own countries.

The Changing Landscape of International Justice

Though exile provided a convenient mechanism for easing leaders out of power and resolving civil wars, the standard practice of bad rulers retiring abroad without ever facing punishment was troubling. By offering an easy escape route for violent, corrupt, and unpopular leaders, exile was a detriment to the pursuit of justice. Indeed, it can hardly be considered a just outcome when a leader pillages and plunders his own country before decamping to a foreign retirement in a posh capital city or an exotic island locale. Partly in response to some of the more egregious examples of golden parachutes, human rights activists and sympathetic policymakers came to realize that ending impunity would require something new.

Since the late 1990s, something new *has* happened. The tradition of using exile as a golden parachute collided with the creation of a robust system of international justice. Nested within the larger trends toward the legalization of international politics and the prioritization of human rights in foreign policy, there has been a "justice cascade" (Sikkink 2011) or "revolution in accountability" (Sriram 2005). A slew of leaders previously considered

22. Looking beyond heads of state, there are other high-profile cases of political elites who fared badly in exile. For instance, the Russian revolutionary Leon Trotsky was murdered as he lived out his days in Mexico, and Israeli "Nazi hunters" assassinated or captured several former Nazi officials hiding abroad (most famously Adolf Eichmann).

23. Cynthia Gorney, "Somoza Is Assassinated in Ambush in Paraguay," *Washington Post*, September 18, 1980.

untouchable have been hauled before international tribunals to account for their crimes. This development may represent "one of the most ambitious judicial experiments in the history of humankind—a global assault on the architects of atrocities" (Scheffer 2012, 2).

This push to end impunity is, in a sense, the result of a battle of ideas pitting long-standing notions of sovereignty and head-of-state immunity against new norms of global accountability. If a norm is a widely shared standard of appropriate behavior, then the new international justice norm is the expectation that legal accountability ought to be pursued whenever and wherever human rights have been massively jeopardized. This is a revolutionary idea because it means that a national border or a head-of-state position should no longer offer protection against prosecution if an individual is responsible for terrible abuses.

The development of the international justice norm largely follows Martha Finnemore and Kathryn Sikkink's (1998) model of "norm entrepreneurs" winning over others to their cause.[24] The key norm entrepreneurs for international justice have been nongovernmental organizations (NGOs) such as Human Rights Watch and Amnesty International as well as victims' groups who refused to forget the crimes of ousted despots living out their days abroad. While these norm entrepreneurs eventually had success, they initially failed to convince a larger audience—particularly the most important audience, powerful states—to adopt their cause. Given the geopolitical tensions of the Cold War, realpolitik strategies consistently trumped concerns about international justice. The end of the Cold War, however, created a more favorable context for international justice.[25] Norm entrepreneurs soon won over a critical mass of actors, ushering in several dramatic developments in world politics.

In this section, I focus on the manifestations of this normative change. I first describe the international legal regime, the set of laws, policies, and institutions that formalize the campaign against impunity. I then discuss the key challenge for this regime: enforcement. International courts lack their own police forces to track down oppressive rulers, but a number of states have helped fill this enforcement gap by apprehending leaders responsible for atrocity crimes. Finally, I summarize how the international justice movement coalesced in 1998 with two key events: the creation of the

24. The nature and origins of this normative shift have already been covered extensively elsewhere (e.g., Sikkink 2011), so I address them only briefly here. My primary focus is on the *effects* of the justice cascade.

25. To be clear, the end of the Cold War was a permissive background condition that enabled the pursuit of international justice, but geopolitical change certainly did not guarantee a shift from impunity toward accountability. I will return to this theme in the empirical chapters and show that the end of the Cold War itself cannot explain the observed patterns of exile, civil war duration, and mass killing onset.

ICC (the first permanent court with potentially global jurisdiction) and the arrest of Augusto Pinochet in the United Kingdom (the first time a leader was arrested on foreign soil for international crimes). These seminal events in 1998 marked the tipping point in a global shift from an era of impunity to an era of accountability, raising profound implications for patterns of exile.

CONSTRUCTING AN INTERNATIONAL LEGAL REGIME

The normative prohibition against impunity has been institutionalized in international criminal law, the "body of international rules to proscribe certain categories of conduct . . . and to make those persons who engage in such conduct criminally liable" (Cassese 2008, 2). International criminal law is closely related to international humanitarian law, the set of laws governing the conduct of armed conflict, because a central concern of both is protecting the lives of civilians. Thus, the proscribed categories of conduct in international criminal law, typically called international crimes, include genocide, crimes against humanity, and war crimes.[26] The seeds of today's legal regime can be traced back to the horrors of World War II, when the Allies created the International Military Tribunal at Nuremberg to prosecute the most prominent surviving Nazi officials.[27] While Cold War dynamics ensured that the Nuremberg Trials remained just a brief moment when the world focused on individual criminal accountability, the so-called Nuremberg principles would later serve as a blueprint for the new international tribunals that were created in the 1990s onward.[28]

26. *Genocide* refers to an attempt to destroy a national, ethnic, racial, or religious group. The archetypical case of genocide is Nazi Germany's attempt to exterminate European Jews before and during World War II. *War crimes* refer to serious violations of the laws of war. An example is the Omar Bashir regime's intentional killing of civilians as a counterinsurgency strategy in the Darfur region of Sudan. *Crimes against humanity* are the broadest category of international crime. Unlike genocide, there is no specific list of potential target groups (crimes against humanity can occur against any civilian population, including political groups). Moreover, unlike war crimes, crimes against humanity can occur during times of peace as well as times of war. An example comes from the early stages of the 2011 uprising in Libya when Muammar Gaddafi's security forces killed civilians protesting against the regime. These three crimes constitute the core international crimes. Other crimes—including torture, aggression, and terrorism—are sometimes considered international crimes, but their status as such is contested.

27. Antecedents of international criminal law can be traced back even further. Those who attempted to combat piracy in the seventeenth century, for example, held that pirates were enemies of mankind who could be punished by any state. After World War I, the Versailles Treaty stipulated that an international tribunal should be set up to try Germany's Kaiser Wilhelm II. However, Wilhelm II fled into exile in the Netherlands at the conclusion of World War I. When the Netherlands declined to extradite the kaiser, plans for the tribunal were quickly dropped (Bass 2000, 58–60).

28. The Nuremberg Trials (and the Tokyo Trials, which applied similar standards to Imperial Japan) helped establish a pair of legal principles that would shape the future

In today's accountability era, the landscape for pursuing international justice is diverse. Prosecutions can and do take place in four different legal venues: ad hoc tribunals, the International Criminal Court, hybrid tribunals, and foreign courts exercising universal jurisdiction.

Ad Hoc Tribunals. The initial impetus for ad hoc international tribunals was the widespread ethnic violence in Bosnia and other parts of the former Yugoslavia.[29] The combination of several factors—new post–Cold War diplomatic flexibility, another genocide on European soil despite claims of "never again," and shocking media accounts of detention camps that evoked the Holocaust—all prompted the UN Security Council to create the International Criminal Tribunal for the former Yugoslavia (ICTY) in 1993. The next year, the Security Council established the International Criminal Tribunal for Rwanda (ICTR) to prosecute those responsible for instigating and carrying out the country's genocide that claimed eight hundred thousand lives in a one-hundred-day killing spree.

Both tribunals got off to slow starts. During their first few years, the ICTY and ICTR were woefully underfunded, suffered from bureaucratic inertia at the UN, and could not count on states to enforce the arrest warrants they issued. Richard Goldstone, the first prosecutor at both courts, summed up the early years by saying, "We had an empty prison. There was a great deal of frustration" (Hagan 2003, 71). After a few years, however, things started to change. The ICTY indicted a total of 161 persons. Every single indicted war criminal—including high-profile targets such as the Serbian president Slobodan Milosevic and Bosnian Serb leaders Radovan Karadzic and Ratko Mladic—has now been apprehended. The numbers for the ICTR are almost as impressive: of the ninety-five individuals the ICTR indicted, only four remain fugitives today.[30]

The International Criminal Court. The tribunal-building process reached its apex with the Rome Statute, the 1998 treaty creating the International

development of international criminal law. First, Nuremberg advanced the doctrine of individual criminal accountability for international crimes. Until then, only states were held accountable in the international realm (e.g., reparations), but individual accountability means that the specific persons guilty of ordering and carrying out the prohibited violence bear criminal responsibility. Second, Nuremberg represents an early example of extraterritorial jurisdiction for international crimes. The conventional wisdom had long been that each state could treat its subjects however it saw fit without facing outside legal interference, but the Nuremberg Trials challenged that idea for the first time with its prosecutions for crimes against humanity.

29. International tribunals created in response to specific cases of mass atrocities are often labeled ad hoc tribunals.

30. Both tribunals eventually became victims of their own success. Having fulfilled their mandates, the ICTR and the ICTY were shuttered in 2015 and 2017, respectively.

Criminal Court (ICC). As Mark Kersten (2016, 2) puts it, "The pinnacle of post–Cold War thinking on international criminal justice came in 1998, as diplomats gathered in Rome to negotiate the Rome Statute of the ICC and created the first-ever permanent institution of international criminal justice." When the delegates traveled to Rome to discuss setting up a permanent international court in the spring of 1998, however, the project was certainly not guaranteed to succeed. Since the end of World War II, there had been several attempts to keep the "Nuremberg principles" alive by creating a permanent international criminal tribunal, but these attempts always failed.[31] Against this background, the Rome Conference was a shocking success for advocates of global justice.[32] By an overwhelming vote of 120 to 7, the delegates created the ICC, the first permanent tribunal with jurisdiction over international crimes (specifically, war crimes, crimes against humanity, and genocide).[33] The Rome Statute granted the ICC automatic jurisdiction under two conditions: if the accused is a national of a signatory party or if the alleged crime took place in the territory of a signatory party. Additionally, the ICC can prosecute individuals outside the court's standard jurisdiction if the UN Security Council refers a case to the court, giving it potentially global jurisdiction.[34]

Two aspects of the ICC are worth highlighting because they marked important changes to the status quo. First, the ICC is a *permanent* court (it sits in The Hague in the Netherlands). Before the ICC, pursuing international justice meant working through the UN Security Council to attempt to build ad hoc tribunals from scratch for each particular case of atrocities. This, however, was a monumental task since a veto from only one of the Security Council's five permanent members was enough to scuttle plans for a new tribunal. On top of that, even when the permanent five agreed to pursue justice, as they did in Yugoslavia and Rwanda, creating new ad hoc

31. In 1946, the newly formed United Nations tasked a panel with investigating how the Nuremberg principles might be codified into a permanent international criminal court. In 1948, the Genocide Convention contained language about creating an international court that would have jurisdiction over the crime. In 1953, the UN's International Law Commission prepared a draft statute for an international court. In 1990, Caribbean nations discussed the creation of an international court to punish drug traffickers regardless of their nationality or area of operations. All these efforts, however, came to naught.

32. For a personal history of the dramatic twists and turns that occurred during the negotiations, see Scheffer 2012.

33. The Rome Statute stipulated that the ICC would enter into force once at least 60 states ratified the treaty, which occurred in 2002. There are presently 123 state parties to the ICC and another 31 states that signed but have not yet ratified the Rome Statute.

34. The ICC also operates according to a complementarity principle (i.e., the court is designed to complement national courts rather than replace them). This means that the ICC should defer to national courts if they make a genuine effort to prosecute international crimes that occur within their jurisdictions. The ICC is only supposed to step in when necessary.

tribunals typically required wading through tedious diplomatic negotiations (e.g., Bass 2000; Hagan 2003). By creating a permanent standing court, the Rome Statute reduced the legal and political barriers to prosecuting international crimes.

Second, the ICC's reach is potentially *global*.[35] This represents a marked change from previous international tribunals like the ICTY and the ICTR. The mandates of these ad hoc tribunals were limited to specific episodes of violence in specific countries during specific periods of time. For example, the ICTY could only prosecute individuals for crimes connected to the conflict in the former Yugoslavia, and the ICTR's purview only included violence linked to Rwanda's genocide. War criminals outside of these narrowly defined conflicts had nothing to fear from the tribunals. But due to the ICC's wide reach, all oppressors are forced to pay attention. Indeed, "a leader whose country has not signed onto the Rome Statute, and who is committing crimes entirely within his own borders, could still find himself in the court's crosshairs" (Bosco 2014, 55). This is not just a hypothetical—a fact that leaders such as Libya's Muammar Gaddafi and Sudan's Omar Bashir discovered when the ICC issued arrest warrants for them even though both leaders had deliberately opted not to sign the Rome Statute.

Beyond these institutional innovations, the signing of the Rome Statute also had signaling value. Just as domestic law serves as a signal of the broader community's values (e.g., Kahan 1997), the Rome Statute served as an indicator of the international community's preferences. By creating a permanent court designed to punish international crimes wherever they occur, the Rome Statute signaled to leaders worldwide the international community's desire to pursue justice globally.[36] As Hans Corell, the UN's top legal officer boldly proclaimed at an ICC ceremony, "A page in the

35. To be clear, the ICC does not by definition have worldwide jurisdiction, but UN Security Council referrals give the ICC the *potential* to reach every corner of the globe.

36. At this point, it is reasonable to wonder about the complicated relationship between the United States and the ICC. For instance, the Clinton administration vacillated on whether to sign the Rome Statute, and the Bush administration later "unsigned" the treaty and pressured other countries to agree that they would not surrender Americans to the ICC (on these Article 98 agreements, see Kelley 2007). One could argue that American actions weakened the signal that the ICC's creation sent to would-be war criminals. There is some merit to this point, but it does not undermine my general claim. The United States had a fraught relationship with the ICC because of the perception that the American military, given its global presence, could be unfairly targeted. The relationship was *not* troubled because the goals of the United States and the ICC differed. In fact, the United States has frequently collaborated with the ICC despite having never ratified the Rome Statute. As David Kaye (2013) puts it, "Although the United States is not a party to the ICC's charter . . . it is arguably doing as much as, if not more than, member states are doing to bolster the work of the court." More broadly, the United States has for the most part been an ardent supporter of the global accountability project writ large. For example, it was ultimately American "military, diplomatic, and financial might" that allowed the ICTY to succeed (Goldsmith 2003, 93).

history of humankind is being turned."[37] One might argue that leaders have good reasons to dismiss such grandiose pronouncements and even the Rome Conference itself as nothing more than diplomatic "cheap talk."[38] While it may often be appropriate to view diplomacy as cheap talk, it is a mistake to do so in the context of the Rome Conference. The creation of the ICC contained credible information about the international community's preferences because it was a costly signal: it exposed the leaders of all states to potential prosecution. Indeed, the ICC "represents a stunning change of course" since it "takes away from sovereign states the discretion to decide when to initiate prosecutions—a right they have heretofore jealously guarded" (Simmons and Danner 2010, 226). The Rome Conference therefore was an informative sign of the value the international community placed on pursuing global accountability.

Hybrid Tribunals. While the ICC's permanent nature and wide reach may make it seem like the obvious venue for every humanitarian crisis, the international community has continued to build other tribunals even after adopting the Rome Statute. These newer courts generally are considered to be hybrid (or quasi-international) tribunals because they mix elements of international and domestic legal processes as well as personnel. The hybrid tribunal model is attractive to many because it can mitigate problems associated with purely national or international courts. Unlike national courts, concerns of bias and victor's justice are relatively low due to the international community's extensive involvement. Compared to international tribunals, criticisms about imposing justice from the outside, ignoring local context, and holding trials far away from victimized populations are less convincing. Prominent examples of hybrid tribunals include the East Timor Tribunal (ETT), created in 2000 to prosecute crimes linked to that country's referendum on independence from Indonesia; the Special Court for Sierra Leone (SCSL), created in 2002 to prosecute atrocities committed during that country's civil war; the Extraordinary Chambers in the Courts of Cambodia (ECCC), created in 2003 to prosecute members of the Khmer Rouge regime; and the Extraordinary African Chambers (EAC), created in 2013 to prosecute crimes committed during the tenure of Hissène Habré, former dictator of Chad.

Foreign Courts Exercising Universal Jurisdiction. In addition to the various international tribunals, foreign courts that make use of universal

37. Barbara Crossette, "World Court Is Ratified," *New York Times*, April 11, 2002.

38. In international relations scholarship, diplomacy is often dismissed as cheap talk because it is considered a costless signal. Only costly signals, such as mobilizing troops or putting one's reputation on the line, are thought to convey credible information. See, for example, Fearon 1997, 69; and Schelling 1981, 150.

jurisdiction laws are important players in the pursuit of global justice. In a foreign prosecution, one state uses its national courts to try an individual from another state after arresting him within its own territory or extraditing him from another country. Foreign prosecutions typically rely on universal jurisdiction, a legal principle holding that some crimes are so heinous that the perpetrator should be punished even if his national courts do not or cannot prosecute the crime. As a result, universal jurisdiction allows foreign courts to claim jurisdiction over international crimes regardless of where the alleged crime took place or the accused's nationality. Universal jurisdiction therefore is "a power that makes every national court a potential policeman for the global community" (Slaughter 1999, 34). Amnesty International (2011) estimates that 145 states have laws allowing universal jurisdiction, although only a few states attempt to use them frequently.

Using universal jurisdiction laws, foreign courts might be able to act as a backup option in the rare cases where it is possible for war criminals to evade the reach of international tribunals for jurisdictional reasons. For instance, the Syrian leader Bashar Assad is unambiguously responsible for war crimes and crimes against humanity (e.g., Taub 2016). Yet Assad has not been indicted because Syria is not a state party to the ICC. Further, Assad's ally, Russia, is able to use its veto power to block a UN Security Council referral to the ICC or the creation of a new UN-sponsored ad hoc tribunal for Syria. It would be possible, however, for another state to use the principle of universal jurisdiction to apprehend and prosecute Assad if and when he falls from power. In fact, several different European countries have already used universal jurisdiction laws to launch prosecutions for war crimes in Syria committed by both the Assad regime and the Islamic State.[39]

A Global System. Taken together, the ad hoc tribunals, the ICC, the hybrid tribunals, and foreign courts exercising universal jurisdiction make up a relatively new, decentralized, and interrelated system of global accountability.[40] To be clear, there are some notable differences between the specific legal venues. But rather than dwell on legal niceties, it is worth emphasizing that

39. On universal jurisdiction and the Syrian conflict, see Anthony Faiola and Rick Noack, "For Syrian Victims, the Path to Justice Runs through Europe," *Washington Post*, March 2, 2017. The most famous universal jurisdiction case, the arrest of the former Chilean leader Augusto Pinochet in the United Kingdom, will be discussed shortly.

40. Readers may wonder why I do not include domestic prosecutions in my description of the international legal regime. For example, several states—such as Greece, Portugal, and Argentina—have held domestic human rights trials of outgoing autocrats as they transitioned to democracy. While these domestic prosecutions are important in their own right, they do not influence the exile as a golden parachute dynamic described earlier. Indeed, if there were only domestic prosecutions, oppressive leaders would have no reason to fear post-tenure punishment since they could always retire abroad with little risk.

these courts and tribunals share important similarities. Specifically, they provide legal mechanisms to pursue justice across national borders and reject the premise that head-of-state immunity should shield political leaders from prosecution.[41] Stepping back to view the various pieces of this regime as parts of the same system yields an important insight: In today's accountability era, there is almost always a potential path to prosecution via at least one of the legal venues.[42]

FILLING THE ENFORCEMENT GAP

Even when a prosecution is theoretically possible in a strict legal sense, politics can still get in the way of pursuing justice. Indeed, sophisticated legal doctrines on ending impunity and fancy new tribunal buildings will have little real-world effect if advocates of justice cannot get tyrants into court. The entire international legal regime faces a common challenge: enforcement. Though international tribunals and foreign courts can issue arrest warrants, they cannot call upon an international police force to bring oppressive leaders to justice. Instead, enforcement depends on the willingness and ability of states to apprehend and transfer indicted individuals. For this reason, some critics of international criminal law have argued that it will have no effect whatsoever.[43]

Recent events, however, have shown that states often (though certainly not always) provide the muscle to make international tribunals work. The turning point for enforcement goes back to the heady days just after the conclusion of the Rome Conference in 1998. Despite the ICC's obvious importance, there nonetheless was ambiguity at the time about whether

41. International and foreign courts treat head-of-state immunity somewhat differently. When international crimes are committed, international tribunals reject head-of-state immunity entirely, whereas foreign courts generally reject it only for former leaders (i.e., foreign courts still recognize immunity for incumbent leaders). However, as I will discuss later in this chapter, the practical implications of this distinction are minimal since both international and foreign courts can typically only get their hands on ousted leaders.

42. In fact, the jurisdictions of multiple different legal venues sometimes overlap and generate competition, such as when a foreign state exercising universal jurisdiction (Belgium) and an international tribunal (the EAC) both indicted the same leader (Chad's Hissène Habré). In this way, the international justice landscape may represent an example of what Karen Alter and Sophie Meunier (2009) call "international regime complexity."

43. Jack Goldsmith (2003, 92) sums up the nature of the enforcement challenge in his critique of the ICC, although it applies more generally to international criminal law: "The ICC is unlikely to punish the Husseins and future Milosevics of the world because it is unlikely to get its grip on them. . . . It depends completely on member states to arrest and transfer defendants." For evidence that is mostly consistent with the perspective that international tribunals have little real-world effect, see Meernik 2005; Meernik, Nichols, and King 2010; and Mendeloff 2004.

heads of state really would face international punishment.[44] When the Rome Conference ended, no leader had ever been arrested on foreign soil.[45] For international justice—whether it was the ICC, other international tribunals, or foreign courts using universal jurisdiction—to pose an unambiguous threat, it was necessary for states to discard the old norm of head-of-state immunity and start apprehending oppressive rulers. Hence, as recently as the late 1990s, the question remained: Would international justice actually target those at the top? The arrest of the former Chilean leader Augusto Pinochet in the United Kingdom, which occurred just a couple of months after the Rome Conference, provided a striking answer.

Augusto Pinochet came to power in Chile in 1973 when he led a military coup against the incumbent leader Salvador Allende. Pinochet's rule was bloody from the beginning. Shortly after taking power, his security forces rounded up and killed those who were perceived to be loyal to Allende's cause. Pinochet also participated in the notorious Operation Condor, a joint effort of several South American right-wing dictatorships to launch a massive campaign of political assassinations against leftist dissidents throughout the region. A report commissioned by the Chilean government after Pinochet's ouster documents that his regime was responsible for over three thousand political murders and nearly thirty thousand cases of torture.[46] The number of undocumented acts of violence is likely considerably higher. Due to this history, Pinochet became an infamous symbol of modern authoritarianism, known worldwide for his iconic look: "eyes hidden behind dark glasses, face set in a scowl, arms folded defiantly across his chest."[47] In 1990, Pinochet formally stepped down from office and presided over a transition to democracy, at least superficially. In reality, the move toward democracy was quite limited, with Pinochet keeping his position as commander in chief of the army and giving himself the new position of "senator for life," which carried immunity from prosecution within Chile.

On September 22, 1998, Pinochet left Chile for London. There initially was nothing special about the trip. Pinochet had traveled to London, his favorite city, several times since giving up the presidency. On this particular trip, Pinochet planned to have back surgery at a renowned London clinic after doing some sightseeing and meeting with a weapons manufacturer.[48]

44. For an analysis of state cooperation with ICC arrest warrants, see Hillebrecht and Straus 2017.

45. At this point, international tribunals had primarily focused on "small fry" war criminals. For instance, the first individual tried at the ICTY was a relatively unknown Bosnian Serb politician named Dusko Tadic.

46. For a detailed documentation of the human rights violations committed by the Pinochet regime, see Kornbluh 2013.

47. Jonathan Kandell, "Augusto Pinochet, Dictator Who Ruled by Terror in Chile, Dies at 91," *New York Times*, December 11, 2006.

48. For a thorough accounting of Pinochet's time in London, see Munoz 2008, 242–73.

On October 16, shortly after his back surgery, Pinochet—and virtually the entire world—was taken by surprise when British police barged into his hospital room and placed him under arrest. The arrest warrant came from a Spanish judge, Baltasar Garzon, and charged Pinochet with torture, crimes against humanity, genocide, and terrorism.[49] The Spanish court requested Pinochet's arrest and extradition so they could try him under the principle of universal jurisdiction for international crimes committed in Chile. Pinochet's fate was then put in the hands of the British Law Lords, who preside over the country's highest court. The issue at stake was whether or not Pinochet, as a former head of state, possessed immunity that protected him from arrest in Britain. The legal proceedings took a number of twists and turns, but the Law Lords ultimately ruled that head-of-state immunity did not protect former leaders charged with international crimes.[50] In short, the arrest was legitimate.[51]

Pinochet's arrest provided a dramatic change to the status quo for leaders: it marked the first time in the modern international state system that a current or former head of state was arrested in a foreign country for international crimes. In the words of one legal scholar, Pinochet's arrest on British soil was "a milestone in the evolution of international law" that had "no precedent over the previous five centuries" (Rabkin 2007, 104).[52] The Pinochet arrest therefore created a powerful demonstration effect that shattered the expectation of impunity leaders had previously enjoyed. The bombshell decision to apprehend Pinochet became "the moment when the technical lawyers' concern with 'universal jurisdiction' made headlines" (Falk 2004, 97) and "sounded the death knell for head-of-state immunity for international crimes" (Tunks 2002, 659). If Pinochet could be nabbed in London, the rules of the game had changed for other tyrants as well. Hence, international justice moved from a hypothetical to a reality with the Pinochet arrest, causing other leaders to update their punishment expectations.

49. Most of these charges were later dropped as the British Law Lords decided to focus on the torture allegations.

50. The legal reasoning used to reach this conclusion was more complicated than the brief summary provided here. For a detailed analysis of the legal proceedings, see Roht-Arriaza 2005.

51. After seventeen months of legal proceedings and house arrest in Britain, Pinochet's health had deteriorated considerably. Home Secretary Jack Straw eventually decided not to extradite Pinochet to Spain due to his ill health. Instead, Pinochet was allowed to return to Chile, where he died in 2006, facing a slew of domestic prosecutions for human rights violations. While Straw's decision not to extradite Pinochet disappointed human rights activists, it did not diminish the significance of Pinochet's arrest in Britain. The Pinochet case remains important because it demonstrated that former leaders could not count on head-of-state immunity as protection against arrest on foreign soil.

52. The precedent from five centuries ago is a reference to when Cesare Borgia hosted the leaders of the Italian city-states for a diplomatic conference. After the other leaders had assembled at the meeting, Borgia promptly had them arrested and killed.

Of course, this assumes that leaders form expectations on the likelihood of international punishment based on what happens to their fellow heads of state. The assumption that rulers update their beliefs after observing their counterparts is intuitively appealing because they commonly do so across a variety of contexts. For example, the fall of rogue leaders without nuclear weapons taught North Korea's rulers the importance of never giving up their nuclear weapons program. Two former American policymakers who participated in negotiations with North Korea in 2017 concluded that Kim Jong Un would never surrender his nuclear weapons because of how past leaders had fared after doing so: "Citing the fates of Iraq's Saddam Hussein and Libya's Muammar Gaddafi, the North Koreans repeatedly said that their nuclear program is the ultimate life preserver for the regime."[53]

In the context of human rights prosecutions, there is ample evidence that leaders closely follow the fates of their peers. After the Pinochet arrest, the former British prime minister Margaret Thatcher lamented, "Pandora's box . . . has been opened" and "all former heads of government are potentially at risk" (Bronner 2014, 37). In response, leaders around the world "began factoring the [Pinochet] precedent into their travel plans" (Roht-Arriaza 2005, 66). The former Guatemalan leader Efrain Rios Montt stopped traveling abroad only after the Pinochet arrest (Sikkink 2011, 175–76).[54] Laurent Kabila of the Democratic Republic of Congo nearly cancelled a trip to France shortly after the Pinochet arrest and only proceeded once French diplomats gave assurances that Kabila would not meet a similar fate (Munoz 2008, 265). Other evidence is more subtle: leaders who once traveled abroad for medical treatment suddenly began viewing hospitals at home as sufficient (Roht-Arriaza 2005, 66). Overall, Pinochet's arrest served as "a wake-up call to tyrants everywhere" (Brody and Ratner 2000, iv) about the possibility of international punishment.[55]

53. Bruce Klinger and Sue Mi Terry, "We Participated in Talks with North Korea: This Is What We Learned," *Washington Post*, June 22, 2017.

54. As mentioned earlier, Rios Montt was eventually arrested in 2012 and charged with genocide in Guatemala.

55. Evidence of leaders updating their punishment beliefs is not confined to the Pinochet case—it moves in step with the broader justice cascade. After Liberia's Charles Taylor was arrested during his exile in Nigeria and sent to the SCSL in 2006, Libya's Muammar Gaddafi complained, "This means that every head of state could meet a similar fate. It sets a serious precedent." See "How the Mighty are Falling," *Economist*, July 5, 2007. Moreover, there was widespread speculation that Zimbabwe's Robert Mugabe might retire abroad after a controversial rigged election in 2008 triggered protests against his rule. However, Mugabe's aides proclaimed that the dictator had closely watched what happened to his friend Charles Taylor and that Mugabe "would only leave Zimbabwe in a coffin." See Christina Lamb, "Trapped in the Palace," *Spectator*, May 28, 2011. Years before that, as the People Power Revolution threatened to overthrow his regime, the Philippines' Ferdinand Marcos ordered his aides to research the last days of other dictators, including the Shah of Iran and Anastasio

Table 1. Fates of leaders indicted in international criminal tribunals

Leader	*Country*	*Court*	*Outcome*
Slobodan Milosevic	Serbia	ICTY	Arrested (died during trial)
Charles Taylor	Liberia	SCSL	Arrested (50-year sentence)
Johnny Paul Koroma	Sierra Leone	SCSL	Killed
Omar Bashir	Sudan	ICC	Arrested (currently being held in Sudan)
Khieu Samphan	Cambodia	ECCC	Arrested (life sentence)
Laurent Gbagbo	Ivory Coast	ICC	Arrested (acquitted after 7 years in prison)
Muammar Gaddafi	Libya	ICC	Killed
Uhuru Kenyatta	Kenya	ICC	Remains in power
Hissène Habré	Chad	EAC	Arrested (life sentence)

The Pinochet arrest was a watershed event not only in its own right, but also because it helped usher in a new period of accountability for leaders (see table 1). If the arrest of a head a state was simply a one-time event, it might have had a short-lived effect on leaders' punishment expectations. However, this was not the case. The Pinochet arrest made it easier to target other leaders in different legal venues by redefining the realm of the possible for international justice. According to one human rights lawyer, the Pinochet case was "the trigger moment" that galvanized prosecutions against other heads of state.[56] An official at Human Rights Watch explained how Pinochet's arrest immediately reoriented their goals: "We wanted to create other Pinochets. It is hard to overestimate the impact of this case on the international human rights movement."[57] Geoffrey Robertson, who served as a judge at the SCSL, had a similar assessment: "It was not until Augusto Pinochet came to London in 1998 . . . that the idea of ending the impunity of political and military leaders seemed possible."[58]

Almost immediately after Pinochet's arrest, foreign courts were flooded with universal jurisdiction cases attempting to bring other brutal leaders to justice in a so-called Pinochet effect (Roht-Arriaza 2005). Few of these foreign prosecutions progressed, but a variety of different international courts have been more effective. While there were no arrests of heads of state for international crimes before 1998, several leaders who were once considered untouchable have since been apprehended and transferred to international

Somoza (leaders who went into exile) and Ngo Dinh Diem and Salvador Allende (leaders who were killed in office). See Bonner 1987, 384. Thus, there is unambiguous evidence that leaders closely monitor the fates of their peers and update their punishment expectations accordingly.

56. Quoted in Sikkink 2011, 123.

57. Quoted in Hicks 2018, 58.

58. Geoffrey Robertson, "War Crimes: Charles Taylor Now, Bashar Al-Assad Next," *Guardian*, May 30, 2012.

tribunals (as shown in table 1). Hissène Habré, Khieu Samphan, and Charles Taylor will spend the rest of their lives behind bars after successful prosecutions at the EAC, ECCC, and SCSL, respectively. Slobodan Milosevic died of natural causes in the midst of his ICTY trial. Laurent Gbagbo was imprisoned in The Hague for seven years during his ICC trial before he eventually was acquitted. Omar Bashir is currently under arrest in Sudan as he waits to learn whether he will be prosecuted in a domestic court or at the ICC. Other leaders, such as Muammar Gaddafi and Johnny Paul Koroma, were killed while trying to evade the wide reach of international justice. The implication of this trend is clear: If these once-powerful tyrants can end up in the dock, other leaders are vulnerable too.

1998 AS A TRANSITION FROM IMPUNITY TO ACCOUNTABILITY

The international justice landscape has changed dramatically over time. In the tug-of-war between respect for sovereignty and head-of-state immunity on the one hand and globalized accountability on the other, new international justice norms first started to prevail in the late 1990s. Since then, a slew of notoriously oppressive leaders have been arrested and transferred to international courts as part of the justice cascade. This rapid change in the likelihood of international punishment provides a unique opportunity to estimate the effects of international prosecutions of political leaders. Though they do not pursue this empirically, Hunjoon Kim and Kathryn Sikkink (2010, 944) go so far as to speculate that "the international realm may provide some kind of natural experiment . . . because a major change in the key variable, the likelihood of sanction, has occurred in a relatively short period of time."

Building on this insight, I view the watershed events of 1998—the ICC's Rome Conference and Augusto Pinochet's arrest—as the tipping point in the quest for globalized justice.[59] Taken together, these events mark the first time leaders faced a well-developed international legal regime backed up by a realistic threat of arrest on foreign soil. To be clear, the Pinochet arrest and the creation of the ICC are certainly not the only events that "matter" for international justice. The justice cascade is far more complicated than

59. Others agree on the revolutionary nature of these developments. Referring to the joint effect of the Rome Statute and Pinochet's arrest, Yitiha Simbeye (2004, 1) notes, "Two very significant events occurred in 1998 . . . that marked a turning point for international criminal law." David Wippman (1999, 473) similarly sees the late 1990s as "a turning point in international legal history." For Daniele Archibugi and Alice Pease (2018, xii), these changes represent "a new deus ex machina . . . in the political landscape."

that.[60] But this pair of events heralds the beginning of a new period where the risk of international punishment is higher than ever before, making 1998 a convenient date for building the theoretical framework and conducting the empirical analysis. I therefore view 1998 as a transition from an era of impunity to one of accountability.

Exile in an Era of Accountability

My claim that the world shifted toward an era of accountability in the late 1990s does *not* mean that every oppressive leader will now be held accountable.[61] It does mean, however, that today's leaders must at least factor the possibility of someday facing international justice into their decision-making. How does this shift from impunity to accountability affect the exile as a golden parachute dynamic described at the start of the chapter? In short, rulers must now grapple with the fact that arrest on foreign soil is a very real possibility. While the justice cascade does not affect all leaders in the same way, the new risk of international punishment creates incentives for certain leaders to try to hold on to power at home when they otherwise would retire abroad.

THE INCREASINGLY COMPLICATED SEARCH FOR A SAFE HAVEN

There historically has been no shortage of potential safe havens for troubled leaders, but the recent pursuit of international justice complicates the practice of granting asylum to outgoing rulers. In the accountability era, there can be a variety of costs associated with hosting exiled leaders. Due to these costs, the pool of potential host states both willing and able to provide credible long-term protection has shrunk considerably.

To start, hosting an exiled leader can entail *domestic costs*. Given the normative shift away from impunity, many states have decided that it is no longer acceptable for them to shelter leaders with unsavory pasts. In some

60. As explained in the previous discussion, the dedication of norm entrepreneurs, new ideas about universal jurisdiction, a weakening of sovereignty and head-of-state immunity, the creation of other international tribunals, and the attitudes of major powers toward pursuing accountability for past abuses all played a role in creating the justice cascade.

61. Kathryn Sikkink (2011, 12) makes a similar point, noting that the existence of a justice cascade does not mean "that all state officials who have committed crimes will be sent to prison. I simply mean that the norm that state officials should be held accountable for human rights violations has gained new strength and legitimacy." For this reason, it may be more accurate to view the post-1998 period as one of weakened impunity rather than as one of perfect accountability. However, to better distinguish the two periods, I refer to the post-1998 years as the accountability era.

cases, policymakers in third-party states may have internalized international justice norms to the point that they never even consider hosting leaders with blood on their hands. In other cases, policymakers might be tempted to set aside normative concerns, but domestic public opinion prevents them from doing so. Either way, the domestic context for hosting ousted rulers is different than it once was. This is especially true for the countries that Emilie Hafner-Burton (2013) calls "steward states."[62] Steward states not only tend to have good human rights practices at home, but they also care about protecting human rights and pursuing justice abroad. Though they are not the only stewards, powerful Western democracies such as the United States, the United Kingdom, and France are the key players when it comes to pursuing international justice. One may notice that these are some of the very same states that traditionally played an outsized role in facilitating exile for dictators in distress.[63] For instance, so many ousted rulers settled in the south of France that the French Riviera was once dubbed "the haunt of exiled royalty" (Tomes 2003, 280). But it is hard to imagine that a country like France would today choose to shelter some of the despots it has hosted in the past.

Even when it might be politically expedient for policymakers to ignore accountability for atrocity crimes, the domestic costs associated with sheltering ousted leaders can loom large. After Pinochet's arrest, for instance, one of Tony Blair's top advisers noted that it would have been "pretty gut wrenching stuff . . . for most people in this country" if Britain decided to shelter Pinochet rather than arrest him.[64] More recently, with Syria mired in conflict in 2012, one European Union official acknowledged that getting Bashar Assad out of Syria was a worthy goal but also stated that there was "no way we'd have him in our countries."[65] Hence, many states—including several that previously played major roles in crafting golden parachutes—are now reluctant to harbor violent rulers. The decreased supply of third-party states willing to grant sanctuary means that the world is a smaller place for oppressive leaders since many exile options are now off the table.

Yet not all states share a strong commitment to accountability. Some states care little about international criminal law and may still offer to

62. To describe a related concept, Alison Brysk (2009) uses the term "global good Samaritans."

63. Abel Escribà-Folch and Daniel Krcmaric (2017) find that the United States, the United Kingdom, and France were among the five most common exile destinations in the post–World War II era.

64. Rory Carroll, Ian Black, and John Hopper, "Pinochet Decision for Straw," *Guardian*, October 19, 1998.

65. Arshad Mohammed and Matt Spetalnick, "US and Allies Exploring Prospects for Assad Exile," *Reuters*, February 2, 2012.

shelter a longtime ally or a like-minded ideologue. This is a crucial point because an embattled ruler, after all, only needs one foreign state to provide sanctuary. However, despite the initial willingness of some states to roll out the welcome mat, providing long-term sanctuary is increasingly difficult.

A variety of actors that prioritize pursuing justice abroad—steward states, NGOs, international courts, victims' groups, and others—can impose *international costs* on a host state. These international costs, while not necessarily massive, can nonetheless be enough to convince the third-party state that it is better off giving up the ex-leader. Though the former leader's survival is at risk, the stakes are considerably smaller for the host, giving it a low cost tolerance for international pressure. Hence, a host state usually has little reason to continue protecting a former leader if international actors can generate even minimal costs of protection.[66]

There are two types of costs international actors can impose on host states: material and normative. International actors typically impose normative costs by calling attention to practices that others would prefer to keep quiet. In the context of exiled rulers, this means ensuring that despots are not allowed to fade into blissful anonymity during their retirements. Over the past couple of decades, both states and nonstate actors, not to mention the world media, have all played a role in "naming and shaming" states that harbor oppressive rulers.[67] Many view this as an effective tactic. As one NGO report put it, "Human rights advocates are adept at leveraging shame to press for change. Once exposed, governments . . . can become so ashamed to be in the spotlight they quickly switch tactics to avoid further criticism" (Kumar 2017, 16). Even if the targets of these naming and shaming campaigns care little about human rights and do not truly "feel the shame," they may nonetheless respond because they worry about their reputation. Indeed, naming and shaming may be especially effective when international actors can advertise the fact that states are failing to live up to their legal commitments. All 123 state parties to the Rome Statute, for example, have a legal obligation to arrest indicted

66. Michael Gilligan (2006) develops a formal model of how one specific international tribunal, the ICC, might shape the decision calculus of leaders. He explicitly rejects the idea that the ICC will create perverse incentives for brutal leaders, arguing that "the reign of atrocity-committing dictators will not be prolonged" (Gilligan 2006, 937). Since Gilligan's model shares some similarities with my theory, it is worth examining why we reach different conclusions. In short, Gilligan's prediction hinges on the assumption that it is costless for third-party states to shelter leaders who flee into exile. Since the ICC has no independent enforcement powers, this may be a reasonable assumption if the ICC is viewed in isolation. However, if we are interested in the broader justice cascade, it is clear that a host of international actors can generate costs for the third parties that shelter brutal rulers.

67. On naming and shaming in international politics, see Hafner-Burton 2008; Keck and Sikkink 1998; Krain 2012; and Lebovic and Voeten 2006.

criminals whenever possible. Invoking the ICC's moral authority, the prosecutor Luis Moreno-Ocampo spent a great amount of effort reminding states of their duty to arrest war criminals on their soil.[68] Hence, states may acquiesce to this sort of pressure because they want to preserve a reputation for keeping international commitments.[69]

International actors can also impose material costs on the host state if normative costs are not sufficient to alter the host's decision to protect an exiled leader.[70] Unlike normative costs, which several different actors can impose, powerful steward states are the primary actors when it comes to imposing material costs because a high coercive capacity is required. For instance, stewards can impose economic sanctions or withdraw diplomatic support from states that provide safe havens. Moreover, there is a flip side to such coercive measures: positive inducements. Steward states can get host states to comply with their wishes by offering "carrots" (or promising to remove existing punishments). In one case discussed later in the book, the prospect of an official White House visit appears to have played a decisive role in convincing the leader of one host state to stop protecting another deposed ruler. While some of these costs may seem relatively minor, recall that much less is at stake for the host state than for the exiled leader, so even small costs can be enough to change a host's calculus about continuing to protect an ousted despot.

A pair of examples illustrates how international pressure on host states can undermine a leader's safety in exile. Let us start by considering the case of Chad's Hissène Habré. From 1982 to 1990, Habré presided over a brutal regime that killed some forty thousand Chadians and engaged in a host of other human rights abuses. When rebels marched on Chad's capital in 1990, Habré fled into exile in Dakar, Senegal. Habré used his ill-gotten wealth to "create a luxurious web of security in Dakar: bribes for politicians, religious leaders, journalists, and police—and two mansions" (Bronner 2014, 36). Comfortably ensconced in Senegal, Habré lived the stereotypical gilded exile for many years and "that is probably the way it would have remained had it not been for the Pinochet case" (Brody 2008). Indeed, everything changed for Habré after Pinochet's arrest in 1998.[71] Looking to build on

68. Luis Moreno-Ocampo explained this approach by noting that the diplomatic community "is crucial for me, because basically, at the end of the day, the impact of my cases will be defined by them, not by me" (Moreno-Ocampo 2010).

69. On the importance of gaining a reputation for keeping commitments in international relations, see Tomz 2012.

70. On coercive diplomacy, see Art and Cronin 2003.

71. The Habré case illustrates an important facet of the justice cascade: even leaders who committed atrocities exclusively during the impunity era can have their violent pasts come back to haunt them in the accountability era.

new momentum for international justice, many in the human rights community decided to target Habré as "the next Pinochet" (Brody 2015, 210).

The legal case against Habré took a number of strange turns, but there was one constant in the quest to bring Habré to justice: increasing the costs on Senegal for sheltering the former Chadian strongman.[72] Working in concert with NGOs such as Amnesty International and Human Rights Watch, several of Habré's surviving former victims personally filed cases against Habré in Senegal's courts, a move that made headlines around the world and cast Habré as an "African Pinochet" in the *New York Times*.[73] Hounded by unwanted attention for sheltering Habré, the Senegalese authorities briefly put him under house arrest in Dakar in 2000, although they soon reversed course and made it clear they had no intention of prosecuting Habré. Over the next decade, international pressure on Senegal slowly escalated. Belgium invoked universal jurisdiction to indict Habré, and the International Court of Justice demanded that Senegal either prosecute Habré or extradite him to a country that would.[74] The United States and France publicly supported prosecuting Habré, a stunning change in political alignment given that they had been some of Habré's staunchest supporters during his time in power.[75] Archbishop Desmond Tutu, a Nobel Peace Prize–winner and respected moral authority throughout much of Africa, lambasted Senegal for the "interminable political and legal soap opera" surrounding its continued protection of Habré.[76] Even the African Union, typically wary of international justice, called on Senegal to ensure that Habré face trial. In 2012, Senegal elected a new president, Macky Sall, who decided it was in Senegal's interests to put an end to the Habré affair. In 2013, Senegal arrested Habré so that he could be tried at the Extraordinary African Chambers (EAC), a hybrid court sponsored by the African Union and located in Senegal. After Habré was sentenced to life in prison, one of his former victims aptly captured the implication for other leaders:

72. For a thorough accounting of the attempts to prosecute Habré, as well as his ensuing trial at the EAC, see Hicks 2018.

73. "An African Pinochet," *New York Times*, February 11, 2000.

74. See the *Belgium v. Senegal* case at the International Court of Justice.

75. Secretary of State John Kerry acknowledged America's about-face in its approach toward Habré: "As a country committed to respect for human rights and the pursuit of justice, this is also an opportunity for the United States to reflect on, and learn from, our own connection with past events in Chad. I strongly commend the Senegalese Government, the Chadian Government, and the African Union for creating the Extraordinary African Chambers that allowed for a fair and balanced trial. Let this be a message to other perpetrators of mass atrocities, even those at the highest levels and including former heads of state, that such actions will not be tolerated and they will be brought to justice. (Press Statement by Secretary of State John Kerry, May 30, 2016, available at https://2009-2017.state.gov/secretary/remarks/2016/05/257811.htm)

76. Souleymane Guengueng, "I've Waited Decades to Write These Words," *CNN News*, August 20, 2015.

"This shows that no matter who the person is, if he commits a crime and runs away, no matter where he is hiding, we . . . can still go for him and bring him to face justice."[77]

The saga of Liberia's Charles Taylor, a case that is analyzed in detail in chapter 3, provides another example. During the civil war in Liberia and neighboring Sierra Leone—where Taylor's forces committed widespread atrocities—Taylor agreed to give up power in 2003 in return for a supposedly safe exile in Nigeria. The Nigerian president Olusegun Obasanjo even explicitly announced that he would not turn Taylor over to an international court. Nigeria, however, soon faced a torrent of pressure from international actors interested in bringing Taylor to justice (e.g., Alter 2014; Tejan-Cole 2009). Human rights groups raised awareness of Taylor's brutality, and powerful Western states demanded that Nigeria hand him over to the UN-sponsored Special Court for Sierra Leone (SCSL). Not surprisingly, the Nigerian government eventually decided sheltering Taylor was not worth the cost. It caved to international pressure in 2006 and extradited Taylor to the SCSL, which sentenced Taylor to fifty years in prison for his role in perpetrating war crimes and crimes against humanity.

The costs associated with sheltering exiled rulers in the accountability era raise profound implications for how leaders view the exile option. Even if a friendly government offers sanctuary, a beleaguered leader may have good reasons to doubt that his potential protector will shelter him over the long haul if it will soon face a barrage of threats or take a major reputational hit for harboring a war criminal. If a leader thinks a third-party state will not be able to withstand international pressure on his behalf, an offer of protection abroad is no longer credible. The pursuit of international justice can therefore reduce the attractiveness of the exile option.

The reach of international justice, however, has its limits. The strategic environment for holding a leader accountable is fundamentally different when the leader is still in office. I make no assumption that foreign states will dislodge oppressive leaders from power and bring them to justice.[78] Indeed, enforcing an arrest warrant against a sitting head of state is an extraordinarily difficult task. Though international actors can issue threats, enact sanctions, and publicly shame current leaders for their abuses, such efforts are unlikely to succeed. Sitting heads of state are highly resolved to

77. Jaime Yaya Barry and Dionne Searcey, "Hissène Habré, Ex-Ruler of Chad, Loses War Crimes Appeal," *New York Times*, April 27, 2017.

78. Such an assumption would be questionable. Even liberal states that care deeply about international law and human rights have generally been unwilling to risk the lives of their own soldiers in military interventions for the sake of bringing war criminals to justice (Bass 2000). Some even view pursuing international justice *after* atrocities as an alternative to military intervention to stop *ongoing* atrocities (K. Anderson 2009).

resist international pressure because their own survival is at risk. Furthermore, current leaders are exceedingly capable since they wield tremendous influence over the state's policies and resources, including having the nation's armed forces at their disposal. Hence, even infamous human rights violators can usually remain safe behind their own borders as long as they remain in power.[79]

As an example, consider the many international attempts to bring Sudan's Omar Bashir to justice. The ICC issued an arrest warrant for Bashir in 2009 for war crimes and crimes against humanity committed in the Darfur region of Sudan. Bashir was not only charged with presiding over a massive campaign of civilian killing but also with using rape as a weapon of war and employing torture regularly. Given this litany of atrocities, international actors tried to put pressure on Bashir. The United States and its allies imposed economic sanctions, the UN sent a peacekeeping force to Darfur, and NGOs raised awareness with popular campaigns such as "Save Darfur." These efforts bore no fruit since Bashir unsurprisingly did not surrender himself to The Hague. Further, Bashir kept a highly curtailed travel schedule for a head of state, only traveling to sympathetic countries and never staying long enough to allow international pressure for an arrest to build.[80] Given this, I predicted the following in an earlier article: "Absent the emergence of a domestic challenger who unseats Bashir, the prospects for justice are bleak" (Krcmaric 2018a, 489). Subsequent events in Sudan have borne out this prediction. A decade of attempts to impose international justice on Bashir failed, but a domestic revolution toppled his regime

79. The threat of international prosecution might also increase the benefits of coming into power in the first place. In a strange example, the ICC indicted two bitter political rivals, Uhuru Kenyatta and William Ruto, for their role in fomenting mass electoral violence in Kenya in 2007. To the surprise of many, Kenyatta and Ruto responded by joining forces, with Ruto agreeing to serve as Kenyatta's running mate for the 2013 presidential election. The two former enemies went on to win the election and, once in office, used the power of the state apparatus to undermine the ICC investigation. The ICC eventually dropped the investigation because it was impossible to collect evidence in Kenya. See Kevin Sieff, "ICC Drops Charges against Kenyan President after Probe into Violence," *Washington Post*, December 5, 2014.

80. In 2015, however, Bashir miscalculated and was nearly arrested when visiting South Africa, an ICC member, for an African Union summit. There was a great deal of confusion over Bashir's visit to South Africa. The country's ruling party, the African National Congress, stated that its decision to grant visiting heads of state immunity took priority over its obligation to the ICC. By contrast, South Africa's High Court dramatically announced during Bashir's visit that South Africa had a legal duty to arrest and extradite Bashir to The Hague. Amid this turmoil, Bashir cut his visit short and made a hasty return to Sudan on his presidential jet. See Norimitsu Onishi, "Omar al-Bashir, Leaving South Africa, Eludes Arrest Again," *New York Times*, June 15, 2015. While Bashir ultimately escaped arrest, this example underscores the relatively long reach of international justice in the accountability era. It is hard to imagine a leader being sufficiently afraid of arrest to flee an international summit for the safety of his own state's borders during the impunity era.

in 2019. Although Bashir's precise fate remains uncertain—he is under arrest in Sudan awaiting a transfer to the ICC at the time of this writing—his ouster was a necessary condition for any potential prosecution.

Overall, there is a timing issue with regard to international punishment. As a ruler's political fortunes change, so too does the possibility of pursuing international justice. Leaders often are vulnerable to prosecution after fleeing abroad, but they typically are safe as long as they hold onto power. As a result, leaders who fear international arrest will have incentives to entrench in office as a way to forestall punishment.

THE ROLE OF LEADER CULPABILITY

The previous discussion addressed the issue of *when* leaders are vulnerable to international punishment and drew a distinction between apprehending current and former leaders. There is also variation in *who* fears international justice. Whether a leader has reason to worry about international arrest upon going into exile depends on the leader's culpability.

Leader culpability refers to whether leaders have committed atrocities that could expose them to international prosecution.[81] Culpable leaders are those who are responsible for atrocity crimes, whereas nonculpable leaders are those who are not. A technical definition of leader culpability is provided in the next chapter, but I briefly describe leader culpability as a concept here. To begin, when I say culpable leaders are those who "commit" atrocities, I do not necessarily mean that leaders personally carry out atrocity crimes. I simply mean that culpable leaders preside over regimes that engage in horrendous abuses. As Antonio Cassese (2008, 246) notes in his discussion of holding state officials accountable under international criminal law, "Most of the time they do not perpetrate crimes directly. They order, plan, instigate, organize, aid and abet, or culpably tolerate or acquiesce, or willingly or negligently fail to prevent or punish international crimes." Thus, even if leaders never personally engage in violence, they can nonetheless be held accountable for the conduct of their state security forces.

It is also worth emphasizing that culpability (or the absence of it) is not meant to imply any sort of normative judgment. It is merely an indicator of a leader's past behavior. One might assume that nonculpable leaders are by definition "good" leaders, but this would be a mistake. Nonculpable leaders are not necessarily exemplary rulers with perfectly clean hands (although some are, of course). A leader's status as nonculpable simply means that

81. Some use the terms "leader culpability" (Croco 2015) and "leader responsibility" (Prorok 2016) to refer to whether specific leaders initiated (rather than inherited) wars. To be clear, these studies use a very different notion of culpability than the one employed here.

the leader is not responsible for the type of atrocity crimes that would potentially lead to an international prosecution. This rather high bar for leader culpability is appropriate since international and foreign courts only have jurisdiction over an extremely limited set of crimes. Indeed, many norms about respecting human rights fall beyond their scope. Article 5 of the Rome Statute, for instance, limits the ICC's jurisdiction to war crimes, crimes against humanity, and genocide, which it deems "the most serious crimes of international concern." Similarly, the idea behind foreign courts exercising universal jurisdiction is that some crimes are so heinous that they affect the entire international community, thereby giving every state the right to prosecute. This means that states are only supposed to exercise universal jurisdiction over a set of "very limited—and very awful—crimes" (Roht-Arriaza 2005, 11). Only the most brutal leaders, which I later define as those responsible for killing large numbers of civilians, should therefore be viewed as culpable.

How does leader culpability shape patterns of exile? During the impunity era, leader culpability had no effect whatsoever on a leader's willingness to go into exile because all leaders, regardless of how they behaved while in power, had nothing to fear from international justice. Some of the previous examples illustrate this point. Juan Peron, a nonculpable leader whose regime never engaged in mass atrocities, fled for the safety of exile when Argentina's conservative Catholics and parts of the military turned against him. Idi Amin, a culpable leader who presided over the killing of some three hundred thousand Ugandans, similarly was able to retire to a secure exile in Saudi Arabia. Thus, exile used to be an attractive exit strategy for all leaders—regardless of their culpability—when the threat of domestic punishment became sufficiently high.

In the accountability era, however, leader culpability matters. In sharp contrast to past oppressive rulers who seemingly went into exile at the first sign of trouble, today's culpable leaders tend to hunker down in office because they have good reason to anticipate international arrest if they go into exile. A thought experiment proposed by Stephen Krasner, an academic who also worked in the policy world, aptly captures this changing standard of accountability for culpable leaders. In a 2003 interview, Krasner suggested a hypothetical involving Idi Amin: "When you think about justice and especially Idi Amin, who killed a lot of people, the question is this: was it better to offer him sanctuary in Saudi Arabia, or would it have been better to say to him when he was still in power, 'We are going to prosecute you'? The reaction of any autocratic ruler under those circumstances would be to hold on to power as long as he possibly can. . . . Threatening these actors with prosecution may make it more difficult to get rid of them" (Krasner 2003). This concern is not confined to the realm of hypothetical thought experiments. Today's culpable leaders, as the case studies and statistical analyses in this book will show, clearly worry about international arrest should they go into exile. Getting away with political mass murder is not as easy as it once was.

The justice cascade undermines the possibility of a pleasant exile for culpable leaders only. Nonculpable leaders—those who do not employ mass violence against civilians—still can safely retire abroad if they are overthrown. Hence, when people mobilize against a leader's regime due to cronyism, the dismantling of term limits, or rapidly declining popularity, exile could very well be the best option available for a nonculpable leader. Even though nonculpable leaders may have numerous flaws and shortcomings, exile remains a viable option for the "merely" corrupt or unpopular because the threat of international arrest is low. As I mentioned earlier, the jurisdiction of international and foreign courts is limited to only the gravest international crimes, and there will be little international pressure on third-party states that provide safe haven to nonculpable leaders. Consequently, even in the accountability era, nonculpable leaders often calculate that a retirement abroad is preferable to remaining at home and facing the wrath of their own people.

Bolivia's Evo Morales provides one example. Morales, who could take credit for reducing inequality and increasing indigenous representation, was popular during his early years in office. But he eventually fell from grace due to his creeping authoritarianism. The final straw for many Bolivians was a rigged election in 2019, which triggered mass protests and strikes that paralyzed the country. After enraged crowds attacked government buildings and the military largely sided with the protestors, the Morales regime was on the verge of collapse. As a nonculpable leader who did not commit atrocity crimes during Bolivia's crisis, Morales opted to look for an escape route and ultimately accepted an offer of safe haven from Mexico.[82] Burkina Faso's Blaise Compaoré, a leader discussed in detail in chapter 5, provides another example. In 2014, Compaoré announced plans to modify the country's constitution to allow himself yet another term, which provoked an immense backlash in Burkina Faso. Compaoré, who held power for twenty-seven years via shrewd co-option rather than brute force, fled for the safety of the Ivory Coast once protestors set fire to the parliament building and marched on his presidential palace.

To sum up, the justice cascade does not affect all leaders in the same way. The possibility of facing international justice in the accountability era makes the attractiveness of the exile option—and consequently whether a leader has incentives to step down or cling to power—conditional on the leader's culpability.

82. Kirk Semple and Elisabeth Malkin, "Mexico, a Haven for Leftists in Exile, Provides Evo Morales with a Landing Spot," *New York Times*, November 12, 2019.

COMPARING DOMESTIC AND INTERNATIONAL PUNISHMENT

An international prosecution is one notable type of punishment that leaders hope to avoid—but it is not the only one. How does the threat of international punishment compare to that of domestic punishment? And what are the implications for leader decision-making?

The literature on the economics of crime provides a starting point for thinking about this issue. The Nobel Prize–winner Gary Becker provided the seminal rationalist model of domestic crime and punishment. In Becker's (1968) framework, crime is essentially the result of individuals making expected value calculations. Since people are assumed to want to avoid punishment, crime is expected to decrease as the likelihood and/or severity of criminal punishment increases. Within this framework, my argument could be restated in the following terms: The justice cascade has increased both the likelihood and severity of international punishment for culpable leaders who go into exile.

Yet it must be acknowledged that the maximum severity of international punishment remains less than that of domestic punishment. International tribunals cannot impose the death penalty on convicted war criminals (life imprisonment is the harshest sentence possible). Domestic punishment, however, might involve a gruesome death. Even if a leader's domestic punishment turns out to be imprisonment rather than death, there are reasons to believe domestic prosecution could be a worse fate than international prosecution. International tribunals at least provide decent prison facilities, guarantee due process, and respect the rights of the accused.[83] In 2019, for instance, ICC judges acquitted the Ivory Coast's Laurent Gbagbo of crimes against humanity charges after deciding that the ICC's prosecution failed to prove its case beyond a reasonable doubt. By contrast, an ex-leader facing a domestic prosecution has to worry about the possibility of a show trial and inhumane prison conditions. This potential discrepancy in the severity of punishment has led some to conclude that the international legal regime will have little, if any, effect since the punishments it doles out are not as harsh at the preexisting alternative of domestic punishment (e.g., Ku and Nzelibe 2006).

Many criminologists, however, push back against this logic. A growing consensus in the field suggests that the severity of punishment matters little for how individuals make decisions compared to the likelihood of

83. At times, international tribunals have come under fire for providing prison facilities deemed too good. A report on the conditions at Scheveningen prison in the Netherlands, which has housed many ICTY and ICC detainees, noted that some prisoners and guards jokingly call it the "Hague Hilton" due to its impressive facilities. See Anna Holligan, "Scheveningen Prison," *BBC News*, May 16, 2012.

apprehension. Mark Kleiman (2009, 74) even asserts that it is now a "maxim of criminology that certainty of punishment is more important than severity." In the US context, for example, there is little evidence to suggest the death penalty reduces the murder rate any more than life imprisonment (Donohue and Wolfers 2005). On the flip side, across a wide variety of issue areas ranging from tax evasion to sexual assault to substance abuse, scholars have found that raising the certainty of facing some sort of punishment—even a relatively weak one—can alter behavior (e.g., Kleiman 2009; Nagin 1998). These results suggest that many individuals make decisions in ways that are not perfectly captured in Becker's model, an insight that might shed light on how leaders view domestic versus international punishment. For heads of state, a unique group of individuals who tend to care profoundly about status and prestige (e.g., Renshon 2017), the prospect of arrest may simply be seen as unacceptable. The thought of ending up in the jail cell of an international tribunal might be so unappealing that leaders are willing to take big risks to avoid it—even if international arrest is a less severe punishment than the domestic alternative.

Ultimately, I do not seek to resolve the debate on certainty versus severity, nor is doing so necessary. The key point of this book is that the threat of domestic punishment has remained relatively constant over time, whereas the threat of international punishment has risen dramatically.[84] Exile used to offer a golden parachute that virtually guaranteed leaders would not face *any* punishment in retirement. But in today's accountability era, exile no longer ensures that culpable leaders will have a secure exit. Embattled culpable leaders therefore may be tempted to try to avoid punishment altogether by digging in their heels.

To be clear, the comparison of domestic and international punishment also suggests that at least some culpable leaders in the accountability era could still prefer retiring abroad to staying at home. If a leader is nearly certain that he will soon be killed at home, for instance, the leader might prefer going into exile even though doing so clearly risks future arrest and prosecution.[85] In this scenario, exile is a bad option—but it might be the

84. One could argue that the justice cascade might increase the threat of domestic punishment as well. One example is the ICTY's indictment of Slobodan Milosevic, which complicated his domestic retirement in Serbia and eventually contributed to his apprehension and transfer to The Hague. In general, though, the justice cascade has only had a marginal influence on the threat of domestic punishment because it was already high for embattled leaders (as described at the start of this chapter, that is usually why leaders consider exile in the first place). For this reason, I primarily focus on how the justice cascade has altered the prospects for international punishment.

85. In another (admittedly extreme) variant of this scenario, a leader might conceivably turn himself over to an international tribunal to avoid suffering an even worse fate at home. While no head of state has ever pursed this strategy, there is at least one precedent involving a rebel leader. Bosco Ntaganda, a Congolese warlord wanted by the ICC, surprised much of

"least bad" option on the table. Overall, though, the rate of exile for culpable leaders should be lower in the accountability era.

Taken together, the preceding discussions—concerning the shift from impunity toward accountability, the timing of international arrests, the role of leader culpability, and the comparison of domestic and international punishment—suggest the following hypothesis:

> ***Exile Hypothesis:*** *A leader's decision to flee into exile is conditional on expectations of post-tenure international punishment. Culpable leaders are significantly less likely to go into exile than nonculpable leaders in the post-1998 accountability era only.*

WHAT ABOUT . . . ?

My main prediction about patterns of exile involves over-time variation: the landscape for prosecuting heads of state has changed dramatically since the late 1990s, making culpable leaders less likely to go into exile. Beyond culpability for atrocity crimes, however, there are a number of other sources of cross-case variation that might plausibly influence each leader's susceptibility to international punishment. While these other factors are not a core part of my theoretical framework, exploring them can add nuance to the argument. Therefore, in chapter 3, I will investigate several different factors that might shape punishment expectations and thus each leader's decision to go into exile. These additional tests will allow me to answer the following questions, among others: Are leaders with major power allies still able to retire abroad regardless of their culpability? Do the leaders of poor, weak, and isolated countries seem most concerned about international punishment? Are African leaders, a group against which some believe the international legal regime is biased, particularly reluctant to go into exile? By exploring these additional factors in the next chapter, I will be able to paint a richer picture of how international justice influences the exile option without undermining the relatively parsimonious theory presented here.

Exit Options and Leader Behavior While in Power

The possibility of facing post-tenure punishment casts a long shadow over the decision calculus of leaders while they are still in office. Rulers know there is a chance—even if it seems remote at the time—that they

the world in 2013 when he showed up at the American embassy in Rwanda and asked to be transferred to The Hague. While Ntaganda's motives remain somewhat murky, many speculate that he surrendered himself to the ICC because he was convinced that continuing to remain at large would virtually guarantee an untimely death.

could be deposed at some point in the future. If and when that day comes, leaders would prefer to have a secure exile option on the table. Since culpable leaders in the accountability era have limited exit options, today's leaders face a unique set of incentives during their time in power. Specifically, by making the availability of a safe exile conditional on how a leader behaves, the justice cascade generates two opposing effects: it both prolongs civil wars and deters mass atrocities.

CIVIL WAR DURATION

During the impunity era, leaders generally had little reason to risk it all on the battlefield. In a typical scenario, a leader such as Mengistu Haile Mariam or Idi Amin would flee abroad for the safety of exile rather than make a final, desperate stand once rebel forces came within reach of the country's capital city. In other cases, a leader like Ferdinand Marcos or Juan Peron would give up power even more easily and flee abroad during a conflict that likely could have been won if the leader had stayed at home to fight.

But since exile is no longer the golden parachute it once was, today's culpable rulers can find themselves trapped in the palace. An international retirement is now perilous because leaders risk landing in the jail cell of an international tribunal. A domestic retirement continues to be fraught with danger because leaders are vulnerable to retribution from their newly empowered adversaries. In other words, punishment—whether at the hands of domestic or international actors—is likely for culpable leaders upon losing power. There is, however, one option that at least offers the possibility of avoiding punishment entirely: Leaders can keep fighting. In fact, culpable leaders in the accountability era have a strong motive to prolong civil wars—even if the prospects for victory are relatively slim—and hope to turn the tide of the conflict. Thus, by reducing the viability of exile as a retirement option, the justice cascade encourages culpable leaders to double down on the battlefield.

This is, of course, a risky option that could end badly for the leader. But if the leader is confident that giving up power will result in severe punishment, he has little to lose by continuing to fight. At a minimum, continuing the war forestalls punishment. In the best-case scenario (from the leader's perspective), it offers a chance to evade punishment altogether if the leader's forces are able to reassert control over the country. It is this tantalizing possibility—that an embattled ruler might turn the war around, eventually win, and thus avoid punishment—which gives today's culpable leaders an incentive to risk a fight to the bitter end. Therefore, the sort of last stands that leaders traditionally tended to avoid by fleeing into exile should be increasingly common for culpable leaders in the accountability era.

For this strategy to be attractive to culpable leaders, doubling down on the battlefield must work at least some of the time. It would be irrational for leaders to take this gamble if it consistently failed (as it did with Muammar Gaddafi, for example). The case of the Syrian leader Bashar Assad, however, shows that risking it all on the battlefield can pay off for the leader.

The Syrian civil war steadily worsened during 2012 for Assad, an unambiguously culpable leader whose regime has violated virtually every law of war. Assad suffered a continuous string of military defections, and rebels killed several of his most trusted advisers when they bombed an intelligence agency building in Damascus.[86] Assad's prospects became so poor that the United States reached out to Israel and Russia to coordinate a response for the complete collapse of the Syrian government.[87] By December 2012, rebel fighters had approached Damascus, and the end appeared in sight for Assad. Given the high likelihood of the Assad regime falling and of Assad personally facing a grisly fate at the hands of his domestic enemies, many expected the besieged leader to flee into exile.[88] Consistent with my argument, however, Assad decided to take his chances on the battlefield, a strategy that has succeeded thus far.[89] Buoyed by military support from Russia, Iran, and Hezbollah, Assad reclaimed control of many of the strategically important suburbs surrounding Damascus and decimated most of the opposition groups who had once challenged him. In other words, doubling down on the war paid off for Assad since the threat to his personal safety is minimal compared to late 2012. As one assessment of Assad's strategy concluded: "Although he remains a pariah to the West . . . even his opponents acknowledge that he has navigated his way out of the immediate threats to his rule. . . . Mr. Assad has succeeded in muddling through, without being held accountable."[90]

If my argument that international justice can exacerbate civil conflict is correct, it begs a question: Why does the international community not simply refrain from prosecuting culpable leaders who are fighting for survival? One might expect international actors, such as the tribunals that issue arrest warrants and the powerful states that provide enforcement, to work their way out of the problematic situation described above by

86. As one analyst described the bomb attack, "It was at the heart of the government's nexus of control. If the regime had a center, that was it." See Neil MacFarquhar, "Syrian Rebels Land Deadly Blow to Assad's Inner Circle," *New York Times*, July 18, 2012.

87. Helene Cooper, "Washington Begins to Plan for Collapse of Syrian Government," *New York Times*, July 18, 2012.

88. Andrew E. Kramer, "In Russia, Exile in Comfort for Leaders Like Assad," *New York Times*, December 28, 2012.

89. Speculating about an ongoing conflict is a risky endeavor. To be clear, my discussion of Assad's gamble paying off applies only to the early stages of the Syrian civil war described here. It would be an overstatement to claim Assad "won" since the Syrian conflict is still ongoing in 2020, but his turnaround has been striking.

90. Ben Hubbard, "His Grip Still Secure, Bashar al-Assad Smiles as Syria Burns," *New York Times*, September 17, 2016.

pledging not to punish culpable leaders who agree to step down without a fight to the end. After all, the international community puts a high priority on ending civil wars. Recall that part of the reason why exile was so common in the past was that the international community explicitly employed it as a conflict management tool to ease violent leaders out of power with soft landings. Could today's policymakers pursue a similar strategy of sacrificing the pursuit of justice for the sake of conflict resolution once a civil war becomes too deadly?

It turns out that this sort of thinking is pervasive. Even in the accountability era, it is not uncommon for third-party states to dangle the possibility of peace-for-exile deals with culpable leaders. The case of Muammar Gaddafi during Libya's 2011 revolution, discussed in detail in chapter 4, provides one example. The international community clearly sought to bring Gaddafi to justice, even referring the Libyan conflict to the ICC. But at the same time, several states discussed coaxing Gaddafi out of office with the promise of a safe exile. According to one commentator, "The tough talk of relentless pressure aimed to oust the unpredictable and brutal despot who has ruled Libya for 41 years didn't entirely drown out hints of possible exile and the possibility of avoiding a war crimes trial."[91] Thus, the problem for culpable leaders in the accountability era is not necessarily a lack of exile offers (although this can happen). Instead, the larger issue appears to be that today's culpable leaders do not trust offers of foreign protection in the same way their peers previously did. Why?

In short, there is a time inconsistency problem when it comes to the leader's fate. The international community might prefer a peaceful transition over pursuing international justice while the leader is still wreaking havoc in his home country. As a result, exile offers may emerge and even states typically committed to international justice might seem to support a peace-for-exile deal. However, once the leader is out of power and no longer presents a threat to his own people, international actors will be tempted to renege on the deal. The very same actors who helped arrange the safe haven might now prefer pursuing justice over letting the culpable leader get off scot-free in a quiet retirement. This presents a problem from the leader's perspective: regardless of any promises made during a crisis, the leader cannot be sure that the long arm of the law will not catch up to him later. Even if, for instance, a culpable leader does not face an indictment at the time of the crisis, international tribunals and foreign courts can issue arrest warrants after the leader steps down. Likewise, powerful states can exert pressure on any third-party state that might shelter the leader. Anticipating

91. Paul Koring, "London Summit Doesn't Rule Out Exile For Gaddafi," *Globe and Mail*, March 29, 2011.

this, culpable leaders in the accountability era will often prefer trying to win the war at home over going into retirement abroad.

To see this dynamic at play, let us continue with the Bashar Assad example. Given the extraordinarily heavy toll of the Syrian civil war, international actors desperately wanted to get Assad out of Syria.[92] Britain's David Cameron, for example, floated the possibility of a golden parachute for Assad by stating that he was willing to do "anything, anything, to get that man out of the country and to have a safe transition in Syria."[93] For its part, the Arab League worked behind the scenes to find an exile destination for Assad.[94] Yet, consistent with my argument, a good exile option never emerged. The problem was finding a third party that was both willing to take Assad and able to provide him with credible long-term protection. When Russia, Assad's most powerful ally, made it clear that it had no desire to host Assad, the only remaining exile options were relatively weak countries in the region.[95] This was not an attractive option for Assad, who had good reason to anticipate a forceful push for justice if he ever left office. Though Western powers certainly wanted Assad to give up power without a bloody fight to the finish, it was also obvious that they hoped to prosecute Assad *after he was out of power*. For instance, Cameron qualified his golden parachute proposal by stating, "Of course I would favor [Assad] facing the full force of international law and justice for what he's done."[96] Similarly, the United States seemed to tacitly approve of a peace-for-exile deal in the region, but senior officials also warned, "No one is getting a free pass here. . . . He has to go, but there are issues of accountability that have to be addressed."[97] Moreover, some officials even spoke as if a trial for Assad was

92. Though estimating casualties from the conflict is a difficult task—especially after the UN gave up counting Syria's dead in 2014—independent observers put the death toll near five hundred thousand, making it the deadliest conflict of the twenty-first century (Taub 2016, 36). On top of that, the Syrian civil war helped produce the world's gravest refugee crisis since World War II and created the instability that facilitated the rise of the Islamic State.

93. Mohammed Abbas and Khaled Yacoub Oweis, "Bombings Rock Damascus, Brother of Parliament Speaker Killed," *Reuters*, November 6, 2012.

94. Arshad Mohammed and Matt Spetalnick, "US and Allies Exploring Prospects for Assad Exile," *Reuters*, February 2, 2012.

95. Rather than provide safe haven, Russia has pursued a strategy of propping up Assad with military assistance, thus maintaining Russia's strategic interests in the region (e.g., Russia's naval facility at Tartus, its only Mediterranean port). Nonetheless, rumors of an Assad exile in Russia continued to surface during the Syrian conflict's first few years. Putin has at times encouraged these rumors, once boasting, "It was surely more difficult to grant Mr. Snowden asylum in Russia than it would be in the case of Assad." See "Putin: The Interview (Part 2)," *Bild*, January 12, 2016.

96. Mohammed Abbas and Khaled Yacoub Oweis, "Bombings Rock Damascus, Brother of Parliament Speaker Killed," *Reuters*, November 6, 2012. Cameron also made it clear that the United Kingdom would never consider hosting Assad.

97. Matthew Lee, "US Aware of Assad Asylum Offers," *Seattle Times*, December 6, 2012.

inevitable, such as when the US ambassador at-large for war crimes Stephen Rapp asserted, "When the day of justice arrives, we'll have much better evidence than we've had anywhere since Nuremberg" (Taub 2016, 39). Given all this, no state willing to grant asylum to Assad could credibly offer protection against the barrage of threats, sanctions, and shaming that would likely follow. With no way out, Assad had incentives to remain in Syria and try to win the war.

Thus, the shift toward global accountability creates a credible commitment problem at the international level that is similar to the more familiar commitment problem at the domestic level. Unlike their predecessors, today's culpable leaders must worry about reversals with regard to their personal fates if and when they retire abroad.[98]

By contrast, exile can still be used as a conflict resolution strategy to facilitate the exits of nonculpable leaders since they have little reason to anticipate international punishment. For example, Michel Djotodia came to power in the Central African Republic in 2013. As the first Muslim leader in a country deeply divided between Muslims and Christians, Djotodia's ascension to the presidency triggered a slow descent toward sectarian violence and civil war. For the most part, Djotodia was viewed as an "impotent" leader who was "ill-suited to the job" and could never break free of the deadly cycle of reprisal attacks between Christian and Muslim militias.[99] At the recommendation of regional leaders and organizations, Djotodia resigned the presidency and left for exile in Benin in 2014. Benin's decision to host Djotodia was clearly part of a regional conflict management strategy. As Benin's foreign minister described it, Benin welcomed Djotodia with open arms because it was their "contribution to the search for peace in central Africa."[100]

Overall, then, patterns of civil war duration should mirror those of exile.[101] During the impunity era, leader culpability should have no effect on civil war duration because all leaders had a reliable exit option if they needed it. In the accountability era, however, civil wars should last longer when culpable leaders are in power. Since it is less likely that today's

98. For culpable leaders, the possibility of the international community reneging on its promises also presents an issue with regard to travel. In 2015, the ICC prosecutor Luis Moreno-Ocampo urged the United States to give Sudan's Omar Bashir a visa to visit the UN in New York City and then, once Bashir set foot on US soil, arrest him. Public calls for this sort of trickery will likely exacerbate credible commitment problems when international actors attempt to negotiate with dictators. See Luis Moreno-Ocampo, "Let Sudan's President Come to New York. Then Arrest Him," *New York Times*, August 24, 2015.

99. David Smith, "Central African Republic President's Resignation Brings Joy and Fear," *Guardian*, January 11, 2014.

100. "CAR Ex-Leader Heads for Exile in Benin," *Al Jazeera*, January 12, 2014.

101. As I will discuss in chapter 4, my argument should apply to center-seeking civil wars fought over control of the government more than secessionist civil wars.

culpable leaders can use exile as a golden parachute, they should be more willing to risk it all on the battlefield. This suggests the theory's second hypothesis:

> ***Civil War Duration Hypothesis:*** *A leader's decision to continue fighting during civil war is conditional on the availability of a safe exile option. Civil conflicts with culpable leaders last significantly longer than conflicts with nonculpable leaders in the post-1998 accountability era only.*

MASS ATROCITY ONSET

The aforementioned dark side of international justice counterintuitively produces a benefit: deterrence. To engage in mass killing in today's accountability era is to step over a bright line. Since leaders know that crossing the line will decrease their exit options if they ever need to flee abroad, the justice cascade effectively increases the cost of wielding mass violence against civilians. Put another way, rulers would prefer not to get trapped in a position where the only way to avoid punishment is to gamble on a desperate fight to the bitter end. Leaders in the accountability era therefore will be less likely to initiate campaigns of mass atrocities than their peers were during the impunity era.

Let me unpack that claim. When it comes to crime and punishment, scholars generally discuss two different types of deterrence: specific and general. Specific deterrence refers to how judicial punishment influences the behavior of the individual targeted with legal sanctions, whereas general deterrence concerns how *others* respond to said judicial punishment (e.g., Akhavan 1998; Drumbl 2007). My claim that international justice can deter atrocities is a claim about general deterrence only.[102] The basic idea is that the trend toward holding culpable leaders accountable has signaled to the broader peer group—that is, other heads of state—that atrocity crimes will now be punished. In other words, deterrence should operate across borders. This logic fits with how policymakers often think about deterrence. For example, the former ICTY and ICTR prosecutor Richard Goldstone speculated that high-profile arrests and trials would be effective because they send "shockwaves into the homes of other leaders" (Goldstone 2000, 136).

One might counter that only a relatively small number of heads of state have been arrested and charged with international crimes. While true, this does not undermine my claim about general deterrence. Effective deterrence should, in theory, mean that fewer leaders need to be prosecuted. To give an example from everyday life, if the drivers on a highway start to

102. In fact, my theory implies that specific deterrence is likely to fail.

slow down after seeing just a couple of other drivers receive speeding tickets, then the police need to hand out fewer tickets. The absence of a large number of speeding tickets does not mean that deterrence is failing. On the contrary, it is a sign of success.

To be clear, I do not aim to advance a new theory on the causes of state-sponsored violence against civilians. There is already a rich literature on this topic. A common theme running throughout much of this work is that violence, even abhorrent violence, can be understood as a rational (though brutal) strategy. In other words, the killing of civilians is a product of a cost/benefit calculation that governments make as they pursue their political and military objectives. Though some have argued that the rational cost/benefit assessments that underpin the logic of deterrence are not applicable to evildoers who engage in horrific abuses (Cobban 2006), a growing consensus suggests violence is a tool states use strategically (e.g., Valentino 2014). Payam Akhavan (2009, 630) gets it right when he argues that "somewhere in the anatomy of genocide lies a cost-benefit calculus, however diabolical its parameters may be."[103]

Mass killing can carry high costs. For starters, killing civilians often ignites resistance to the government among the domestic population. Large-scale violence against civilians tends to generate grievances that motivate individuals to strike back against the hated government (Petersen 2002; E. J. Wood 2003). Moreover, when mass atrocities are indiscriminate in nature, the connection between a civilian's behavior and the likelihood of punishment is broken. Facing a violent and capricious state, people who otherwise would stay loyal to the government might throw their support behind the opposition simply to increase their odds of survival (Goodwin 2001; Kalyvas 2006). Yet another cost associated with mass killing can come from international constituencies (Stanton 2016), who may pull their support from violent regimes. In some cases, international actors go so far as to launch military interventions or impose economic sanctions. Overall, the domestic and international costs of mass killing can be substantial.

Mass killing can also yield strategic benefits for a government. This makes civilian targeting a tempting strategy for incumbent regimes bent on staying in power. Violence is thought to benefit the regime in two distinct ways. First, states can use violence to control, coerce, or intimidate the civilian population so that they will behave in a manner consistent with the state's political or military goals (e.g., Arreguin-Toft 2005; Balcells 2010; Downes 2008; Kalyvas 1999, 2006; Valentino 2004; Valentino, Huth, and

103. The idea that even mass killers make cost/benefit calculations is an important one. If violence is a means to an end—and not the end itself—then the threat of international prosecution should influence the decision calculus of leaders as they weigh whether to commit atrocity crimes.

Balch-Lindsay 2004). Second, states may turn to violence that is more genocidal in nature. Rather than influencing the behavior of civilians, the goal here is the complete elimination of a subset of the population that either threatens the regime's rule or whose very existence calls into question the regime's ideology (e.g., Semelin 2007; Straus 2015).

My claim about the deterrent effect of international justice is meant to complement, not challenge, existing research on violence against civilians. My aim is to supplement the insights of prior work by calling attention to a new cost associated with brutality in the accountability era. For some leaders, knowing that atrocities will foreclose exile possibilities may be enough to tip the cost/benefit calculus in favor of restraint.

An analogy using stoplights illustrates my point. In the past, by not prosecuting leaders who were responsible for mass atrocities, the international community essentially gave a green light to the next round of potential mass killers. One ICTY judge, for instance, concluded that the absence of any international punishment for the Ottoman leaders who engineered the Armenian genocide during World War I "gave a nod and a wink to Adolf Hitler and others to pursue the Holocaust some twenty years later" (Cassese 1998, 2).[104] In another example of this logic, the director of America's War Refugee Board warned in 1944: "The failure to punish the criminals of World War I may well have removed a deterrent to the commission of brutalities against civilian populations in this war."[105] More broadly, Samantha Power (2003, 522) documents how the "historic 'forgetting' of atrocities was a phenomenon noted by many a brutal regime" which convinced them that they too could kill without repercussions. But in today's era of accountability, there is something like a red light—or at least a yellow one—in the lane of would-be mass killers. Even though culpable leaders are unlikely to face international punishment until after they are ousted, forward-thinking leaders will be reluctant to commit atrocities because they prefer to keep the exile escape route open should they ever need to flee abroad to avoid domestic punishment. In other words, leaders now have a good reason to think twice before killing civilians because culpability carries a real cost.[106]

104. While this may seem like an extraordinary statement, Hitler's own words appear consistent with this view. On the eve of the Holocaust, Hitler is widely reported to have said, "Who, after all, speaks today of the annihilation of the Armenians?"

105. Quoted in Bass 2000, 290.

106. Beyond reducing a leader's post-tenure exit options, there are other potential costs associated with becoming a culpable leader in the accountability era. Many of today's culpable leaders are forced to maintain limited international travel schedules, which can be costly if leaders need to travel abroad for top-notch medical care. Moreover, culpable leaders sometimes are not invited to international summits and other high-prestige events, which may be especially grating to heads of state, a select group of individuals who tend to care a great deal about status (e.g., Renshon 2017).

Of course, even a robust system of international justice will not deter all atrocities.[107] There are two conditions under which leaders in the accountability era likely will *not* be deterred. First, if a leader is already culpable, there is no marginal cost to committing more atrocities. Imagine a leader who engaged in mass killing during the impunity era because there were few repercussions to doing so at the time. If that leader is still in office during the accountability era, he knows that he is already culpable. Due to his sordid behavior in the past, a secure exile is likely off the table today. This sort of leader has already "crossed the Rubicon" and therefore will not be deterred from targeting civilians with violence because the constraint identified in my theory—foreclosing one's future exit options—is missing.

Second, a leader will not be deterred if he believes using violence against civilians provides a sufficiently large advantage. If the benefits of mass killing are enough to keep the leader in power, the leader may decide to commit atrocities even though he knows that doing so will limit opportunities for exile down the road. Put differently, a nonculpable leader might strategically decide that becoming culpable is worth the risk.[108] In such a case, sacrificing a safe exile option might not be too troubling to the leader since he probably will not need to retire abroad anyway. By contrast, if a leader believes that the advantage atrocities provide is relatively small, then the threat of post-tenure international punishment can deter the leader from committing mass atrocities when he otherwise would have done so. No leader wants to become culpable and sacrifice the possibility of receiving a future golden parachute for only a tiny increase in the odds of remaining in power.

Thus, the deterrent effect stemming from international prosecutions of heads of state will be far from perfect. In general, however, the preceding discussion implies that the overall rate of mass atrocity onset in the accountability era should be lower (conditional on the other factors that incentivize states to use violence against civilians) than it was in the impunity era. This suggests the theory's final hypothesis:

> ***Mass Killing Onset Hypothesis:*** *A leader's decision to commit mass atrocities is conditional on whether doing so limits the availability of a safe exile option. Leaders*

107. This would be an unreasonable expectation for international criminal law since even the strongest domestic legal systems do not deter all crime.

108. Identifying which specific leaders are likely to believe the advantages of atrocities are large enough to justify the risks is a tricky business. A case-by-case analysis that uses detailed knowledge of the leader under study is likely the most promising approach. For instance, Bashar Assad may have calculated that mass killing could work given that his father Hafez used a similar strategy to decimate an uprising in Hama in 1982. I return to this general issue in chapter 5 with the case study of Muammar Gaddafi.

are significantly less likely to initiate campaigns of mass killing in the post-1998 accountability era.

This chapter developed my justice dilemma theory with four main claims. First, exile should be understood as a golden parachute exit strategy for embattled leaders. Second, the landscape for pursuing international justice has changed dramatically over time, with the late 1990s marking a transition from an era of impunity to an era of accountability. Third, this justice cascade has made exile a risky retirement option for culpable leaders, the subset of leaders responsible for atrocity crimes. Fourth, by making a safe exile conditional on how a leader behaves, international justice influences whether and why leaders use violence while they are still in office. In particular, deterring atrocities and prolonging conflicts are two sides of the same coin in today's accountability era. The justice cascade therefore is helpful in some ways but harmful in others, producing a dilemma.

The rest of the book is devoted to testing, using both quantitative and qualitative methods, the hypotheses developed in this chapter. The next chapter, chapter 3, presents evidence on how the threat of international justice influences patterns of exile. Chapters 4 and 5 then turn to the conflicting effects of the justice cascade. Chapter 4 investigates how the recent push for international justice affects civil war duration, while chapter 5 examines how it shapes the onset of mass killings.

CHAPTER 3

The Mechanism

Exile

On May 3, 1814, history's most famous exile, Napoleon Bonaparte, stepped off the *Undaunted* onto the shores of Elba. Taking in his surroundings, Napoleon must have been sorely disappointed. Not long before, he had been the world's most powerful man: the emperor of France on the cusp of achieving hegemony in Europe. Now, under British guard, he was forced to live in a modest home on a tiny island with little economic development.[1] As one historian described it, "Less than two years had elapsed since the Emperor had led an army of half a million men across Europe. He was now forming brigades consisting of two mules and a Corsican horse" (Young 1914, 150). How did it come to this for the great Napoleon Bonaparte?

Following a string of victories in the Napoleonic Wars, France's success eventually provoked a balancing coalition that included Great Britain, Russia, Prussia, and Austria, among others. Napoleon's army was critically weakened after his disastrous decision to invade Russia in 1812, and the Quadruple Alliance finally defeated the French in 1814. Yet the allies disagreed on what to do with Napoleon. Prussia preferred simply shooting him, but the British objected. Executing the former emperor both offended the British and risked turning Napoleon into a martyr. The British wanted the newly restored Bourbon monarchy to put Napoleon on trial in France, but the Bourbons worried that France was too weak for such a controversial trial—it might plunge France into another civil war. Czar Alexander of Russia eventually proposed the winning compromise: Napoleon should be kept alive but removed from France.[2] Naturally, this produced more quibbling among the allies regarding Napoleon's exile destination. Corsica and

1. For a thorough description of Napoleon's days on Elba, see McLynn 2002, 590–604.

2. On the allies' discussion of Napoleon's post-ouster fate, see Bass 2000, 37–39; and McLynn 2002, 590–91.

Sardinia were proposed but then rejected because the islands were large enough that Napoleon could conceivably transform them into strongholds. The allies ultimately selected Elba, a small Mediterranean island located between Italy and France. With great prescience, Lord Castlereagh, the British foreign secretary, objected to Elba on the grounds that it was too close to France, but he was overruled (McLynn 2002, 590). On April 11, 1814, the allies signed the Treaty of Fontainebleau, which banished Napoleon to Elba.

Napoleon's exile on Elba was short-lived. After less than one year on the island, he secretly left Elba and sailed for France. After landing near Cannes, Napoleon's party quickly marched toward Paris, and its ranks swelled with war veterans disgruntled with the Bourbon restoration. Within twenty days of landing on French soil, all opposition to Napoleon's return had melted away. The unpopular Bourbon king Louis XVIII fled the Tuileries Palace for the safety of Belgium, and Napoleon entered Paris to the sound of cheering crowds. The return of the emperor, however, revived the old balancing alliance. Russia, Great Britain, Prussia, and Austria each committed 150,000 soldiers to crushing Napoleon before his army regained its full strength (McLynn 2002, 607), and the allies succeeded in their task at the Battle of Waterloo on June 18, 1815. Perhaps surprisingly, the allies once again decided to exile Napoleon. This time, however, they selected the exile destination more strategically: Saint Helena, a desolate volcanic island under British control in the middle of the Atlantic Ocean (the nearest landmass was the western coast of Africa, located over one thousand miles away). Napoleon lived out his days in exile on Saint Helena and died there in 1821.

In the academic literature, political scientists have had little to say about exile, preferring for the most part to leave the topic to historians. The small amount of political science literature on the subject is inspired by the example of the Quadruple Alliance "punishing" the already defeated Napoleon by sending him into exile. As a result, exile is often viewed as a mild form of punishment for leaders. In fact, quantitative studies of war and punishment in international relations typically lump exiled leaders together with leaders who endured severe punishments such as imprisonment or death.[3]

The shortcoming of this approach is that Napoleon's exile is an outlier: exile is rarely employed as a form of punishment for defeated leaders. Far more often, exile is the result of the opposite dynamic. Fleeing abroad is

3. See the multitude of studies that use the Archigos dataset (Goemans, Gleditsch, and Chiozza 2009) without justifying why exile is a fate comparable to death or imprisonment. To their credit, however, Giacomo Chiozza and Henk E. Goemans (2011, 52) accurately acknowledge that "there is undoubtedly a qualitative difference between the three forms of punishment of exile, imprisonment, and death."

an appealing exit strategy for unpopular leaders because it allows them to *avoid punishment* such as imprisonment or death.[4] I am not alone is this assessment. The great Roman statesman Cicero described exile as "a refuge for men in danger," and the political philosopher Thomas Hobbes concurred that exile is "an escape" that allows one to "avoid punishment by flight" (Hobbes [1651] 1996, 209). This is why my theory views exile as a golden parachute: leaders who fear punishment at home can go into exile abroad and obtain foreign protection.[5] External exit options provide incentives for rulers, particularly those facing domestic unrest, to step down and leave the country. In this sense, exile can be a substitute for domestic safety that allows political leaders to avoid the costs of losing power.

This chapter tests my hypothesis on patterns of exile. My main claim is that international justice reduces the attractiveness of a foreign retirement for culpable leaders. Specifically, I expect that there is no relationship between leader culpability and exile during the impunity era because all leaders—regardless of how they behaved while in power—had a reliable exile option if they were overthrown. In the accountability era, however, culpable leaders should be significantly less likely than nonculpable leaders to go into exile since culpable leaders now have good reason to fear post-tenure international punishment. To test this prediction, I proceed in two parts. First, I conduct a statistical analysis of patterns of exile using a dataset of all political leaders worldwide over the past fifty years. Relying on a variety of statistical techniques, I find robust support for my hypothesis. Most notably, culpable and nonculpable leaders went into exile at nearly identical rates during the pre-1998 impunity era, but culpable leaders are about six times less likely to go into exile during the post-1998 accountability era. Second, I provide a case study of Liberia's Charles Taylor, one of the very few culpable leaders to go into exile after 1998, because it allows me to investigate a key question: Do culpable leaders who go into exile in the accountability era actually get punished? As I show, the Taylor case illustrates how an important part of the theory—costly international pressure on the states that host culpable leaders—unfolds in practice.

4. Even within the Napoleon example, we can see this is the case. After Napoleon's return to France from Elba, King Louis XVIII viewed exile as a way to avoid punishment at the hands of his domestic enemies. Once it became clear that it would be dangerous for him to remain in France (i.e., when the Bonapartists marched on Paris), Louis XVIII fled abroad to the safety of Belgium.

5. See also Krcmaric 2018a. For another paper that views exile as a golden parachute, see Bennett, Hagh, and Ritter 2020.

Exile Statistical Tests

In this section, I use statistical tests to evaluate general trends in the empirical record: Has the recent justice cascade made culpable leaders less likely to go into exile? In what follows, I first describe the quantitative data and then provide a number of results that bolster my theoretical claims.

DATA

Identifying Leaders. Assessing my hypothesis on when leaders are likely to flee into exile first requires identifying the relevant population of individual rulers. I identify political leaders using the Archigos dataset (Goemans, Gleditsch, and Chiozza 2009). Archigos codes the "effective ruler" of each country, which is "the person that de facto exercised power in a country" (Goemans, Gleditsch, and Chiozza 2009, 272). Thus, the effective ruler is defined as the individual who actually holds political power rather than as the formal head of state (although these are almost always the same person). For example, in some countries a monarch is a ceremonial head of state, but political power is delegated to an elected prime minister. In such cases, the prime minister is coded as the effective ruler. Moreover, in some countries a strongman may not technically hold an official position or may step down on paper without actually ceding power (e.g., Muammar Gaddafi after 1979). In these cases, the strongman is recognized as the effective ruler.[6]

The unit of analysis is the leader year.[7] There is an observation for each leader who held power for at least part of one year, which means there can be multiple leader years for a country in a given year (i.e., years with leadership transitions). The Archigos data (version 2.9) covers the 1875–2004

6. Henk E. Goemans, Kristian Skrede Gleditsch, and Giacomo Chiozza (2009) provide a nearly nine-hundred-page case description document that gives the justification for each coding decision.

7. This is preferable to using the leader as the unit of analysis (i.e., only having one observation for each leader's entire tenure) for two reasons. First, using the leader as the unit of analysis would mask the fact that leaders have many opportunities over time to go into exile. Indeed, if the unit of analysis was the leader, a ruler who stayed in power for less than a year and then went into exile would be treated the same as a leader who clung to power for a decade before finally decamping for a foreign retirement. Second, using the leader as the unit of analysis raises an issue concerning the time-varying independent variables. One seemingly reasonable option would be to average all the time-varying covariates over the course of the leader's tenure. This strategy, however, has a major shortcoming. Consider the leader culpability variable. Say, for example, that a leader's tenure lasted ten years before he fled into exile. Also assume that the leader became culpable in the ninth year. Averaging the time-varying covariates would treat this as a case of a nonculpable going into exile, which is clearly incorrect. By contrast, my decision to use the leader year as the unit of analysis allows for time-varying covariates, which provides a more accurate coding.

period.[8] However, I made a pair of changes to the temporal coverage of the data when it comes to my analysis. Since there is no reliable data, if any, for some of the covariates before 1960, I excluded leader years before then from the analysis. Further, the Archigos data were only available through 2004, so I extended the data on the entry/exit dates of leaders through 2010 using the coding rules set forth in Goemans, Gleditsch, and Chiozza 2009 to ensure a post-1998 sample large enough for statistical analysis.[9] Hence, the sample used in most of the statistical tests is comprised of leader years between 1960 and 2010.

Measuring Leader Culpability. Having constructed the sample of leaders, the next task was to determine whether each leader should be considered culpable. At the conceptual level, culpability simply refers to whether leaders have previously committed mass atrocities. This means leader culpability is distinct from whether a leader is indicted in an international tribunal or foreign court (i.e., a culpable leader may or may not face an indictment at any given time). It would be a mistake to focus solely on indictments because doing so ignores the time inconsistency problem: even if a brutal leader does not face an indictment at the time of a crisis, the leader knows that he may be prosecuted after giving up power and will adjust his behavior accordingly. I therefore focus on a behavioral indicator by coding whether leaders have presided over mass atrocities in the past.

Of course, this raises the issue of identifying and measuring cases of state-sponsored mass atrocities. This is no easy task. For one thing, states typically are not eager to share information about their misdeeds—if anything, states sometimes try to engage in strategic cover-ups.[10] Moreover, judging what counts as a mass atrocity might differ across countries or time periods. Fortunately, however, there already is a carefully researched and relatively objective source of data on state-sponsored mass atrocities, Jay Ulfelder and Benjamin Valentino's (2008) Mass Killing Dataset. They define mass killing as "any event in which the actions of state agents result in the intentional death of at least 1,000 noncombatants from a discrete group in a period of sustained violence" (Ulfelder and Valentino 2008, 2). This mass killing dataset forms the basis of my leader culpability variable. Specifically, in my dataset, *Culpable Leader* is a dummy variable that equals 1 starting in the leader year in which the mass killing episode begins and every year thereafter during the leader's tenure (i.e., once a culpable leader,

8. An updated Archigos dataset (version 4.1) now covers an even longer time period.

9. My data collection for the 2005–2010 period yielded 1,120 additional leader year observations.

10. On states' efforts to strategically cover up massacres, as well as a discussion of how information and communication technologies can make such strategies difficult, see Krcmaric 2019. For a broader discussion of secrecy in international relations, see Carson 2018.

always a culpable leader). To give an example of how I coded leader culpability, Ahmed Sekou Toure of Guinea ruled from 1958 to 1984 and presided over a campaign of mass killing that lasted from 1960 to 1980. He is coded as culpable starting in 1960 and lasting until his tenure ends in 1984.

It is worth highlighting three points about the leader culpable variable. First, consistent with the conceptual discussion of culpability in chapter 2, this variable measures the actions of the leader's regime, not the individual leader.[11] In other words, a leader does not need to engage personally in the killing to be considered culpable in my dataset. This coding scheme for leader culpability is consistent with international law, where criminal responsibility extends beyond direct, personal perpetration of international crimes (e.g., Cassese 2008, 161–205). In other words, leaders are liable for the conduct of their state security forces. For example, Article 25 of the Rome Statute makes clear that a head of state can be held responsible for violence conducted by forces under his command if the leader played a role in ordering the crime or in aiding and abetting the direct perpetrators of the crime.[12]

Second, a very high level of brutality is required to become a culpable leader in my dataset. One might even argue that the bar for leader culpability is too high. According to my definition, some leaders who have engaged in dubious, perhaps even repulsive, behavior may nonetheless be coded as nonculpable. This, however, is not problematic. As discussed in the previous chapter, culpability (or its absence) is not meant to imply any sort of normative judgment. Culpability simply refers to whether leaders have engaged in the sort of behavior that could trigger an international prosecution—and that requires a very high threshold. For instance, the ICC was created to "prosecute the worst perpetrators responsible for the worst crimes" and therefore needs "a high threshold of gravity" before it intervenes (Moreno-Ocampo 2009, 12). A concrete example illustrates this point. The human rights situation in Venezuela deteriorated substantially under the rule of Hugo Chavez, which prompted public calls for an ICC investigation. In a 2010 speech, however, the ICC prosecutor Luis Moreno-Ocampo reminded his audience that the court's "jurisdiction is [limited to] crimes against humanity, war crimes, and genocide. . . . [Therefore] we'd reject Venezuela, because whatever you think about Venezuela, these crimes are not committed there" (Moreno-Ocampo 2010).

11. Note that this would be true for any measure of leader culpability derived from data on state-sponsored violence.

12. This leader-centric approach to international justice is also consistent with the view of national-level policymakers. As the United States' first ambassador-at-large for war crimes put it, the task of international justice is not to prosecute "foot soldiers," but rather the "political and military leaders" who enable mass atrocities (Scheffer 2012, 3).

Third, the threshold of 1,000 civilian deaths is, of course, arbitrary. One would be hard pressed to distinguish between the crimes of one leader responsible for 999 deaths and another responsible for 1,001 deaths. Moreover, the law does not play a numbers game in which some magical switch goes off once a ruler kills a certain number of noncombatants. Tribunals instead have jurisdiction over specific international crimes. The issue, however, is that defining and measuring these crimes is extremely difficult. Since genocide requires the "intent to destroy" the targeted group, coding cases of genocide forces researchers to make tough judgment calls on the ultimate intentions of the perpetrators. Vague definitions of crimes against humanity and war crimes have long vexed researchers as well. Even today, legal scholars continue to debate seemingly basic questions such as "What is a war crime?" (Hathaway et al. 2019). Given the challenges of identifying cases of international crimes in the real world, it makes sense to turn to an objective numerical threshold. The 1,000-death threshold is as reasonable as any since it aptly captures the high bar required for culpability (i.e., if a ruler is responsible for killing over 1,000 civilians, we can be reasonably confident that at least one of the core international crimes has occurred).

To be clear, the goal here is not to create a perfect indicator of leader culpability that accounts for the subtleties of each ruler's individual history. Instead, the goal is to construct a variable that provides a clear-cut standard for making comparisons across the full universe of cases in the statistical analysis. I show empirically that this indicator—despite its somewhat blunt nature—is a powerful explanatory variable.[13] A more nuanced view of leader culpability would also consider (1) a broader range of potential government abuses and (2) how leaders and other key actors perceive culpability. This is possible only with a qualitative approach that accounts for the unique context of each situation, which is exactly the approach I take in the book's case studies.[14]

13. While using the mass killing data to capture leader culpability is preferable to alternative indicators, I will show later in the chapter that my results are robust to other ways of measuring leader culpability.

14. For instance, the case studies allow me to consider civilian massacres that come close to the one-thousand-death threshold as well as other large-scale human rights abuses beyond killing civilians. Yet another way to add nuance to the notion of culpability is to think about the status of leaders who take power in regimes that have already committed atrocities. Specifically, when a leader with relatively clean hands (e.g., Bashar Assad in 2000 or Kim Jung Un in 2011) takes over for a family member with very dirty hands, does the new leader have to worry about being associated with the sins of the father? From an international law perspective, this seems unlikely since a key part of the justice cascade has been a shift away from collective guilt toward individual accountability. But it is possible that domestic regime opponents might attempt to settle old scores with new leaders who are closely connected to brutal predecessors.

Cases of Exile. The dependent variable is a binary indicator for whether each leader goes into exile in a given year. I use the Archigos coding of each leader's post-exit fate, which records the fate of each leader during the first full year after the leader is out of power, to identify cases of exile.[15] Since Archigos's coverage does not extend beyond 2004, I coded the exile variable for the last six years of the data using news reports, secondary sources, and leader biographies according to the criteria established in the Archigos codebook. Between 1960 and 2010, the time period covered in the main statistical analyses, there were 132 cases of exile.

Control Variables. For additional covariates, there are no established conventions due to the dearth of research examining exile as a dependent variable. However, I attempt to control for additional factors that might influence a leader's decision to flee abroad. Since the decision to go into exile is largely a function of the degree to which the domestic opposition threatens the leader, I capture the threat the opposition presents by controlling for conflict intensity. I proxy conflict intensity with battle deaths, a measure of people killed in direct combat situations. Importantly, one-sided state violence against civilians is excluded from this measure. Measuring battle deaths provides a good indicator for conflict intensity because it "answers the question of how many people were killed in military operations during a war and, therefore, it is the best measure of the scale, scope, and nature of the military engagement that has taken place" (Lacina and Gleditsch 2005, 148). Therefore, the variable *Conflict Intensity* takes the value of 2 if there are over 1,000 battle deaths in a given year; 1 if there are between 25 and 999 battle deaths; and 0 otherwise.[16]

An opposition movement can also threaten a leader's hold on power outside the context of organized armed conflict. For example, mass protests demanding regime change have been sufficient to drive leaders into exile, such as when the People Power Revolution in the Philippines toppled Ferdinand Marcos or the Euromaidan Revolution in Ukraine ousted Viktor Yanukovych. To account for this dynamic, *Revolutionary Activity* is a variable from the Banks Cross-National Time-Series Data (Banks and

15. In addition to coding exile as a post-tenure fate, Archigos also records other outcomes such as "death," "imprisonment," and "OK."

16. The battle deaths data are from the UCDP/PRIO armed conflict dataset. Other datasets attempt to code the exact number of battle deaths (e.g., Lacina and Gleditsch 2005). These datasets, however, have two limitations for my purposes. First, none cover the entire period under study here. Second, there is a substantial amount of missing data for the best estimate of battle deaths. Therefore, I use the ordinal variable provided in the UCDP/PRIO dataset, which avoids both problems. For a discussion of the methodological challenges of estimating precise numbers of battle deaths, see Spagat et al. 2009.

Wilson 2013) that measures the number of attempts in a year, if any, to change the ruling elite through irregular means.

I also control for two variables that are meant to capture the degree to which leaders might need the exile option. The first is *Leader Tenure*, which measures the number of years each leader has spent in office. The intuition behind this variable is that leaders who are good at holding on to power are presumably less likely to need to flee abroad when facing domestic threats. For instance, a leader who has held power for decades is more likely than a newly installed leader to have an established internal security apparatus to fend off challengers. Hence, the leader tenure variable serves as a proxy for the extent to which each leader has consolidated power. The second is a dummy variable for *Democracy* (Geddes, Wright, and Frantz 2014). Regime type could be relevant because it is an indicator for domestic institutions and norms that increase the credibility of guarantees concerning the leader's post-tenure domestic security (e.g., Chiozza and Goemans 2011; Riker 1982). In general, democracies provide ex-leaders with better retirement options and a lower risk of domestic punishment, so democratic leaders may think they are less likely to need to seek safety abroad compared to autocratic rulers.[17]

Finally, I account for how international context might influence each leader's decision calculus regarding exile. Since powerful Western states play a dominant role in enforcing international criminal law, it is possible that leaders more closely aligned with the West are less likely to face international justice. For example, NATO's 1999 bombing campaign that was meant to force Serbia out of Kosovo ended up killing a large number of innocent civilians (including when a bomb hit the Chinese embassy in Belgrade). The ICTY prosecutor Carla Del Ponte initially considered investigating NATO's targeting practices since they fell under her jurisdiction, but she soon backed off because she realized "that I had collided with the edge of the political universe in which the tribunal was allowed to function" (Del Ponte 2009, 60). Similarly, the ICC initially "sought to reassure the United States" and "selected uncontroversial early investigations" that did not threaten the interests of Western powers (Bosco 2014, 78). Some policymakers have even accused the ICC of being "hijacked by powerful Western countries."[18] To address the possibility of preferential treatment

17. Even an unpopular leader typically has little reason to fear domestic punishment in a fully consolidated democracy. For instance, despite very low approval ratings near the end of his second term, George W. Bush did not worry about domestic punishment. In his own words, Bush's postpresidency plans included relaxing at his ranch in Texas and "[giving] some speeches, just to replenish the old coffers." See Jim Rutenberg, "In Book, Bush Peeks Ahead to His Legacy," *New York Times*, September 2, 2007.

18. Jina Moore, "Burundi Quits International Criminal Court," *New York Times*, October 27, 2017.

for leaders aligned with the West, the variable *Western Affinity* uses data on voting patterns in the UN General Assembly to control for how friendly each leader is toward the US-led liberal international order (Bailey, Strezhnev, and Voeten 2017).

CHANGE POINT ANALYSIS

The main statistical results presented in this chapter will involve a comparison of leader behavior across two relatively large time periods (the impunity era versus the accountability era). But before proceeding to these tests, it is useful to conduct a change point analysis. This analysis allows us to answer the following question: When, exactly, did culpable leaders stop going into exile? This is an important first test because it provides an opportunity to validate the research design used throughout the book (specifically, that the late 1990s represent a transition from an era of impunity to one of accountability). My research design was based on theoretical expectations about the effects of the Rome Conference and the Pinochet arrest, as well as the aforementioned qualitative evidence that showed leaders updating their punishment expectations in response to these events. Nonetheless, one might wonder whether the evidence of updating presented in chapter 2 was somehow unrepresentative. Were the events of 1998 really internalized by other leaders around the world in such a way that it shaped their calculations about exile?

The change point analysis helps address this issue. Instead of taking it as a given that 1998 represents a meaningful transition from impunity to accountability (as the tests presented later in this chapter must do), the change point analysis makes no assumption about when the change should occur or even whether a change occurred at all. As Janet Box-Steffensmeier et al. (2014, 206) point out, "For some problems it may be better to let the data speak for itself and to identify which point or points are statistically most likely to represent a break in the underlying process." Hence, if 1998 really was a watershed year for international justice, we should see a noticeable break in the rate of exile for culpable leaders around that time.

To check, I use the method developed by Eric Zivot and Donald Andrews (1992), which is applied to a single panel of time-series data. Therefore, I collapse my data into a panel measuring the proportion of culpable leaders worldwide going into exile for every year from 1960 to 2010.[19] The change point analysis suggests that the best-fitting model (by Bayesian Information Criterion) contains exactly one break occurring at 1998. This result

19. To be clear, the change point analysis includes culpable leaders only. Both my theoretical expectations and the results presented later in this chapter indicate that the likelihood of exile for nonculpable leaders has remained relatively constant over time.

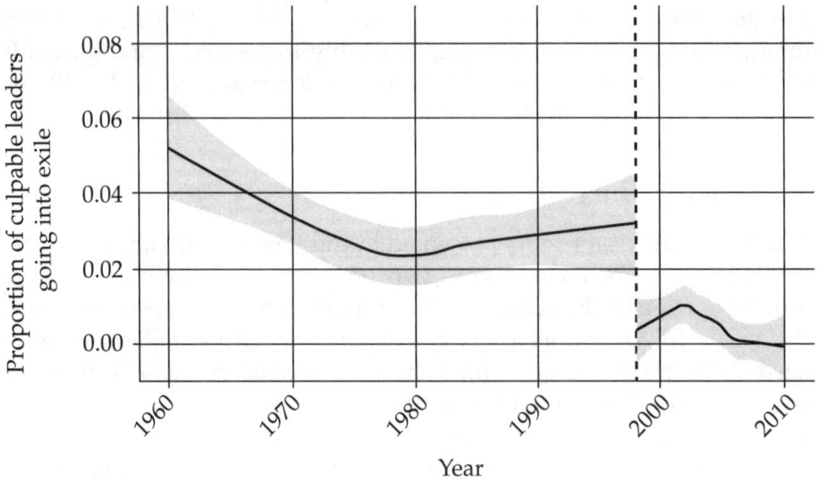

Figure 1. Rate of exile for culpable leaders over time

reaffirms my empirical strategy and lends considerable support to the argument. To visualize how the rate of exile for culpable leaders changes, I use a loess function—which employs a locally weighted nearest neighbor smoothing method—to fit a line on either side of the break.[20] The black line represents the estimate, and the shaded area captures the 95 percent confidence interval (see figure 1). This visualization offers striking prima facie support for my claim that the justice cascade affected leader calculations about exile.

Yet, as encouraging as the results from the change point analysis are, it is important to note that the simple relationship depicted in figure 1 does not account for potentially confounding variables. To offer a more systematic test, I now turn to regression analysis.

MAIN RESULTS

Using the data described previously, I estimate logistic regression models of exile with standard errors clustered on the leader. Given my argument that culpability for mass atrocities inhibits a leader's ability to retire to a safe exile in the accountability era only, there are two reasonable strategies for structuring the models. The first option is to split the data at 1998

20. To estimate the loess functions and their confidence intervals, I used the ggplot2 package in R (Wickham 2009), employing a first degree polynomial and the default bandwidth.

into two samples representing the impunity and accountability eras, respectively, and then estimate the effect of leader culpability in each time period. The advantage of the split samples approach is its flexibility. More specifically, this approach allows the effects of the other covariates to vary across the two periods.[21] Since it is quite possible that factors other than the threat of international justice vary over time (and my argument is agnostic on this point), the subsamples approach is advantageous. The second option is to estimate an interaction model for the entire 1960–2010 period that interacts the leader culpability variable with a post-1998 dummy variable. This approach gives up flexibility because it forces the effects of the other covariates to be equal across the two periods, but it offers a higher degree of statistical efficiency. In what follows, I show that both modeling strategies produce similar conclusions, which should increase our confidence in the results.

The results are reported in table 2. I start by disaggregating the data into two periods: the impunity era (pre-1998) and the accountability era (post-1998). If my argument is correct, *Culpable Leader* should be statistically insignificant in the impunity era but statistically significant and negative in the accountability era. Model 1 probes the relationship between leader culpability and exile in the pre-1998 period. I find that the estimated parameter for *Culpable Leader* is well outside any reasonable threshold of statistical significance ($p = .69$). Thus, the effect of leader culpability on exile is statistically indistinguishable from zero in the pre-1998 sample. Model 2 examines the effect of leader culpability on exile in the post-1998 period. As predicted, *Culpable Leader* is statistically significant and negative. In other words, the results support my theory's prediction: culpable leaders are less likely to go into exile in the accountability era only.[22]

Model 3 reports the results with the interaction term, which is statistically significant. The marginal effect of leader culpability during the impunity era is estimated by the lower-order term for culpability in model 3, *Culpable Leader*. The linear combination of β*Culpable Leader* + β*Culpable Leader × Post-1998* estimates the effect of leader culpability during the accountability era. The results show that the estimate for the lower-order term *Culpable Leader* is not significant, whereas the coefficient for the linear combination is negative and significant. Hence, the interaction model yields

21. By virtue of estimating a separate coefficient for every variable across the two time periods, the subsamples approach approximates a fully interactive model (i.e., it is comparable to using the full temporal span and interacting every variable with a post-1998 dummy, but it is advantageous because interpretation is more straightforward). See Marinov and Goemans 2014 for a similar point.

22. A test for equality of the coefficients for leader culpability between models 1 and 2 suggests that they are not equal ($p < .03$).

Table 2. Logit models of exile

	(1)	*(2)*	*(3)*
	Pre-1998	*Post-1998*	*Both*
Culpable Leader	–0.006	–2.944**	–0.020
	(0.302)	(1.117)	(0.295)
Conflict Intensity	0.426**	–0.585	0.305
	(0.214)	(0.850)	(0.216)
Revolutionary Activity	0.809**	2.165**	0.967**
	(0.280)	(0.492)	(0.286)
Leader Tenure	0.019	0.020	0.019
	(0.016)	(0.034)	(0.014)
Western Affinity	0.215*	–0.515**	0.086
	(0.117)	(0.262)	(0.109)
Democracy	–0.611*	0.578	–0.360
	(0.353)	(0.654)	(0.306)
Culpable Leader × Post-1998			–2.223**
			(1.044)
Post-1998			–0.041
			(0.273)
Constant	–4.557**	–5.746**	–4.671**
	(0.253)	(0.648)	(0.248)
β*Culpable Leader* + β*Culpable Leader × Post-1998*			–2.243**
			(1.049)
N	5094	2184	7278
AIC	825.72	196.63	1031.85
BIC	871.48	236.46	1093.89

Note: Standard errors clustered by leader in parentheses.
* $p < 0.10$, ** $p < 0.05$ (two-tailed)

the same conclusion as the split sample models: it is only after 1998 that culpable leaders are less likely to go into exile.

While the regression estimates are all consistent with my argument, it is difficult to interpret the magnitude of effects with logistic regression models. To remedy this, I calculate substantive effects that can be understood more easily. I use the estimates obtained in model 3 to generate the predicted probability of culpable and nonculpable leaders fleeing into exile in a given year during the impunity and accountability eras, respectively, while all the other variables are held constant. The results, which are shown in figure 2, are compelling.[23] Before 1998, culpable and nonculpable leaders go into exile at nearly identical rates. After 1998, however, there is a substantively large difference between culpable and nonculpable leaders, with culpable leaders being about six times less likely to go into exile.

23. The simulations are conducted using Clarify (King, Tomz, and Wittenberg 2000).

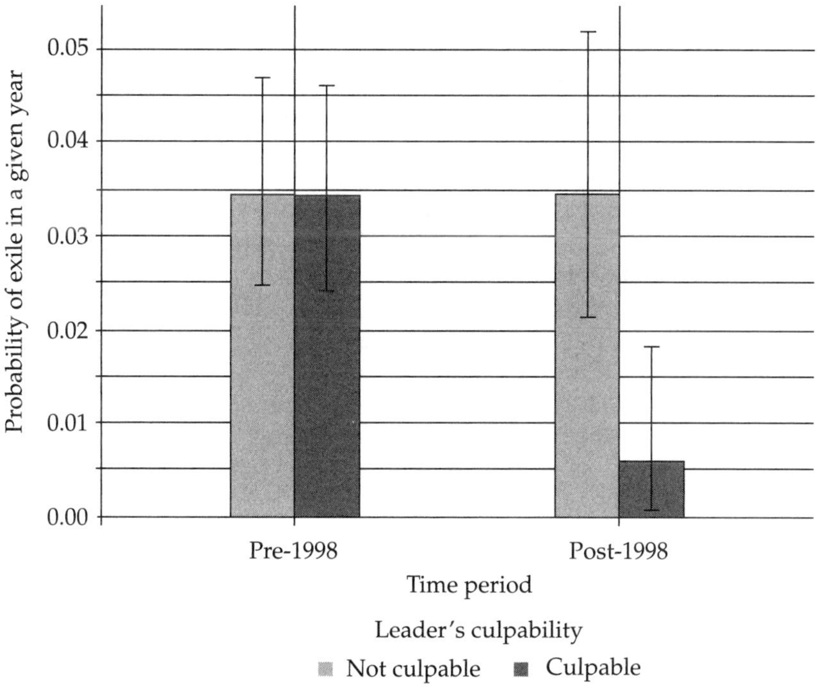

Figure 2. International justice and the probability of exile

One might notice that the predicted probability of a culpable leader going into exile in the accountability era is close to zero. Digging deeper, this number is so low because there are only two cases of culpable leaders fleeing abroad after 1998: Alberto Fujimori and Charles Taylor. Each leader's fate after going into exile offers further support for my theory. Fujimori ruled Peru from 1990 to 2000, when he claimed to have won an election that was widely considered stolen. Mass protests against Fujimori's rule erupted in Peru, prompting him to flee to the safety of Japan (where he had longstanding family connections). However, in 2005, Fujimori miscalculated by traveling to Chile, where he was arrested and then extradited back to Peru. In 2009, Fujimori was sentenced to twenty-five years in jail for supporting anticommunist death squads during his time in office. The story of Liberia's Charles Taylor, covered in detail later in this chapter, shares an important similarity. Taylor fled to exile in Nigeria in 2003 after it became clear that his forces were on the verge of losing Liberia's civil war. Despite initially promising to protect Taylor in retirement, Nigeria later decided to hand Taylor over to the Special Court for Sierra Leone, which sentenced Taylor to fifty years in prison. Thus, the two culpable leaders who fled abroad upon their ousters in the accountability era both eventually ended up behind bars. As these examples illustrate, the recent pursuit of international justice truly has made the world a smaller place for culpable leaders.

Overall, the statistical results—both the regression estimates and the substantive effects—offer support for my theory's predictions about patterns of exile. During the impunity era, embattled leaders went into exile regardless of whether they had previously committed atrocities. During the accountability era, however, leaders' decisions to flee into exile are conditional on their past behavior.

But how robust are the results? The regressions reported in table 2 offer, in my view, the most appropriate manner in which to model exile. However, a number of different modeling strategies and variable definitions offer reasonable alternatives. To the extent that these various quantitative techniques produce similar results, our confidence in the findings should increase. Therefore, I subject my results to several robustness checks.[24]

To begin, I guard against rare events bias by using an estimator specifically designed to handle infrequent events.[25] Next, I address whether the end of the Cold War is a confounding factor. The impunity era mostly consists of leader years during the Cold War, whereas the accountability era exclusively contains leader years after the Cold War. It is therefore possible that factors associated with the end of the Cold War—and not the justice cascade—drive patterns of exile over time. To ensure that changes linked to the Cold War do not distort the findings, I limit my analysis to the post–Cold War era. Specifically, I compare the last nine years of the impunity era (1989–97) to the first nine years of the accountability era (1998–2006).[26] I also check whether the results hold when using an alternative definition of leader culpability that codes whether leaders presided over a genocide or politicide identified by the Political Instability Task Force.[27] Finally, I consider a potential source of endogeneity bias. If leaders commit atrocities with expectations of the exile option in mind, it is plausible that the

24. The results are reported in the appendix, which can be found at https://hdl.handle.net/1813/69640.

25. Rare events bias can occur in datasets with many times more zeros (i.e., nonevents) than ones (i.e., events) and causes the standard logistic regression model to underestimate the probability of the rare events.

26. I examine the same amount of time in the impunity and accountability eras (i.e., nine years) to create a comparable number of observations on either side of the break in 1998, which should eliminate the possibility of sample size bias.

27. This dataset codes genocides and politicides as events which "involve the promotion, execution, and/or implied consent of sustained policies by governing elites or their agents . . . that result in the deaths of a substantial portion of a communal group or politicized non-communal group" (Marshall, Gurr, and Harff 2014, 14). The difference between the two categories rests on the identity of the victimized group. Genocide victims include ethnolinguistic or religious groups, whereas politicide victims are political opponents of the incumbent regime.

leaders who still decide to initiate campaigns of mass killing in the post-1998 accountability era are substantively different (e.g., they might be particularly risk acceptant). To address this possibility, I estimate a bivariate probit model that simultaneously estimates a selection equation (whether leaders engage in mass killing) and an outcome equation (whether leaders go into exile) while controlling for the correlation in errors between the two equations.[28] In every robustness check, my conclusions remain unchanged.

WHAT ABOUT . . . ?

The theory outlined in the previous chapter was premised on the assumptions that (1) leaders weigh the relative risks of facing domestic punishment and international punishment and (2) leaders are more likely to flee abroad when the likelihood and costs of domestic punishment are high compared to those of international punishment. The results presented thus far have all been consistent with this framework. In the impunity era, when the threat of domestic punishment almost always outstripped the threat of international punishment, exile was a common post-tenure fate for all leaders. But in the accountability era, culpable leaders—the subset of leaders who have good reason to fear international punishment—have been reluctant to go into exile.

Beyond culpability for atrocity crimes, are there other factors that influence each leader's susceptibility to international punishment? Indeed, it sometimes appears that certain leaders are protected from international justice, while others—such as the leaders of weak, isolated, or African states—seem especially likely to be targeted with prosecutions. In this section, I explore additional factors that might plausibly shape punishment expectations, which in turn would influence the likelihood of certain types of leaders going into exile. While these factors were not a core part of my argument, they all fit within the broader punishment expectations framework. By exploring these other variables here, I aim to paint a more nuanced picture of the many factors leaders might consider when deciding to flee into exile or cling to power.

One potential source of variation in punishment expectations is alleged bias against African leaders. This critique is lodged most forcefully against the ICC in particular (rather than the international justice movement in

28. The bivariate probit model covers the post-1998 accountability era only because this is the time period in which an endogenous relationship might threaten my inferences. The outcome equation is identical to model 2 in table 2, and the selection equation includes the variables from the main model of mass killing in chapter 5. I find that the correlation in errors is not statistically significant, meaning that endogeneity bias is unlikely. Moreover, leader culpability remains significant and negative in the bivariate probit model.

general) because the clear majority of the ICC's official investigations have been in Africa.[29] This pattern is striking enough that the *Washington Post* published an op-ed asking the provocative question: "Why is the International Criminal Court picking only on Africa?"[30] Many view the ICC's record of investigations as proof of bias against African leaders. For instance, one African Union (AU) official lambasted the ICC's "glaring practice of selective justice"[31] and Rwanda's prime minister warned that "Westerners who don't understand anything about Africa should stop trying to import their solutions."[32] On the other hand, a large share of civil conflicts and human rights violations have taken place in Africa, so the higher rate of investigations is not necessarily evidence of bias. Regardless of the precise reason for the large number of ICC investigations in Africa, I explore whether African leaders are less likely to flee into exile than their peers from other parts of the world.

Another possibility is that the leaders of weak, poor states have to worry about international justice while the leaders of powerful, wealthy states do not. After all, a small handful of influential states are primarily responsible for funding international tribunals and for enforcing the arrest warrants those tribunals issue.[33] Hence, there is a common perception that international courts are unable or unwilling to target leaders of powerful states since doing so would be equivalent to biting the hand that feeds.[34] Using a market analogy, some even assert that the world's powerful and stable states are the "producers" of international justice whereas weak and unstable states are the "consumers" (K. Anderson 2009). At the same time, however, all leaders know there is some chance (even if it is extremely remote) that they could be held accountable for human rights violations. For instance, George W. Bush cancelled a visit to Switzerland in 2011 amid

29. Official ICC investigations in Africa include Uganda, the Democratic Republic of Congo, Sudan, the Central African Republic, Libya, Kenya, the Ivory Coast, Mali, and Burundi. The ICC's two formal investigations outside of Africa involve violence in Georgia and Myanmar's targeting of the Rohingya (though there are currently several preliminary investigations outside of Africa). By contrast, ad hoc international tribunals (e.g., the ICTY), hybrid tribunals (e.g., the ECCC), and foreign courts exercising universal jurisdiction have been more active outside of Africa.

30. David Bosco, "Why Is the International Criminal Court Picking Only on Africa?," *Washington Post*, March 29, 2013.

31. "African ICC Members Mull Withdrawal Over Bashir Indictment," *Voice of America News*, November 2, 2009.

32. Alfred de Montesquiou, "African Leaders Denounce International Court," *Associated Press*, July 3, 2009.

33. The ad hoc tribunals were direct creations of the UN Security Council, whereas the ICC receives much of its funding from wealthy European powers, which often seem to get their way at the court (Bosco 2014, 82–83).

34. Recall, for example, the ICTY prosecutor Carla Del Ponte's claim that it was politically impossible to investigate NATO's bombing practices in Yugoslavia.

reports that he might be detained to face a human rights trial related to his policies on torture, extraordinary rendition, and Guantanamo Bay.[35] If the former leader of the world's most powerful state has to worry about international arrest, every leader is at least somewhat vulnerable. Nonetheless, it seems likely that the leaders of strong, wealthy states face a lower risk of international prosecution, making exile a relatively more attractive option (should they need it).[36]

International alliances represent another factor that could influence the degree to which leaders fear punishment in exile.[37] In particular, leaders with major power allies may believe they can safely retire abroad even if they have an unsavory personal history because their powerful patrons will help shield them from international justice. In a discussion of cases where the ICC did *not* get involved despite massive human rights violations, one scholar notes: "China has a veto over Security Council action and wants the court to stay well away from North Korea. Russia will not permit an ICC investigation in Syria. And when violence in Iraq was at its most intense, the United States would have blocked any move to give the court jurisdiction there."[38] Moreover, even if international tribunals and human rights campaigns attempt to bring an exiled leader to justice, major power allies are better positioned than other potential host states to withstand foreign pressure on the leader's behalf. Not surprisingly, major power allies have historically been popular retirement destinations for exiled rulers (Escribà-Folch and Krcmaric 2017). To address this dynamic, I investigate whether leaders with powerful allies are more likely to go into exile.

While the first three sources of variation in punishment expectations all concerned international punishment, regime type could shape the degree to which leaders anticipate domestic punishment. I have already discussed how democratic leaders generally face a lower risk of domestic punishment than autocratic leaders, which could give democratic rulers weaker

35. Ewen MacAskill and Afua Hirsch, "George Bush Calls Off Trip to Switzerland," *Guardian*, February 6, 2011.

36. Note that there is also a countervailing pressure: leaders of weak countries may be more likely to need exile in the first place since they presumably are poorly equipped to respond effectively to domestic challenges to their rule. Thus, interpreting the effect of state capacity is difficult.

37. In the previous results, I already accounted for international context to some degree by controlling for Western affinity (the idea was that powerful Western states play a dominant role in enforcing international criminal law, making it conceivable that leaders more closely aligned with the West are less likely to face international punishment). However, this is not the only international context variable that might help capture the availability of a safe exile abroad.

38. David Bosco, "Why Is the International Criminal Court Picking Only on Africa?" *Washington Post*, March 29, 2013.

incentives to flee to the safety of exile. Over the past decade, scholars have moved beyond the simple democracy/autocracy dichotomy by unpacking the various forms of autocracy (e.g., Escribà-Folch and Wright 2015a; Geddes, Wright, and Frantz 2014; Weeks 2014). An important insight is that leaders in one specific type of autocracy—personalist regimes—are worst positioned to extract credible exit guarantees regarding their post-tenure fate (e.g., Escribà-Folch 2013).[39] So while there never is a perfect domestic exit guarantee for outgoing leaders (as argued earlier, this is precisely why exile used to be such a common post-tenure fate), personalist dictators may be especially likely to need to flee abroad since the odds of domestic punishment are particularly high.

To test these propositions, I add several additional variables to my post-1998 accountability era model of exile (model 2 of table 2).[40] Specifically, I include a dummy variable for Africa, each country's Composite Index of National Capability (CINC score) to proxy state power (Singer 1988), a dummy variable for whether each leader's country has an alliance with one of the permanent five members of the UN Security Council (Gibler 2009), and a dummy variable for personalist dictators (Geddes, Wright, and Frantz 2014). Rather than report a large regression table, figure 3 graphs the first difference associated with each new variable.[41] This graph shows how changing the value of an independent variable (from 0 to 1 for the dummy variables and from the 25th to the 75th percentile for the continuous variables) influences the probability of a leader going into exile (expressed in percentage points) while every other variable is held constant.

Figure 3 offers mixed support for the aforementioned expectations. Consistent with the predictions, leaders with major power allies and personalist dictators appear somewhat more likely to go into exile. However, African leaders are more likely to flee into exile than their peers from other world regions—the opposite of what the Africa bias argument would suggest. Similarly, the results do not support assertions that only the leaders of weak states need to worry about international punishment. Yet the most notable aspects of figure 3 are the null results: none of the variables have a

39. By contrast, military and single-party autocracies possess mechanisms (however imperfect) for retaining at least some domestic leverage after leaving office. For instance, the military can return to politics by staging a coup and the party can compete in future elections. This ability to wield political influence after leaving office may be enough to deter incoming governments from punishing outgoing elites. Personalist leaders, however, are not so fortunate when it comes to their post-tenure fates.

40. This test only includes the post-1998 accountability era since all leaders could safely retire to exile in the pre-1998 impunity era. The variables are added to the baseline model individually (rather than collectively) to avoid multicollinearity concerns.

41. The first difference approach is also advantageous because it allows the magnitude of the effects to be compared in a more meaningful way than regression coefficients. The regression results that underpin these first differences are reported in the appendix.

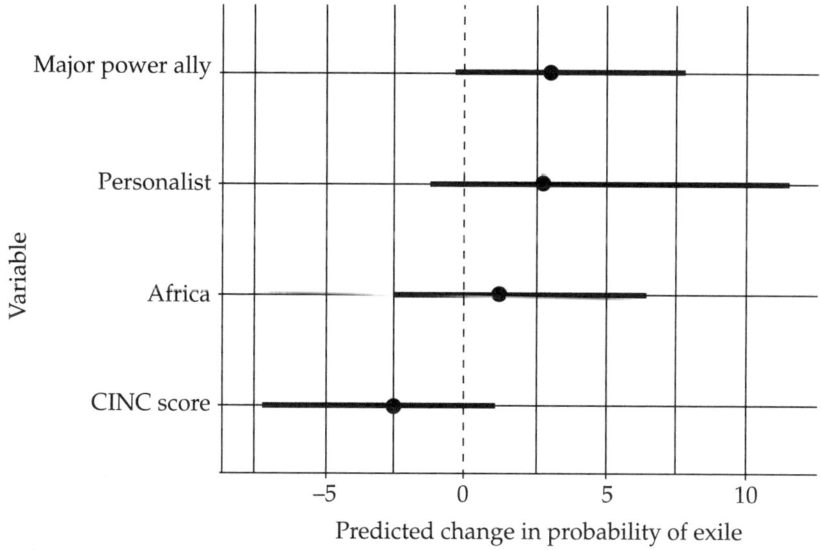

Figure 3. Other potential determinants of exile

statistically significant effect on the probability of exile (the confidence intervals all cross zero). This suggests that other factors do not, on average, have a meaningful effect on the punishment expectations of leaders. To be clear, these other variables sometimes matter (as I discuss in the case studies). But my core theoretical framework that focuses on how the justice cascade interacts with leader culpability remains a compelling, parsimonious explanation for patterns of exile.

Charles Taylor and Punishment in Exile

In this section, I move beyond the statistical correlations and delve into a case study of the Liberian leader Charles Taylor. Why focus on Taylor? At least initially, Taylor might seem like a strange case to examine because he is one of the very few culpable leaders to retire abroad in the accountability era. However, the Taylor case is valuable precisely because Taylor bucks the general trend of recent culpable leaders refusing to go into exile.[42] For starters, the case is theoretically interesting because it allows me to explore why at least some culpable leaders still might choose to retire abroad despite the risk of international arrest. But even more importantly, the

42. Note that in the next chapter I examine a case consistent with the general trend of culpable leaders spurning the exile option and instead risking it all on the battlefield (Muammar Gaddafi during the 2011 Libyan Revolution).

Taylor case allows me to evaluate a part of the theory that was outside the scope of the statistical analysis. While I have already shown that the justice cascade has reduced the likelihood of exile for culpable leaders, a key question remains unanswered: Do the few culpable leaders who go into exile in the accountability era actually get punished?[43] Taylor's fate after going into exile (i.e., his arrest in Nigeria and prosecution at the SCSL) vividly illustrates my argument that international pressure on a host state can undermine its ability to protect a culpable leader.[44]

BACKGROUND

Charles Taylor was born in the Republic of Liberia in 1948 to a father with Americo-Liberian heritage and a mother from a native ethnic group.[45] This mixed heritage would later help Taylor present himself to the country as a leader who represented all Liberians. Taylor's big break came when he was admitted to Bentley College in Waltham, Massachusetts, making him one of the relatively few Liberians with university-level education in the West. After graduating with a degree in economics in 1977, Taylor remained in the United States and became active in the politics of Liberia's expatriate community. Taylor soon established himself as a vocal and charismatic critic of the Liberian president William Tolbert.[46]

In April 1980, a military coup toppled the Tolbert regime and replaced him with Samuel Doe, a twenty-eight-year-old illiterate army sergeant. Taylor, along with many others in the Liberian expatriate community in the United States, returned to their homeland. Since the newly installed Doe regime lacked advisers with expertise in politics and business, many of these expatriates initially were appointed to important positions in the regime. Taylor became the director of Liberia's General Services Agency, a position that put him in charge of the country's procurement policies. Eventually, however, the military power base on which Doe relied became suspicious of "imported" advisers such as Taylor. In 1983, he was removed from his post at the General Services Agency as a result of a politically motivated (though probably accurate) embezzlement accusation (Waugh 2011, 97–99). Realizing that he was no longer safe in Liberia, Taylor returned to the United States.

43. Answering this question is important because my argument rests on the claim that the fear of international punishment is the reason why the rate of exile for culpable leaders has fallen so dramatically. The Taylor case therefore allows me to get at the causal mechanism in a different way.

44. Moreover, due to Taylor's high-profile trial at the SCSL, there is an abundance of rich data on Taylor that enables a thorough investigation of his decision-making.

45. Americo-Liberians are the descendants of freed slaves who founded Liberia in 1847 and later dominated the country's politics.

46. On Taylor's early years and time in the United States, see Waugh 2011, 63–75.

After a brief stint in the United States, Taylor made his way back to Africa in 1985.[47] Though he stayed under the radar for several years, he was far from inactive. Taylor traveled widely in West Africa—including a period of guerrilla training in Libya—as he built regional alliances and founded the National Patriotic Front of Liberia (NPFL), a group dedicated to the overthrow of the Doe regime (Huband 1998, 45–62). On Christmas Eve 1989, Taylor's NPFL forces entered Liberia from the Ivory Coast, starting the First Liberian Civil War. Doe's forces crumbled against the NPFL onslaught, and the NPFL soon controlled the entire country except for the capital city, Monrovia (Ellis 2007, 75–80). At this point, the conflict splintered from a straightforward government–rebel group conflict into a multiparty civil war. One of Taylor's top commanders, Prince Johnson, broke away from the NPFL and formed his own rebel group, the Independent National Patriotic Front of Liberia (INPFL). Additionally, the Economic Community of West African States (ECOWAS) deployed a military unit called ECOMOG, which developed into an independent fighting force whose interests temporarily aligned with those of the Doe regime. In the chaos surrounding Monrovia in 1990, Prince Johnson's INPFL forces captured and murdered President Doe (Waugh 2011, 149–52).

The war, however, did not end with the killing of Doe. Instead, the various factions turned on each other and Liberia descended into a period of warlordism.[48] No single group was able to win a decisive victory that would give it control of all of Liberia, but Taylor became the "richest, most powerful, and best connected of all the warlords" during the early 1990s (Ellis 2007, 105). At some points in the conflict, Taylor's forces controlled as much as 90 percent of Liberia, a swath of territory that many dubbed "Taylorland" (Reno 1998, 92).

47. Taylor's time in the United States between 1983 and 1985 was full of unusual twists and turns. The Doe regime, one of America's Cold War allies, asked the United States to extradite Taylor back to Liberia. Taylor was temporarily held in a prison in Massachusetts, but the extradition request proved to be more complicated. Taylor called on his powerful contacts in the United States, such as the former attorney general Ramsey Clark, to block extradition on the grounds that Taylor would be summarily executed upon his return to Liberia. As the extradition proceedings dragged on, Taylor somehow escaped from prison, reacquired his passport, and drove across the Mexican border without any trouble (Ellis 2007, 67; Waugh 2011, 110). For some, Taylor's escape seemed too miraculous to be an ordinary prison bust. Eric Stover, Victor Peskin, and Alexa Koenig (2016, 252) even liken it to the prison escape in the film *The Shawshank Redemption*. Speculation was rife that the US intelligence community—with whom Taylor allegedly developed secret ties during the early 1980s—intentionally turned a blind eye to Taylor's escape or perhaps even played a role in it. See Bryan Bender, "Former Liberian Dictator Charles Taylor Had US Spy Agency Ties," *Boston Globe*, January 17, 2012. Years later, at his SCSL trial, Taylor would claim that the Central Intelligence Agency helped orchestrate his escape.

48. On warlordism in Africa, see Reno 1998.

After years of fighting, the various warring groups in Liberia eventually seemed ready to make peace. In August 1995, Taylor and the other warlords signed the Abuja Accord, which created a Council of State to share power among the factions. At the last minute, however, Taylor surprised his adversaries by reigniting the conflict. In August 1996, a new peace agreement that was more favorable to Taylor, the Supplement to the Abuja Accord, was struck (Ellis 2007, 105–9). This time, peace really did come to Liberia. After a disarmament and demobilization program, an election was held in July 1997. In what international observers recognized as a relatively free and fair election, Taylor won the presidency with an overwhelming 83 percent of the vote. The International Crisis Group speculated that many Liberians voted for Taylor because they feared the consequences of him losing, noting that "Liberians voted with their heads, not their hearts, in part because Taylor openly threatened to return the country to war if not elected" (International Crisis Group 2002, 13). The terrifying Taylor campaign slogan "He killed my Ma, he killed my Pa, but I will vote for him" seems to support this claim.[49] Thus, after being the most powerful man in Liberia for several years, Charles Taylor was now officially its president. He would remain in office until 2003.

EVIDENCE OF CULPABILITY

Within my theoretical framework, Taylor should be regarded as a culpable leader. This section provides evidence of Taylor's culpability for mass atrocity crimes. While the potential pool of evidence is overwhelming, I focus here on atrocities committed in two contexts: Taylor's actions during the civil war in Liberia and his support for rebels in neighboring Sierra Leone.

The Liberian civil war may have killed as many as two hundred thousand people, about 8 percent of the country's population (Reno 1998, 79). Atrocities were committed on all sides of the conflict, but the behavior of Taylor's NPFL was particularly heinous. During the march on Monrovia and the subsequent period of warlordism, the NPFL indiscriminately massacred civilians in towns and villages across Liberia.[50] In the words of Colin Waugh (2011, 137):

> What had begun as sporadic incidences of atrocities against civilians by the advancing NPFL troops in the insurgency's early days now became their horrific modus operandi. Unpaid, unruly and undisciplined, they had been

49. Sarah Left, "War in Liberia," *Guardian*, August 4, 2003.

50. See Waugh 2011, 132, for a detailed description of precisely where mass killings took place.

> promised by their commanders that they would have the right to loot in enemy areas as compensation, and many had by now been in the campaign for months—it was time to get paid. As the rampaging band of young fighters claiming affiliation to the NPFL approached the capital, their brutality against civilians intensified, and the rebels pillaged and raped their way southwards.

Liberia's Truth and Reconciliation Commission, which attempted to document all war crimes at the conclusion of the hostilities, reports that Taylor's NPFL was responsible for an astounding 63,843 violations of international human rights and international humanitarian law (Truth and Reconciliation Commission of Liberia 2009). While the specific number should be interpreted with a healthy dose of caution, the general conclusion is clear: Taylor's forces committed war crimes on a massive scale.

Taylor was also linked to atrocities committed in neighboring Sierra Leone, where he championed the cause of a rebel group called the Revolutionary United Front (RUF). There are two theories as to why Taylor intentionally brought the fighting across the border from Liberia into Sierra Leone. The first is that Taylor hoped to destabilize his neighbor. Taylor's hatred for Sierra Leone, particularly its leader Joseph Momoh, stemmed from the fact that Momoh had allowed ECOMOG to launch its incursion into Liberia from Sierra Leone's territory. Taylor thus viewed Sierra Leone as partly responsible for his failure to capture Monrovia outright in the early phases of the Liberian conflict. As retaliation, Taylor infamously announced that Sierra Leone would soon "taste the bitterness of war" (Ellis 2007, 93). Taylor made good on his promise by funding, arming, and at times directing the RUF and its nominal leader, a former Sierra Leone corporal named Foday Sankoh. The second explanation is economic. With Sankoh leading the charge against Momoh's central government in Freetown, Sierra Leone descended into an archetypal resource war with the country's huge reserves of diamonds as the ultimate prize.[51] The relationship between Taylor and Sankoh became one of mutual benefit, with Taylor receiving valuable blood diamonds in exchange for the weapons he funneled to Sankoh's forces.[52]

The RUF quickly gained global notoriety for using tactics that were arguably even more brutal than those employed by the NPFL in Liberia. When the RUF captured Sierra Leone's capital city of Freetown, for example,

51. The behavior of both the NPFL and the RUF comports with Jeremy Weinstein's (2006) prediction that rebel groups relying on "economic endowments" are likely to engage in looting and civilian victimization. One particularly brutal NPFL offensive was even called Operation Pay Yourself (Ellis 2007, 108).

52. The UN estimated that the arms-for-diamonds trade between Taylor and the RUF was worth between $25 million and $125 million annually (Tejan-Cole 2009, 209).

atrocity crimes were commonplace: "The [RUF] occupation of Freetown was characterized by the systematic and widespread perpetration of all classes of gross human rights abuses against the civilian population. Civilians were gunned down within their houses, rounded up and massacred on the streets, thrown from the upper floors of buildings, used as human shields, and burnt alive in cars and houses. They had their limbs hacked off with machetes, eyes gouged out with knives, hands smashed with hammers, and bodies burned in boiling water" (Gberie 2005, 130). On top of the killings, the RUF "reveled in imaginative torture techniques" (Tejan-Cole 2009, 208). An executive director of Human Rights Watch summed up the tragic situation in Sierra Leone by noting, "This is not a war in which civilians are accidental victims. This is a war in which civilians are the targets" (Human Rights Watch 1999).

Some have questioned the extent to which Taylor can and/or should be held responsible for the behavior of the RUF in Sierra Leone (e.g., Heller 2013). After all, Foday Sankoh at least nominally led the RUF. While true, this misses the on-the-ground dynamics of the conflict in Liberia and Sierra Leone. The RUF was "functionally a faction of [Taylor's] NPFL" (Tejan-Cole 2009, 209) and was used as "Charles Taylor's foreign legion" (International Crisis Group 2002, i). More specifically, "From the outset, Charles Taylor acted as mentor, patron, banker, and weapons supplier for this motley collection of Sierra Leonean dissidents, bandits, and mercenaries" (Tejan-Cole 2009, 208). In the end, Taylor's close relationship with the RUF would prove to be crucial at his SCSL trial. The SCSL mandate was rather restrictive: to prosecute the individuals most responsible for human rights violations in the territory of Sierra Leone. Hence, the atrocities committed by Taylor's NPFL in Liberia were outside the court's jurisdiction. Nonetheless, the SCSL had plenty of evidence to charge Taylor with war crimes and crimes against humanity associated with his role in aiding and abetting the RUF in Sierra Leone.

In sum, Taylor was unambiguously culpable for mass atrocity crimes. By the time his regime ended in 2003, he had helped perpetrate infamous campaigns of civilian killing in both Liberia and Sierra Leone. My theory would therefore expect Taylor to be reluctant to go into exile because, as a culpable leader in the accountability era, he faced a high risk of arrest.

Taylor's Behavior during the 2003 Crisis

As I noted earlier, Taylor assumed the presidency of Liberia in 1997 after the warring factions agreed to lay down their arms. Peace, however, did not last long. Taylor struggled to make the transition from warlord to national leader. Indeed, he ran the country like a "personal fiefdom" (International Crisis Group 2002, 21), and discontent within Liberia began to build. Furthermore, some of Taylor's neighbors were no longer willing to put up with his meddling in regional affairs. The Guinean president Lansana Conte responded to a major RUF incursion into his country by providing support to a new anti-Taylor rebel group, Liberians United for Reconciliation and Democracy (LURD). In July 2000, LURD invaded Liberia from Guinea and established a foothold in northern Liberia. As LURD slowly began to move toward the capital, its ranks swelled with dissatisfied Liberians ready to take up arms against Taylor. Another rebel group, the Ivory Coast–backed Movement for Democracy in Liberia (MODEL), attacked Taylor from the south. By early 2003, rebels controlled most of the country outside Monrovia, and Taylor's regime was in deep trouble.

The international community was also fed up with Taylor. He had embroiled not only his country, but also the entire region, in war. Moreover, blood diamonds had become a cause célèbre, and Western democracies were under enormous pressure from their own publics to end the war and stop the flow of blood diamonds.[53] As a result, the "growing recognition that Taylor and his regime lay at the heart of the widening spiral of fighting in the region developed into a movement to confront him" (Ward 2003, 8). In May 2002, the UN Security Council adopted Resolution 1408, which included sanctions against Liberia, prohibitions on diamond sales, and travel bans on Taylor and his associates. Additionally, the United States and the United Kingdom seemed to move toward a policy resembling regime change in Liberia, albeit unofficially and indirectly. As one off-the-record US official explained, "You put Taylor in a box, drain his finances, and wait for somebody to remove him" (International Crisis Group 2002, 22).

Around the same time that the international community was confronting Taylor and the two rebel groups were pushing toward Monrovia, another notable development occurred. In 2002 the UN and Sierra Leone jointly created the Special Court for Sierra Leone (SCSL).[54] The origins of the SCSL go back to 2000, when the government of Sierra Leone managed to arrest the RUF leader and Taylor protégé Foday Sankoh.[55] Convinced that they lacked the capacity to try Sankoh, Sierra Leonean authorities contacted the UN about creating a court to address the RUF's atrocities. This process eventually produced the SCSL, whose mandate was to prosecute the individuals

53. In fact, public consciousness about blood diamonds reached new levels thanks to Taylor's trial. A media firestorm erupted when the supermodel Naomi Campbell and the actress Mia Farrow were summoned to testify at the SCSL regarding Taylor's practice of giving blood diamonds as gifts. See, for example, Owen Bowcott, "Charles Taylor and the 'Dirty-Looking Stones' Given to Naomi Campbell," *Guardian*, April 26, 2012.

54. The SCSL is an example of a hybrid tribunal that mixes components of international and national courts.

55. Amazingly, Sankoh was captured in Freetown while trying to hail a taxi to take him to the Nigerian embassy. See "The Strange Tale of Sankoh's Capture," *BBC News*, May 18, 2000.

most responsible for war crimes and other serious violations of international humanitarian law committed in the territory of Sierra Leone after November 30, 1996. The SCSL began its operations in late 2002.

Despite Taylor's constant meddling in Sierra Leone, it was far from obvious that the SCSL would attempt to target Taylor in his capacity as Liberia's president (e.g., Alter 2014, 268). Nonetheless, it was clear that the SCSL at least in theory had the legal authority to pursue Taylor. Beyond its mandate to prosecute the individuals responsible for violations of international humanitarian law, the SCSL statue stated, "The official position of any accused persons, whether as head of state or government or as a responsible government official, shall not relieve such person of criminal responsibility nor mitigate punishment."[56] On March 7, 2003, the presiding judge of the SCSL indicted Charles Taylor on seventeen counts of war crimes and crimes against humanity and signed the concomitant arrest warrant. However, David Crane, the prosecutor at the SCSL, kept the indictment sealed (i.e., secret) for strategic reasons. The SCSL later explained that because "Taylor was a sitting head of state and the subject of a United Nations Security Council travel ban, [the Court] waited for one of Taylor's infrequent known trips out of Liberia in hopes that the country he visited would assist the Court in executing the warrant" (Ward 2003, 9). As a result of the sealed indictment, nobody outside of a select few at the SCSL knew that Taylor was now a wanted war criminal.

Facing adversity at home and abroad, Taylor traveled to Accra, Ghana, in June 2003 to participate in a peace conference with the two main rebel groups, LURD and MODEL, as well as key stakeholders throughout the region (including several heads of state from other West African countries and representatives from the AU). This was the moment the SCSL prosecutor David Crane had been waiting for since getting the sealed indictment in March: a rare chance to arrest Taylor while he ventured outside Liberia's borders. Shortly after Taylor and his entourage arrived in Accra, Crane authorized the unsealing of the international arrest warrant for Taylor. Notably, Crane did not give advance warning to any of the participants in the peace process in Accra. Crane would later say that this was necessary because he had good reason to worry that if he shared his plan, the information would have leaked to Taylor, who then would have avoided traveling to Accra in the first place (Hayner 2007, 8).

Crane's dramatic move proved to be controversial. First off, it put Ghana in a difficult position. Ghana's leadership had invited Taylor to their country to participate in negotiations and explicitly guaranteed his safety (as it did for all the peace conference's participants). Now Ghana was

56. Statute of the Special Court for Sierra Leone, Article 6(2).

suddenly ordered to arrest Taylor. Ghana's president John Kufuor explained his frustration with the indictment:

> Five African presidents were meeting in Accra to find ways of kick-starting the Liberian peace process, and Mr. Taylor had been invited as president of Liberia. We were not even aware that a warrant had been issued for his arrest. Incidentally, the African leadership had taken the initiative to convince Mr. Taylor to resign and allow all the factions in Liberia to negotiate. It was when Mr. Taylor was expected to make a statement that word came in that a warrant had been issued for his arrest. I really felt betrayed by the international community.[57]

Exactly what happened with the communication of the arrest warrant from the SCSL to the Ghanaian authorities remains a mystery, but Taylor somehow managed to fly back to Monrovia before an arrest could be made. The SCSL said it had given the Ghanaians twenty-four hours' notice before publicly revealing the arrest warrant, but the Ghanaians claimed the warrant was not officially delivered in time for them to act.[58] Regardless of whether the mistake was bureaucratic or intentional, Crane's gambit failed to produce an arrest. Charles Taylor escaped to the safety his own national borders provided.

Unsealing the indictment was also controversial because of the effect on the Liberian peace process. Revealing the arrest warrant on the day the warring parties finally entered into negotiations virtually guaranteed that Taylor would back out of the peace conference. This prompted many to doubt Crane's judgment. The Liberian civil war had already featured fourteen failed peace agreements (Stedman, Rothchild, and Cousens 2002, 599–630), most of which lasted just days or weeks, but many observers had hoped Accra might provide a long-lasting solution. According to Kathy Ward (2003, 8), "When news of the indictment broke, Taylor rushed back to Liberia . . . [and] accusations flew that the Court had ruined the best chance for a quick peace in Liberia." Similarly, Abdul Tejan-Cole (2009, 213) noted, "Some diplomats considered the Accra talks the best chance in years to create a peaceful, durable solution for Liberia that would also remove Taylor by allowing him a graceful exit from the presidency as part of a negotiated settlement."

For his part, Taylor was certainly worried about the prospect of facing international justice. He announced that he would heed the growing calls to step down from power and depart Liberia only if the SCSL withdrew its

57. Lansana Gberie, Jarlawah Tonpoh, Efam Dovi, and Osei Baoteng, "Charles Taylor: Why Me?," *New African*, May 2006, 3.

58. On the confusion surrounding the delivery of the SCSL arrest warrant to Ghana, see International Crisis Group 2003, 8.

arrest warrant. In an address to the nation, Taylor said: "People are asking me why I'm afraid to go to Sierra Leone and appear before the court. Why are American officials afraid to appear before the World Court in The Hague? I am willing . . . to give up my constitutional right to a second term but the international community must do the same. They must make a sacrifice and withdraw the indictment" (Waugh 2011, 270). Not surprisingly, the SCSL refused to budge on the issue of Taylor's arrest. The court's mandate was an exclusively legal one that left no room for political considerations. The SCSL Statute made it clear that the prosecutor "shall not seek or receive instructions from any Government or from any other source."[59] Thus, striking a bargain with Taylor would have been beyond the SCSL's authority (Ward 2003, 9). With negotiations about the SCSL arrest warrant going nowhere, fighting resumed between Taylor's forces and the rebels on the outskirts of Monrovia.

As my theory would expect, Taylor appeared increasingly boxed in to a strategy of battling to the end in Liberia. The possibility of prosecution at the SCSL "sent into disarray diplomatic efforts to coax Mr. Taylor to retire."[60] John Blaney, the US ambassador to Liberia, certainly anticipated that Taylor would entrench himself in power. In a cable sent to Secretary of State Colin Powell, Blaney predicted, "Taylor is under intense pressure but will cling to power longer because he fears the UN's War Crimes Tribunal in Sierra Leone."[61] Another diplomat lamented that the SCSL arrest warrant meant that Taylor "now had every incentive to stay in office" (Paradiso 2016, 12). Taylor himself certainly gave Blaney and others good reason to fear a long and bloody fight to the bitter end. After fleeing the Accra conference and returning to Monrovia, Taylor boldly proclaimed, "I will not leave this city. I will remain to encourage my combatants to fight all the way" (Waugh 2011, 274).

To prevent a disastrous final battle for Monrovia, the international community went into overdrive to try to convince Taylor to leave the country during the summer of 2003. The international community's approach included both carrots and sticks. For instance, the UN secretary-general Kofi Annan openly called for the Security Council to consider an intervention.[62] President George W. Bush publicly stated that it was time for Taylor to go. To make the seriousness of the US position absolutely clear to Taylor, Bush even diverted the USS *Kearsarge*, an amphibious assault ship returning

59. Statute of the Special Court for Sierra Leone, Article 15(1).

60. Jess Bravin, "Peace vs. Justice: A Prosecutor Vows No Deals for Thugs in Sierra Leone War," *Wall Street Journal*, July 28, 2003.

61. US Department of State, "Liberia's Opposition Requests Immediate Peacekeeping Force, States Threats Increased since Indictment," Case No. 200604067, June 18, 2003.

62. Colum Lynch, "Annan Requests U.S. Peacekeepers to Liberia," *Washington Post*, July 2, 2003.

from Iraq, to the Liberian coast (Waugh 2011, 274). In addition to these threats, the search was on for a decent exit option that might coax Taylor out of office. As the American diplomat Richard Williamson recalls, "Behind the scenes, the U.S. government and others engaged in frantic diplomacy to arrange for Taylor's exit."[63]

The breakthrough came when the Nigerian president Olusegun Obasanjo offered Taylor safe haven in Nigeria. Importantly, Obasanjo explicitly announced that he would not turn Taylor over to the SCSL or any other international court. In response to a reporter's question about whether he might hand Taylor over to face trial, Obasanjo stated, "No, I will not. That is made clear. . . . The international community understands [the] conditions."[64] While this stopped short of Taylor's initial desire for the SCSL to drop the indictment, it was the next best thing: a promise of protection from Nigeria, the regional power in West Africa. Given the desperate circumstances in which he found himself, this was probably the closest Taylor could get to a post-exit security guarantee.

On top of Nigeria's promise of safe haven, many interactional actors also signed off on the Nigerian exile plan. In fact, virtually every key player—including the United Nations, the United States, the United Kingdom, the African Union, and ECOWAS—supported the Nigerian exile deal when it was struck (Alter 2014, 271; Stover, Peskin, and Koenig 2016, 268). In his 2004 congressional testimony, Howard Jeter, the American ambassador to Nigeria at the time of the deal, stated that Nigeria "acted with our full knowledge and concurrence" (Lizza 2005, 10). This acknowledgment accords with Taylor's claim at his SCSL trial that he had discussed the exile deal with other heads of state in the region and the United States, obtaining consent from all of them before accepting Nigeria's offer (International Justice Monitor 2010). Not only did a multitude of international actors consent to the deal, some of them went further and praised Nigeria for giving Taylor asylum. For instance, President Bush publicly lauded President Obasanjo's commitment to peace in West Africa, and the former State Department official Susan Rice described Nigeria as "taking a bullet" for the rest of the region by sheltering Taylor.[65]

Facing the wrath of two strong rebel groups virtually knocking on the door of the presidential mansion in Monrovia and staunch pressure from the international community, Taylor decided it was time to go. On August 11, 2003, Charles Taylor resigned the presidency and boarded a plane for exile in Nigeria. This was a shocking outcome to many. As one member of the US

63. Richard Williamson, "Charles Taylor and Closing the Gates of Hell," *American Enterprise Institute*, June 5, 2012, available at https://www.aei.org/articles/charles-taylor-and-closing-the-gates-of-hell/.

64. "Nigeria Would Shield Taylor from Trial," *CNN News*, July 10, 2003.

65. "Liberia's Taylor Not Ready to Leave," *CNN News*, July 7, 2003.

embassy staff in Monrovia described it, "Of all the ways people imagined President Charles Taylor's term might end, to the extent they even dared imagine it, a resignation and peaceful transfer of power . . . was certainly one of the least likely. . . . That he would go gently into the night was unthinkable" (Paradiso 2016, 290). Yet Charles Taylor did go gently into the night, which allowed peace to come to Liberia. Only a week after Taylor fled the country, the warring parties signed the Comprehensive Peace Agreement that ended the civil war. Gyude Bryant, a respected businessman, led a transitional government until national elections could be held. In 2005, Liberians selected Ellen Johnson Sirleaf, a Harvard-educated economist who had previously worked at the World Bank, as president in a free and fair election.[66] Sirleaf's tenure—highlighted by the 2011 Nobel Peace Prize for her work on the role of women in peace building—has been widely hailed as a success.[67] If Taylor had not gone into exile, it is hard to imagine how such a smooth transition could have occurred in Liberia.

EVALUATING TAYLOR'S DECISION TO GO INTO EXILE

My theory suggests that culpable leaders in the accountability era should generally view exile as an unattractive post-tenure option. Such leaders will typically prefer to cling to power in hopes of turning the tide of the conflict, thereby avoiding punishment altogether. So why did Taylor go into exile? Two different factors help explain why Taylor chose a foreign retirement over fighting it out in Liberia.

The first reason Taylor opted for exile is that he had virtually no chance of winning the war. This part of the explanation for Taylor's behavior is consistent with my theory. While my main claim was that the justice cascade makes exile less attractive for culpable leaders, I also pointed out that at least some culpable leaders in the accountability era might still prefer retiring abroad over staying at home. Drawing on a discussion of differences in the severity of domestic and international punishment, I argued that if a leader faces near-certain death by continuing to fight, he might be willing to take a chance on exile even though doing so clearly risks future arrest and prosecution. In other words, if a leader has almost no chance of turning the war around, exile might be the "least bad" option—even if the leader is culpable. This is exactly the situation Charles Taylor was in by the late summer of 2003. By that time, LURD and MODEL controlled almost all of Liberia except for Monrovia. Furthermore, the two rebel groups were

66. On the topic of how Western education might influence the governing style of leaders, see Gift and Krcmaric 2017.

67. See, for example, Ty McCormick, "Ellen Johnson Sirleaf Is Ready for Retirement," *Foreign Policy*, September 13, 2016. See also Sirleaf's autobiography, Sirleaf 2010.

making preparations to take the capital when Taylor fled abroad. Taylor's army was clearly a spent force and could not hold off LURD and MODEL for much longer. As one observer in Monrovia put it, "Taylor's boys had no ammunition left, he could keep sending them to the front but then they had nothing left to fire at the rebels. It was over" (Waugh 2011, 276).

Moreover, if history is any guide, Taylor had good reason to worry that ending the war on losing terms would led to a gruesome death. Consider the personal fates of Liberia's two leaders prior to Taylor. As part of the 1980 coup that brought him to power, Samuel Doe personally murdered the previous president, William Tolbert, in his bed in the presidential mansion. Doe proceeded to humiliate Tolbert's family and closest advisers by parading them naked through the streets of Monrovia and then executing them in front of a cheering crowd of soldiers.[68] A decade later, Doe suffered an arguably even worse fate when Prince Johnson's forces captured him. In a killing captured on video, Johnson—seen sipping a Budweiser as a young woman fans him—tortures Doe, eventually cutting off both of his ears and causing him to bleed to death (Ellis 2007, 1–11; Waugh 2011, 151–52). Given this history of previous Liberian leaders meeting horrific ends, Taylor's decision to flee abroad—and thus avoid a grisly fate at the hands of his domestic adversaries—is consistent with my argument's general claim that leaders attempt to avoid post-tenure punishment.

My theory, however, has a harder time explaining the second reason why Taylor retired abroad. Recall that, in the theory chapter, I discussed time inconsistency problems in the context of peace-for-exile deals. The basic idea was that the international community might dangle the possibility of a safe exile to coax a violent leader into an early retirement. But once the leader is out of the country and no longer wreaking havoc on his own people, the international community would be tempted to renege on the deal. The very same international actors who previously preferred exile over continued war might now prefer justice over allowing a brutal leader to get off scot-free. As I elaborate in the next section, this is exactly what eventually happened in Taylor's case. In fact, it was possible to see the looming time inconsistency problem even before Taylor left Liberia. One senior American official asserted that justice for Taylor was "on the back burner" while they negotiated his exile, which implied that the United States would return to the issue of accountability for Taylor's crimes at some later date.[69] Moreover, Taylor failed in his efforts to get the SCSL to drop its indictment, so it was reasonable to expect that the SCSL and human

68. Leon Dash, "Liberian Soldiers Taunt, Shoot 13 Former Leaders," *Washington Post*, April 23, 1980.

69. "Liberia's Taylor Not Ready to Leave," *CNN News*, July 7, 2003. Another American official, Assistant Secretary of State Walter Kansteiner, was even more open about his wishes regarding Taylor's fate: "We want to see Charles Taylor in leg irons in front of the court in

rights advocacy groups would not let the issue of justice disappear simply because Taylor had left Liberia.

Despite this—and this is where Taylor's decision-making is not quite consistent with my argument—Taylor appeared relatively confident that he could evade punishment in exile. To be clear, there is no evidence suggesting that Taylor naively believed that Western powers would respect the exile deal. Rather, Taylor thought that he would be safe because he trusted President Obasanjo's promise of sanctuary in Nigeria. Even if Western powers tried to renege on the deal in the future, Taylor was confident his foreign protector would never turn him over to an international tribunal such as the SCSL.

Taylor's trust in Obasanjo was partly a product of the broader pan-African context in which they operated. Many African leaders shared a common struggle against colonialism, creating tight bonds among leaders in the region. Even among the next generation of leaders, "Loyalty to members of the heads of state club is still strong" (Baker 2004, 1496). This is especially true when it comes to international justice, which many African leaders view as a form of neocolonialism whereby the Western powers infringe on the sovereignty of their weaker African counterparts.[70] This is exemplified by the fact that, as a sign of solidarity, the presidents of Ghana, South Africa, Mozambique, and Nigeria personally accompanied Taylor on his flight from Liberia to Nigeria to begin his exile (Tejan-Cole 2009, 215). Thus, when Obasanjo put his own reputation on the line by publicly promising to protect Taylor from the SCSL, it carried a high level of credibility. Turning Taylor over to the court would have been a blatant violation of the so-called African hospitality Nigeria had offered him (Hayner 2007, 8).

Given this, it was unthinkable to many observers at the time of Taylor's exile that Nigeria would not live up to its word to shelter Taylor. As the International Crisis Group noted just after Taylor went into exile in 2003, "In a region where solidarity and brotherhood links are strong among heads of state, the scenario of one president handing another over to the Court was implausible" (International Crisis Group 2003, 9). Writing around the same time, Kathy Ward (2003, 10) similarly argued, "Strong links of solidarity and brotherhood among West African heads of state mean that one West African president would not easily hand another over to the Special Court." Taylor himself thought along the same lines. He put a

Sierra Leone." See Jess Bravin, "Peace vs. Justice: A Prosecutor Vows No Deals for Thugs in Sierra Leone War," *Wall Street Journal*, July 28, 2003.

70. Taylor himself tapped into this dynamic when describing his indictment: "This is not about Taylor. . . . It is about the question: can Africa be free? It sets an unhealthy precedent. Tomorrow it could be Museveni, Kagame, Mugabe, or Gbagbo." Quoted in Waugh 2011, 274. It turned out that Taylor was partly correct. In 2011, the Ivory Coast's Laurent Gbagbo was arrested and extradited to the ICC.

great deal of faith in Obasanjo's offer of protection, proclaiming that "my brother will never betray me" (Waugh 2011, 284). Thus, despite the SCSL indictment and the outstanding arrest warrant, Taylor appears to have believed that he could safely live out his days in a splendid exile as so many past culpable leaders had done. As Bruce Baker (2004, 1490) summarizes, "When Taylor finally left Liberia for Calabar City in eastern Nigeria in August 2003, he believed politics had triumphed over justice: that he was under the 'protective custody' of the presidents of Nigeria, South Africa, and Namibia; and that he had the international community's approval."

Overall, my theory offers a partial but imperfect explanation for why Taylor went into exile. Since Taylor almost certainly would have faced a gruesome death if he had stayed in Liberia, the theory can account for why Taylor was willing to retire abroad even though he was culpable. However, my argument is not up to the task of explaining the fact that Taylor believed he could entirely avoid punishment in exile. Indeed, Taylor's high level of personal trust in Obasanjo is a unique aspect of the case that my theory—which aims toward generalizability—does not capture adequately. Despite this shortcoming, the great value of examining the Charles Taylor case lies in what happened *after* Taylor retired to Nigeria. Precisely because Taylor broke with the general trend of culpable leaders in the accountability era avoiding exile, we can observe how international pressure on Nigeria ultimately undermined Taylor's safety and led to his prosecution at the SCSL.[71]

INTERNATIONAL PUNISHMENT: TAYLOR'S ARREST AND TRIAL AT THE SCSL

As time passed, it became clear that Taylor had erred by putting so much faith in Nigeria's Obasanjo. In fact, subsequent events in the Charles Taylor saga vividly illustrate my theory's causal mechanisms. Recall that I argued that third-party states sheltering culpable leaders will generally have a low cost tolerance for international pressure. While a host state may prefer to shelter an old friend or an ideological ally, an ex-leader provides few benefits to his host. Therefore, if international actors can generate even minimal costs of protection, the host state has little incentive to continue sheltering the culpable leader. This dynamic would eventually be Taylor's undoing.

After his flight to Nigeria, Taylor initially settled into a comfortable exile in a seaside villa in the town of Calabar, prompting one journalist to label Taylor's exile "an extended holiday."[72] Almost immediately, however, the

71. It is worth pointing out that if culpable leaders in the accountability era *never* went into exile, it would be impossible to observe the effects of international pressure on host states.

72. The report also suggested Taylor was living a luxurious lifestyle in Calabar: "The exiled Liberian president sleeps in a rambling, red-roofed mansion, travels in a pair of Land

Nigerian leadership began to face a torrent of international pressure due to their new guest. The SCSL desperately wanted to apprehend Taylor and sought ways to convince Nigeria to renege on the asylum deal. The court reached an arrangement with Interpol in which it issued a high-profile "red notice" requesting that all national governments cooperate with arresting Taylor.[73] The SCSL's objectives also overlapped considerably with international human rights groups such as Amnesty International, Human Rights Watch, the Soros Foundation, and No Peace Without Justice, which all brought international attention to Taylor's five-star retirement home by naming and shaming Nigeria (Alter 2014, 271). Moreover, local civil society groups in Nigeria, led by journalists who had suffered amputations at the hands of the RUF while reporting in Sierra Leone, initiated a civil lawsuit against the Nigerian government. The journalists argued that Nigeria's international legal obligations meant that the country had to turn Taylor over to the SCSL.[74] The case ultimately failed, but not before it went all the way up to the Nigerian Federal High Court, drawing plenty of attention in the process. Hence, by tapping into new norms of global accountability, NGOs and activists made sure that Charles Taylor could not quietly disappear in exile as so many brutal leaders had previously done.

While NGOs kept the issue of Taylor's exile alive, powerful Western states and international institutions played an arguably even more important role. In fact, many of the same states that helped facilitate Taylor's peace-for-exile deal changed course and later pressured Nigeria to give Taylor up to the SCSL. For example, the European Parliament and the US Congress both passed resolutions urging Nigeria to turn over Taylor so that he could face justice (Stover, Peskin, and Koenig 2016, 269). The US Congress also authorized a $2 million dollar reward for Taylor's capture.[75] At the UN, the Security Council froze Taylor's assets and made the unusual move of expanding the mission of the UN peacekeeping force in Liberia to include the arrest and transfer of Taylor to the SCSL.[76] A Security Council spokesperson added, "It is a matter of time. In due course, Taylor will face justice. There cannot be impunity for Charles Taylor."[77] The proverbial noose around Taylor was slowly beginning to tighten.

Rovers with tinted-glass windows and buys food and electronic gadgetry in such abundance that residents complain he has caused inflation." See Craig Timberg, "A Warlord's Exile Divides His Hosts," *Washington Post*, October 9, 2005.

73. "Charles Taylor Wanted by Interpol," *BBC News*, December 4, 2003.

74. "Nigerians Challenge Taylor Asylum," *BBC News*, July 14, 2004.

75. "In $87.5 Billion Bill, $2 Million Bounty for Exiled Liberian," *New York Times*, November 10, 2003.

76. See UN Security Council Resolution 1532, March 12, 2004; and UN Security Council Resolution 1638, November 11, 2005.

77. Quote from Emyr Jones Parry on June 24, 2004. See "Taylor, Stubborn since his Childhood," *IRIN News*, March 29, 2006.

For his part, President Obasanjo at first remained steadfast in his promise of protection for Taylor. Yet Nigeria was certainly getting more than it had bargained for when it offered to shelter Taylor as a way to facilitate a transfer of power in Liberia. Less than two years after receiving heaps of praise for taking Taylor, Nigeria now found itself in the opposite position. Obasanjo was frustrated at the international community's 180-degree turn, later telling CNN:

> People's memories are short when they want it to be short. People have forgotten that if Charles Taylor had not moved out, there would never have been peace in Liberia. And the election that had taken place, which brought Ellen Johnson Sirleaf, would never have taken place. . . . So we have played the role we believed we should play, and whether it's appreciated or not, believe that we have played our role in the interests of peace in that area, in the interests of peace in our subregion of West Africa, and in the interests of peace in the international community.[78]

In an attempt to stave off the growing international pressure, Obasanjo made a partial concession in May 2005. He stated that Nigeria would turn Taylor over *if* the newly elected Liberian government (elections were scheduled for October 2005) formally requested Taylor's extradition. Looking back, this was a notable turning point in the quest for justice for Taylor, yet it was not considered particularly consequential at the time. As one observer noted, "It was generally agreed that it would be politically difficult for Nigeria to revoke the hospitality it had extended to Taylor, and the Liberian elections were still months away" (Tejan-Cole 2009, 216).

Ellen Johnson Sirleaf was elected president of Liberia in October 2005. Given Obasanjo's prior claim that he would only extradite Taylor if the new president of Liberia requested it, Taylor's fate was now partly in Sirleaf's hands. To the dismay of many human rights advocates, Sirleaf quickly made it clear that bringing Taylor to justice was not a priority. In her first news conference as Liberia's leader, Sirleaf stated that she did not want "the Mr. Taylor issue to be the issue that constrains us or the issue that causes us not to be able to do what we have to do here for the Liberian people. So we want to see it as a secondary issue, even though it may be of utmost concern to the international community."[79] Instead, Sirleaf said she planned to focus on rebuilding Liberia's economy and consolidating the country's still precarious security situation.[80]

78. "Taylor Arrested; Interview with Olusegun Obasanjo," *CNN News*, aired April 1, 2006, transcript available at http://transcripts.cnn.com/TRANSCRIPTS/0604/01/i_if.01.html.

79. "Taylor 'Not Priority' for Liberia," *BBC News*, January 27, 2006.

80. At the time of Sirleaf's election, Liberia did not have a standing army and was still in the process of demobilizing some militias.

Sirleaf's desire to downplay the "Mr. Taylor issue" did not sit well with the international community, who were now adamant that Taylor should be prosecuted. As a result, the international lobbying campaign to end Taylor's impunity began to pressure Sirleaf almost as much as Obasanjo. The Campaign Against Impunity, a coalition of several hundred civil society groups, wrote an open letter to Sirleaf demanding that she request that Nigeria hand Taylor over.[81] The US secretary of state Condoleezza Rice communicated to Sirleaf that the United States thought it was time for Taylor to stand trial at the SCSL (Tejan-Cole 2009, 217). Most strikingly, the United States threatened to withhold aid to Liberia if she did not request Taylor's extradition.[82] In an interview, Sirleaf admitted that this international campaign to apprehend Taylor was hard for her to ignore: "We also are facing . . . pressure—I must use that word—from the UN, from the US, from the European Union, who are all our major partners in development, on the need to do something about the Charles Taylor issue."[83] For Sirleaf, who had hoped to draw on Western connections made during her time at Harvard University and the World Bank to finance development in Liberia, this international pressure proved decisive. On March 17, 2006, Sirleaf formally requested that Nigeria extradite Taylor.

Now the ball shifted back into Obasanjo's court. Would he, as previously stated, comply with Liberia's request? Obasanjo initially delayed, hoping to find a way to avoid handing Taylor over, which would violate his promise of sanctuary. Obasanjo finally issued a cagey statement that Sirleaf was "free to come and take President Taylor into her custody."[84] Obviously, Sirleaf could not personally arrest Taylor nor could she send a force into Nigeria to make the arrest. Liberia and Nigeria appeared to be headed toward a standoff over Taylor's fate, and human rights groups around the world loudly condemned Nigeria.[85]

The standoff was interrupted by one last surprise from Taylor: he disappeared from his villa in Calabar just days before Obasanjo was set to visit the United States. Rumors swirled that Taylor was on the run, while other reports suggested that Nigeria was helping Taylor slip into Cameroon to

81. "Taylor 'Not Priority' for Liberia," *BBC News*, January 27, 2006.

82. Lydia Polgreen, "Nigeria Says Ex-President of Liberia Has Disappeared," *New York Times*, March 29, 2006.

83. "Johnson-Sirleaf Describes Attempts to Come to Terms with Liberia's Violent Past," *Newshour with Jim Lehrer*, March 23, 2006, transcript available at www.pbs.org/newshour/bb/africa/jan-june06/liberia_3-23.html.

84. "Dispute over Taylor Extradition," *BBC News*, March 27, 2006.

85. Lydia Polgreen, "Nigeria Says Ex-President of Liberia Has Disappeared," *New York Times*, March 29, 2006; "Dispute over Taylor Extradition," *BBC News*, March 27, 2006; Robyn Dixon, "Wanted Ex-President of Liberia Missing," *Los Angeles Times*, March 29, 2006.

spare itself the embarrassment of reneging on its pledge of safe haven.[86] To this day, Taylor's activities for a twenty-four-hour window remain a mystery. Regardless, the United States threatened "consequences" for Nigeria if Taylor was not immediately apprehended and transferred to the court.[87] Moreover, Bush administration officials told Obasanjo that his meeting with the American president—a prized opportunity for any foreign leader, especially one who sought to present himself as a regional leader and elder statesman in Africa—would be cancelled if Taylor was not arrested (Tejan-Cole 2009, 218). At this point, the Nigerian government finally decided sheltering Taylor was not worth the cost. Speaking at the White House the next day, Obasanjo announced to the world that Taylor had been apprehended in Nigeria. Taylor was flown to Liberia on a Nigerian plane, where he immediately boarded a UN helicopter that took him into the custody of the SCSL in Freetown.

Taylor's SCSL trial was ultimately relocated from Freetown to The Hague in the Netherlands because of fears that a local trial might destabilize a region that had only recently reached a state of peace.[88] The original indictment for Taylor included seventeen counts of war crimes, crimes against humanity, and other serious violations of international humanitarian law, but the SCSL prosecution team had reduced this to eleven counts by the opening of the trial. Given the court's mandate, Taylor was charged for his role in aiding and abetting RUF atrocities in Sierra Leone rather than for the abuses associated with the NPFL in Liberia. Some of the specific charges against Taylor included terrorizing the civilian population, murder and unlawful killings, rape and sexual slavery, and the recruitment and use of child soldiers.[89]

In April 2012, the SCSL found Taylor guilty and sentenced him to fifty years in prison. One reporter at Taylor's trial vividly described the scene: "Once the commanding and charismatic warlord, Charles Taylor cut a distant, bewildered, even pathetic figure in the courtroom." After the SCSL chief justice delivered the verdict, "the 64-year-old Taylor blinked nervously and seemed lost. He tried to speak afterwards, but his microphone was cut off and his appeals were ignored as the justices filed out of the

86. "Nigeria Faces Anger over Taylor," *BBC News*, March 29, 2006. According to John Campbell, the US ambassador to Nigeria during the 2006 standoff over Taylor's fate, Obasanjo also worried that going back on his word would weaken his standing as a regional leader (J. Campbell 2013, 157).

87. Felix Onuah, "Wanted Liberian Warlord Disappears in Nigeria," *Reuters*, March 28, 2006.

88. Despite the relocation of Taylor's trial to The Hague, the trial was entirely an SCSL affair and was not affiliated with the ICC.

89. For a legal analysis of the Taylor sentencing, see Heller 2013.

courtroom."[90] It was an inglorious end for Liberia's former warlord president, and one that guaranteed he would spend the rest of his life behind bars.[91]

The evidence presented in this chapter supports my claim that international justice shapes patterns of exile. The quantitative tests showed that there is no relationship between leader culpability and exile during the impunity era because all leaders had a viable exile option if they were overthrown. During the accountability era, however, I found that culpable leaders—those who have a compelling reason to fear post-tenure international punishment—are less likely to flee abroad. The results are not only statistically significant but also substantively meaningful. Whereas culpable and nonculpable leaders went into exile at nearly identical rates before 1998, culpable leaders have been about six times less likely to go into exile after 1998. In addition to the quantitative tests, I offered a case study of Charles Taylor's exile. This case enabled me to assess one of my theory's assumptions that was not tested in the statistical model: Do culpable leaders in fact get punished when they go into exile in the accountability era? Not only did the Taylor saga provide an answer, it also convincingly illustrated the theory's causal mechanisms at work: international pressure on Nigeria undermined its ability to shelter Taylor over the long haul. Thus, both the quantitative and qualitative evidence bolster my theoretical claims.

What should we make of these findings? From a normative perspective, almost everyone would agree that a world with fewer tyrants escaping to comfortable safe havens is a welcome development. Yet if we care about the political consequences of limiting retirement options for bad leaders, things are not so straightforward. Since a credible threat of international justice makes the availability of a safe post-tenure exile conditional on a leader's behavior while in power, I expect the justice cascade will produce a pair of indirect effects: it should both prolong civil conflicts and deter mass atrocities. In the next two chapters, I will explore these opposing effects, one positive and one perverse, in detail.

90. Leo Cendrowicz, "Warlord Convicted: Liberia's Charles Taylor Found Guilty of War Crimes," *Time*, April 26, 2012.

91. Taylor appealed the SCSL decision, but the verdict was upheld in 2013.

CHAPTER 4

The Perverse Effect

Prolonging Civil Wars

This chapter tests a second observable implication of the theory. If culpable leaders in the accountability era are reluctant to go into exile because they fear post-tenure international punishment, they should also be more willing to keep fighting during civil conflicts. Put differently, if a ruler thinks there is no other way out of trouble, he has an incentive to risk it all on the battlefield—even if the prospects for victory are slim—and hope to turn the tide of the conflict. Consequently, I expect that leader culpability has no effect on civil war duration during the impunity era. During the accountability era, however, conflicts with culpable leaders should last longer than those with nonculpable leaders.

Civil war duration is an important topic because civil war is one of the greatest catastrophes a country can experience. In addition to the immediate cost in terms of human lives lost, a civil war can decimate a country in more subtle ways. Scholars have found that civil wars retard economic growth (Collier 2008), undermine public health and facilitate the transmission of infectious diseases (Ghobarah, Huth, and Russett 2003), exacerbate sexual violence (Cohen 2016), displace civilians and generate massive refugee flows (Weiner 1996), and even spread conflict into neighboring countries (Krcmaric 2014; Salehyan 2009; Salehyan and Gleditsch 2006). The costs of civil wars are so high that one prominent economist argues that they should be understood as "development in reverse" (Collier 2008, 27).

Yet civil wars show substantial variation in how long they last and, consequently, how costly they are. For instance, David Cunningham (2006) found that about a quarter of civil wars are resolved within a few months, but 8 percent of civil wars last over two decades. Scholars have proposed numerous theories to explain this variation in conflict duration. One set of explanations calls attention to a rebel group's capacity to resist the state. This point of view highlights how variables such as the military strength of the rebels and whether the rebels have external sources of support can affect war duration. A different school of thought focuses on the state's ability to target rebel groups. Factors that enhance or limit state capacity, such as economic development and mountainous terrain, are used to explain conflict duration. Yet another set of arguments explores the nature of the bargaining environment between the government and the rebels. A key finding from this perspective is that civil wars tend to last longer when there are multiple veto players who can block the implementation of a peace agreement.

The argument advanced here does not directly contradict or aim to undermine any of the theories in the existing literature. The factors just mentioned are doubtlessly important in many cases. The existing literature, however, is missing an important dynamic that influences the incentives of belligerents to keep fighting or make peace. By focusing on the international environment (impunity era versus accountability era) and leader characteristics (culpable leaders versus nonculpable leaders), my argument generates a new set of predictions that help us understand patterns of civil war duration.

Before testing these predictions, it is worth briefly noting how the evidence presented in this chapter relates to previous research. I am not the first to suggest that international justice might conceivably exacerbate civil conflicts (recall the pessimist viewpoint discussed in chapter 1).[1] Existing work on this topic, however, can be critiqued for lacking a strong base of evidence. Some scholars start with a specific arrest warrant and then assess how it influenced a conflict's resolution, but this is an indeterminate research design because it selects only cases where international courts are involved. To their credit, others have examined differences between conflicts where international courts get involved and conflicts where they do not (e.g., Prorok 2017; Snyder and Vinjamuri 2003). But this strategy also has some potential downsides. In addition to endogeneity concerns, this empirical strategy risks zeroing in on the individual trees so much that it loses sight of the forest.[2] A study that only examines cross-case variation in ICC arrest warrants, for example, would fail to capture the dramatic over-time variation in the international justice landscape. Partly due to these shortcomings, Kathryn Sikkink (2011, 133–34) reasonably concludes that "there is not yet systematic empirical evidence that prosecutions block

1. There is also some related research on amnesties, legal mechanisms that shield combatants from prosecution for war crimes or other human rights violations. Geoff Dancy (2018), for example, offers a useful discussion of the conditions under which formal amnesties might help end civil wars.

2. If international courts are more likely to get involved in particularly difficult and intractable conflicts, then an observed correlation between international prosecutions and prolonged conflict duration could be spurious.

peace processes or exacerbate conflict." I seek to rectify this gap in our knowledge by providing evidence that international justice can in fact prolong civil wars under certain conditions.

Evaluating an explanation of conflict duration—why some civil wars last so long while others end quickly—presents a tricky set of empirical challenges. One option is to specify a threshold for what constitutes a long civil war (say, for example, five years). This is problematic, however, because the choice of the threshold is arbitrary. Additionally, it would treat a conflict that lasts only a couple of weeks the same as a conflict that lasts a couple of years. Another option is to draw a distinction between wars that have been resolved and wars that are still ongoing. Yet this is also a dubious technique because it does not handle so-called censored data well. Civil wars that are still ongoing now may continue for a very long time or they may be nearly over. At this point, however, it is impossible to know.

To avoid the aforementioned problems, I turn to event history models (sometimes called duration models or survival models). Originally developed by statisticians to determine how medical interventions (e.g., various cancer treatments) influence patient health (e.g., time until the next relapse), event history models have several advantages. First, they are designed specifically to estimate how independent variables influence the length of time something lasts. Second, duration models handle censored data well because they explicitly incorporate uncertainty about how long something will last into the future.

The event history analysis offers compelling support for my hypothesis: civil wars last significantly longer when culpable leaders are in power during the accountability era only. Moreover, I pair the statistical tests with a qualitative case study of Muammar Gaddafi's behavior during the 2011 Libyan conflict. As I will discuss later in the chapter, the Gaddafi case offers a vivid illustration of how the changing landscape of international justice undermines the viability of a safe retirement abroad for culpable leaders, which in turn produces incentives to keep fighting at home.

Civil War Duration Statistical Tests

DATA

Since the dependent variable for this test is civil war duration, the first step is to identify the relevant population of civil wars. I identify civil conflicts and their duration with the widely used UCDP/PRIO armed conflict dataset. This dataset defines a civil conflict as "a contested incompatibility that concerns government and/or territory where the use of armed force between two parties, of which at least one is the government of a state, results in at least 25 battle-related deaths" (N. P. Gleditsch et al. 2002, 619).

The dataset has an event history structure and includes civil conflicts between 1960 and 2010.[3] Each subject in the data is a conflict dyad, meaning that the unit of analysis is a specific government–rebel group pairing, not the country as a whole. Conflicts are considered to be ongoing as long as the dyad produces at least twenty-five battle deaths annually. Conflicts are coded as over when there is a clear-cut termination event (such as a military victory or a peace agreement) or when there is a lull in fighting that falls beneath twenty-five battle deaths for two consecutive calendar years. This conflict dyads approach follows recent advances in modeling war duration and usefully differentiates between several contemporaneous conflicts in the same country.[4]

Given my theory, it is important to establish scope conditions on precisely which types of civil conflict I seek to explain. At a broad conceptual level, my argument should help explain civil war duration when two conditions are met: the conflict at least minimally threatens the leader's personal safety and the leader has an opportunity to double down on the battlefield. These conditions are generally met when an armed opposition group fights the incumbent regime for control of the government (often called center-seeking civil wars). One example of such a conflict occurred in 1979 as Ugandan rebels marched on the capital city, Kampala, and the Ugandan leader Idi Amin decided to flee into exile rather than continue the war.

There are, however, three types of civil conflict that show up in the UCDP/PRIO dataset that fall beyond the scope of my theory and therefore are excluded from the analysis.[5] The first set of conflicts that I drop from the civil war duration dataset are coups d'état, which occur when elites attempt to unseat the sitting head of state using illegal means. Even though they are typically considered to be a phenomenon distinct from civil war, coups are included in the UCDP/PRIO dataset since it aims to include the full universe of organized armed conflicts. However, because coups often begin with the arrest or killing of the leader (and commonly are over in a single day), their connection to my argument's predictions on civil war duration is tenuous.[6] Indeed, in many coups, the leader never

3. This is the period for which I have reliable data on the covariates.

4. For a more detailed take on the merits of studying civil conflict dyads, see Cunningham, Gleditsch, and Salehyan 2009.

5. To be clear, my starting point for identifying the relevant population of civil wars was the list of conflicts that the UCDP/PRIO armed conflict dataset codes as civil wars or internationalized civil wars. I then excluded the three types of civil conflict that fall outside the scope of my theory (described earlier). Given my interest in civil war duration, I uniformly excluded conflicts that the UCDP/PRIO armed conflict dataset classifies as interstate wars or extrasystemic (i.e., colonial) wars from the analysis.

6. See Thyne 2017 for a compelling argument that scholars should generally remove coups from models of civil war duration.

even has the chance to decide between fleeing abroad and risking it all on the battlefield.

The second excluded category is secessionist civil wars, conflicts where a particular region tries to break away from the rest of the country and create an autonomous state. Since the fighting in secessionist wars almost always takes place on the periphery of the country and does not directly threaten the leader's safety, my theory's ability to explain these conflicts is limited. To be sure, secessionist conflicts can undermine a leader's ability to remain in office via political processes if the war is unpopular (e.g., a leader might get voted out of office for waging an unpopular counterinsurgency campaign). But the dynamics identified in my theory will be less relevant since the conflict itself does not threaten the leader's personal security in the same way as, say, rebels approaching the capital city in a center-seeking civil war. This move to focus only on wars fought over control of the central government builds on developments in conflict scholarship to disaggregate civil wars according to the nature of the fighting and/or the goals of the belligerents (e.g., Kalyvas and Balcells 2010; Krcmaric 2018b; Paine 2016; Valentino, Huth, and Balch-Lindsay 2004).[7]

The third and final excluded category of conflict is extraterritorial warfare, conflicts in which most of the fighting does not take place on the government's territory. One prominent example of an extraterritorial conflict from the UCDP/PRIO dataset is the United States–al Qaeda dyad, which for the most part was not fought on American soil.[8] Even more so than secessionist wars, extraterritorial conflicts do not typically threaten the leader's personal well-being and thus my argument is not particularly germane.

Overall, then, the preceding three types of conflict are omitted from the analysis since they fall outside the scope conditions under which my theory should help explain civil war duration. All other civil conflicts, which we might think of as stereotypical civil wars that pit a rebel group against the incumbent regime in a fight for control of the government, are included in the statistical models.

The independent variable of interest once again is leader culpability, which is defined in the same manner as in the previous chapter. As a reminder, culpability simply refers to whether leaders have previously presided over mass atrocities (defined as the state-sponsored killing of at least one thousand civilians). A leader becomes culpable starting in the year in which the mass killing episode begins and the culpability lasts throughout

7. As Jack Paine (2016, 728) points out, "Disaggregating types of civil war . . . provides needed theoretical and empirical clarifications" for long-standing debates in the civil conflict literature.

8. Following a similar logic, I exclude the wars in Iraq and Afghanistan during the American occupations there.

the rest of the leader's tenure. Thus, in the event history analysis in this chapter, *Culpable Leader* is a dummy variable that equals 1 for conflict dyads with a culpable leader and 0 otherwise. Note that the leader culpability variable can change over the course of a conflict depending on the specific leader in power.[9]

In addition to the leader culpability variable, I also control for several other factors that are thought to influence civil conflict duration. One set of explanations for war duration focuses on a rebel group's ability to resist the state. Almost by definition, a rebel group must possess the capability to resist the state's coercive forces for a conflict to continue. I proxy *Rebel Strength* with the Non-State Actor dataset's (Cunningham, Gleditsch, and Salehyan 2009) measure of the military strength of the rebels relative to the government.[10] Based on a qualitative assessment of each conflict, this variable provides information on whether rebels are weaker than, stronger than, or at parity with the government. Additionally, rebel groups can continue fighting when they would otherwise face defeat if they receive war materiel and cross-border sanctuary from foreign states (e.g., Salehyan 2009). Therefore, I include *Rebel External Support*, a dummy variable from the Non-State Actor dataset indicating whether each rebel group receives explicit support from the government of a foreign state.

Another set of explanations for conflict duration involves the state's capacity to target rebel groups. The classic indicator for state capacity in cross-national research is GDP per capita, which is thought to reflect a state's military, financial, and bureaucratic competencies (e.g., Fearon 2004; Fearon and Laitin 2003).[11] As a result, *Development* measures the natural log of each country's GDP per capita using data from K. S. Gleditsch 2002. Moreover, state capacity may be enhanced when states receive support from foreign backers, such as when the superpowers helped prop up weak governments during the Cold War. Hence, I control for *Government External Support*, a dummy variable indicating whether each government receives explicit support from a foreign state (Cunningham, Gleditsch, and Salehyan 2009). Rough terrain, by contrast, is expected to increase conflict duration because it limits the reach of the state and offers insurgents geography that is conducive to asymmetrical warfare. Consequently, I include

9. More generally, I use time-varying covariates to account for the fact that the values of some independent variables change over the course of the same conflict.

10. The Non-State Actor dataset (Cunningham, Gleditsch, and Salehyan 2009) supplements the standard UCDP/PRIO armed conflict data with information on the characteristics of all rebel groups involved in intrastate conflicts.

11. It is worth mentioning, however, that interpreting the meaning of GDP per capita in conflict studies is controversial. While many have used economic development to proxy state capacity, others believe it captures the opportunity cost of engaging in rebellion (Collier and Hoeffler 2004).

Mountains, a variable that measures the percentage of each country's territory that is mountainous (Fearon and Laitin 2003).

Finally, the bargaining environment during a conflict might influence war duration. Cunningham (2006), for example, shows that civil wars tend to last longer when there are multiple veto players who can block the implementation of a peace agreement. To control for this dynamic, *Multiparty War* is a dummy variable indicating whether each conflict dyad is part of a multiparty civil war involving more than one rebel group.

MAIN RESULTS

Using the data just described, I estimate event history models of civil war duration. To account for the possibility of dependence among dyads that are part of the same broader conflict, I cluster standard errors on the UCDP/PRIO war identification code. Of the various event history models available, I estimate Weibull models to evaluate my predictions on conflict duration.[12] The advantage of the Weibull model is that it gives precise estimates in relatively small datasets like the one used here (Box-Steffensmeier and Jones 1997, 1434), making it a popular choice in studies of civil conflict (e.g., Balcells and Kalyvas 2014; Fortna 2008).

As before, I pursue two different strategies for modeling the effects of the justice cascade. The first option is to disaggregate the data into the impunity era (pre-1998) and the accountability era (post-1998). For the impunity era, I use data on conflicts that begin anytime between the start of 1960 and the end of 1997. The dyads enter the data when the conflict starts and exit when the conflict ends (the dyad "fails"). Some dyads never experience failure during the observation period and are right censored at the end of 1997. For the accountability era, I use data on conflicts that begin anytime between the start of 1998 and the end of 2010. Dyads enter the data in the same process just described and are right censored at the end of 2010 if the conflict is still ongoing at that time. The second option is to estimate an interaction model for the entire 1960–2010 period that interacts the leader culpability variable with a post-1998 dummy variable. For this model, I use data on conflicts that begin anytime between the start of 1960 and the end of 2010, and dyads are right censored at the end of 2010 if fighting is still raging at that point.

These different modeling strategies present the same flexibility/efficiency trade-off discussed in the chapter on exile (chapter 3). However, when examining conflict duration, there may be an additional reason to favor the models with the disaggregated data. In the split sample models, long-running conflicts that began in the pre-1998 period are *not* included in

12. As I will discuss later, my results do not hinge on the choice of event history model.

the post-1998 sample. Instead, they are right censored at the end of 1997. This is important because allowing such conflicts to stretch into the accountability era sample might bias the results if particularly intractable conflicts are both more likely to generate mass atrocities and less likely to terminate before 1998. Limiting the accountability era sample to conflicts that begin after 1998 mitigates this concern. By contrast, with the interaction model, long-running conflicts that start in the impunity era are included in the accountability era sample if they last beyond 1998. Regardless of which modeling strategy one prefers, both the split samples approach and the interaction approach produce similar results.

The results are shown in table 3. In the survival analysis, a negative coefficient means the independent variable is associated with a decreased likelihood of failure (i.e., longer civil wars). Conversely, a positive coefficient means the independent variable is associated with an increased likelihood of failure (i.e., shorter civil wars).

Table 3. Weibull models of civil war duration

	(1)	*(2)*	*(3)*
	Pre-1998	*Post-1998*	*Both*
Culpable Leader	–0.235	–0.941**	–0.204
	(0.207)	(0.263)	(0.217)
Multiparty War	0.079	–0.708**	–0.085
	(0.251)	(0.342)	(0.222)
Mountains	–0.005	–0.004	–0.005
	(0.004)	(0.005)	(0.004)
Development	–0.072	–0.396**	–0.174*
	(0.119)	(0.116)	(0.099)
Gov't. External Support	–0.023	–0.077	–0.044
	(0.198)	(0.236)	(0.153)
Rebel External Support	–0.537**	–0.346	–0.443**
	(0.169)	(0.231)	(0.148)
Rebel Strength	0.194	–0.082	0.105
	(0.118)	(0.223)	(0.118)
Culpable Leader × Post-1998			–0.547*
			(0.319)
Post-1998			0.648**
			(0.269)
Constant	–4.959**	–4.468**	-5.012**
	(0.486)	(0.649)	(0.400)
β*Culpable Leader* + **β***Culpable Leader × Post-1998*			–.751**
			(0.233)
N	1076	337	1414
Log lik.	–352.559	–118.908	–478.400

Note: Standard errors clustered by UCDP/PRIO war code in parentheses.
* $p < 0.10$, ** $p < 0.05$ (two-tailed)

I start with the two models that disaggregate the data into the impunity era and the accountability era. If my argument is correct, *Culpable Leader* should be insignificant in the pre-1998 period but statistically significant and negative in the post-1998 period. Model 1 assesses the relationship between culpability and conflict duration in the impunity era and finds that *Culpable Leader* is statistically insignificant even at the 90 percent level. In other words, the effect of leader culpability on conflict duration is statistically indistinguishable from zero during this time period. Model 2 examines whether leader culpability influences conflict duration in the accountability era. As predicted, *Culpable Leader* is negative and statistically significant, meaning that civil conflicts last longer when culpable leaders are in power. The results from these two models support my theory's predictions: culpable leaders fight longer civil wars in the accountability era only.[13]

In model 3, I turn to the regression with the interaction term, which is significant. The lower-order term *Culpable Leader* estimates the effect of leader culpability on conflict duration in the pre-1998 period. The linear combination of **β***Culpable Leader* + **β***Culpable Leader* × *Post-1998* estimates the effect of leader culpability on war duration in the post-1998 period. The interaction model reveals that the lower-order term *Culpable Leader* is not statistically significant. The coefficient for the linear combination, by contrast, is statistically significant and negative. Therefore, the interaction model yields the same conclusion as the split sample models: it is only during today's accountability era that civil wars with culpable leaders last significantly longer.

I also conduct a number of robustness checks to investigate whether my results hold up when using different modeling strategies and variable definitions.[14] For starters, I estimate a different type of event history model. In the previous results, I used the Weibull model, which assumes the underlying hazard rate is monotonic.[15] To ensure that my findings do not rely on this assumption, I use a Cox proportional hazards model, which makes no assumption about the shape of the baseline hazard rate. Next, I explore whether my results might simply pick up a post–Cold War effect.[16] To parse out the effect of the end of the Cold War from the justice cascade, I use a temporally truncated sample which limits the impunity era to the nine years that fall within the post–Cold War period (1989–97) and compare it to

13. A test for equality of the coefficients for leader culpability between models 1 and 2 suggests that they are not equal ($p < .03$).

14. The results are reported in the appendix.

15. A monotonic function is entirely nonincreasing or entirely nondecreasing. In the context of war duration, this means that the risk of war termination does not change signs over the course of the conflict.

16. The Cold War is a potential concern because Stathis Kalyvas and Laia Balcells (2010) show that the end of the Cold War altered the "technology of rebellion" used in civil wars, and subsequent research finds that the technology of rebellion influences the duration of civil conflicts (Balcells and Kalyvas 2014).

the first nine years of the accountability era (1998–2006). Finally, I test whether a different measure of leader culpability yields similar results. Specifically, I create an alternative leader culpability variable that codes whether leaders presided over a genocide or politicide identified by the Political Instability Task Force (Marshall, Gurr, and Harff 2014). In every robustness check, my conclusions are consistent.

The previous results all support the theory's predictions, but statistical significance does not always translate into substantively meaningful results. In real-world terms, how much does the justice cascade help explain conflict duration? To understand the substantive effect of leader culpability on civil war duration, I estimate hazard ratios (using the results from model 3) that measure how leader culpability shapes the risk of a civil war ending. Hazard ratios are interpreted relative to a baseline of 1. Thus, a hazard ratio of 2 would suggest that the risk of conflict termination is doubled (i.e., wars are twice as likely to end), whereas a hazard ratio of .5 would indicate that the risk of termination is halved (i.e., wars are half as likely to end). The results, reported in figure 4, show that leader culpability has little effect on war duration in the pre-1998 period. While the hazard ratio for this period is a little below 1 (implying that culpable leaders fight slightly longer wars), the hazard ratio's confidence interval overlaps considerably with the baseline of 1. In other words, we cannot meaningfully distinguish between culpable and nonculpable leaders in the impunity era. In the post-1998 period, however, leader culpability matters. The hazard ratio falls to .47 and the confidence interval does not cross 1. In plain

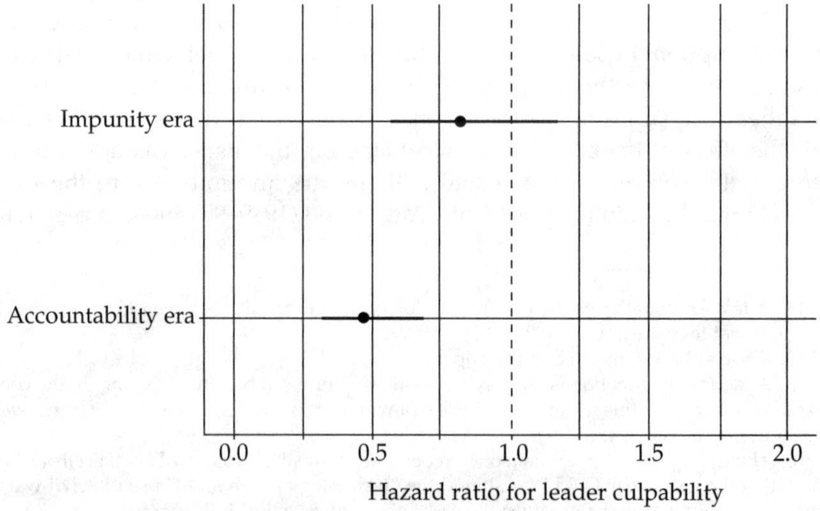

Figure 4. International justice and the hazard of civil war termination

English, this means that having a culpable leader in power reduces the likelihood of a civil war ending by about half.

Overall, the quantitative results lend considerable support to my second hypothesis. During the impunity era, leader culpability did not influence conflict duration because exile was an attractive exit strategy for all leaders. With a safe and often luxurious foreign retirement always on the table, there was little reason for rulers to risk a fight to the bitter end. In the accountability era, however, culpable leaders fight longer civil wars because they have constrained exit options. With nowhere to go, doubling down on the battlefield may well be the best option available to a culpable leader. Hence, the evidence suggests that the quest for international justice—despite the best intentions of advocates—produces a perverse effect on conflict resolution.

Muammar Gaddafi's Fight to the Finish

The statistical results reported in the previous section confirmed that the general patterns of civil war duration are consistent with the theory's predictions. In this section, I delve into one case—Muammar Gaddafi during the 2011 Libyan uprising—to illustrate the causal link between exile options and conflict duration. My argument can provide a compelling account of why Gaddafi decided to keep fighting rather than flee abroad even after it became apparent he would likely end up on the losing side of Libya's conflict.

BACKGROUND

Little is known about Muammar Gaddafi's early years. He was born sometime between 1940 and 1943 into an impoverished Bedouin family in a desert oasis outside of Sirte, Libya. Gaddafi's father was an illiterate goat herder, but he apparently was determined that his son would receive an education, something rather unusual for a poor Bedouin youth. After progressing through a series of elementary and religious schools, Gaddafi joined the military, the primary source of upward mobility in Libya at the time.

While at the Royal Military Academy in Benghazi, Gaddafi formed the Free Unionist Officers Movement, a secret group of young military officers who were critical of the rule of Libya's King Idriss.[17] In their view, Idriss was little more than a Western lackey because he allowed the American and British militaries to use Libyan territory for their Mediterranean bases and

17. On Gaddafi's early years and the coup that ousted Idriss, see Vandewalle 2012, 76–88.

permitted Western companies to control Libya's oil. The Free Unionists eventually decided that Libya was ripe for a revolution. When Idriss traveled to Turkey for specialized medical treatment, Gaddafi and his group of like-minded officers launched a bloodless coup. On September 1, 1969, Gaddafi took to the national radio to announce the beginning of a new regime in Libya. He would rule with an iron fist for the next forty-two years.

Anti-imperialism and pan-Arabism, two of Gaddafi's preferred ideologies, dominated the early years of the Gaddafi regime. Gaddafi began his long-standing anti-imperialist stance by expelling the last of the Italian settlers, Libya's former colonial masters, from the country. He next shut down the British military base at Tobruk and the American base at Wheelus. Finally, Gaddafi nationalized the holdings of foreign oil companies working in Libya and created the National Oil Company, which would later finance much of his foreign adventurism.[18] Thus, by the early 1970s, all the main signs of imperial power in Libya were gone. Gaddafi also promoted pan-Arab nationalism throughout the region. Inspired by the earlier efforts of his hero, the Egyptian president Gamal Abdel Nasser, Gaddafi aimed to establish a single Arab nation spanning North Africa and the Middle East. Within a year of taking power, he sought political unification with Egypt and Syria, but the plans never materialized as other Arab leaders grew wary of Gaddafi. Eventually, Gaddafi's relationship with the other Arab leaders became so bad that he supported (ultimately unsuccessful) attempts to assassinate at least three of them, including Jordan's King Hussein, Morocco's King Hassan, and Saudi Arabia's King Abdullah.

Searching for purpose after his failed attempt at Arab unification, Gaddafi delivered a speech in 1973 that would define the rest of his tenure. In his infamous Zuwara speech, Gaddafi proclaimed that the spirit of the 1969 Libyan revolution was in danger and announced the start of a new popular revolution.[19] According to Alison Pargeter (2012, 78), "This speech—which was to serve as a blueprint for the rest of his four decades in power—represented the real beginnings of the intense personalization of politics that was to characterize Libya under the endlessly eccentric Gaddafi." Gaddafi's new popular revolution essentially eliminated the preexisting political bureaucracy in Libya and marginalized any potential challengers to the regime. Instead of the old bureaucracy, Gaddafi established thousands of popular committees, an effective mechanism for spreading Gaddafism at

18. Libya was the first country in the Middle East or North Africa to secure a majority of its oil revenues. After Libya's success in this endeavor, other nations in the region quickly followed suit, ushering in an era of petropolitics in the Middle East that continues today. On Libya as a petrostate, see Colgan 2013b, 123–51.

19. The Zuwara speech contained many of the concepts that Gaddafi propounded in his *Green Book*, which appeared a few years after the speech.

the local level. The creation of the popular committees unleashed a wave of repression across Libya, leading to the arrests and sometimes even summary executions of broad sectors of society, such as university students and underground political groups, whose loyalty to Gaddafi was questioned.

Gaddafi also sought to export his popular revolution abroad, a task made easier by the fact that Libya's government coffers were flush with oil money. Indeed, Gaddafi represents a stereotypical case of "petro-aggression," the potent combination of a revolutionary leader with plenty of oil wealth at his disposal (Colgan 2013b). Gaddafi's foreign adventurism covered much of the African continent. He either instigated or interfered in conflicts in Sudan, Egypt, Uganda, the Central African Republic, South Africa, Zimbabwe, Angola, Mozambique, Guinea Bissau, and Chad, among others.[20]

Gaddafi's foreign meddling and support for international terrorism put him on a collision course with the West, particularly the United States. During the Carter administration, Libya joined North Korea and Cuba on a new list of enemy states, and the United States refused to sell Libya weapons. Antagonism between the United States and Libya, however, came to a head during the Reagan administration. The two leaders engaged in an entertaining war of words, with Reagan labeling Gaddafi "the mad dog of the Middle East," and Gaddafi in turn referring to Reagan as "that second rate actor" (Pargeter 2012, 137). The conflict also had a more serious side. In the early 1980s, the United States shot down two Libyan planes over the disputed Gulf of Sirte and instituted an embargo on Libyan oil (Vandewalle 2012, 131). The conflict escalated again in 1986, when Gaddafi carried out a terrorist bombing at a discotheque in Berlin, killing two American military members and injuring several hundred civilians. The United States responded by sending fighter jets to bomb military targets in Libya and, more controversially, Gaddafi's Bab al-Aziziya residential compound.

By the late 1980s, Gaddafi had already alienated much of the world, but he acquired true international pariah status with the Lockerbie bombing. On December 21, 1988, a Pan Am passenger airline flight from London to New York blew up over the Scottish town of Lockerbie, killing all 259 passengers as well as eleven people on the ground. Investigators linked the

20. Though the details in several cases remain murky, Gaddafi is believed to have supported "approximately thirty revolutionary groups and foreign insurgencies" during his time in power (Colgan 2013b, 140). See also Vandewalle 2012, 130. This foreign meddling often ended badly for Gaddafi. In Chad, for example, Gaddafi began by funding a rebel group, the Chad National Liberation Front (FROLINAT). Over time, Gaddafi's deteriorating relationship with the FROLINAT leadership—combined with his decision to annex the Aozou Strip, a stretch of mineral-rich land in northern Chad—actually drove FROLINAT to collaborate with the Chadian government to oust Libyan forces from their country. All told, around ten thousand Libyan soldiers died in the ill-fated conflict (Pargeter 2012, 132–33).

terrorist attack to Libya, and the Gaddafi regime was universally condemned. As punishment, the UN Security Council passed Resolution 748, which imposed harsh international sanctions on Libya that significantly weakened its economy.

Facing enemies abroad and a crumbling economy at home, Gaddafi eventually decided that he needed to change the status quo by rehabilitating his international image. In 1999, he handed over the Lockerbie bombers to face trial under Scottish law and offered a massive financial settlement to the families of the Lockerbie victims. As a reward for Gaddafi's improved behavior, the United States removed Gaddafi from its list of State Sponsors of Terrorism, and the UN dropped the extensive sanctions package that had ravaged the Libyan economy for the past several years. The terrorist attacks of September 11, 2001 marked another turning point for Gaddafi's foreign relations. Rather than applaud the 9/11 attacks, as he once might have done, Gaddafi immediately shared counterterrorism intelligence with the United States and the United Kingdom. This newfound level of cooperation not only put him in the good graces of the Western powers but also offered an opportunity to reframe his regime's brutal repression of Islamist extremists as part of the global war on terror.[21] The journal *Foreign Affairs*, a bellwether for establishment foreign policy thinking, even published an article labeling Gaddafi "the rogue who came in from the cold" (Takeyh 2001).

But before Gaddafi could truly shed the pariah label, he needed to address Libya's weapons of mass destruction (WMD) program. As early as 1987, the United States had strongly suspected that Gaddafi was building a chemical weapons program using a facility at Rabta (St. John 2011, 201). Even more troubling, the Gaddafi regime had developed a relationship with A. Q. Khan, the father of Pakistan's nuclear program turned rogue scientist, who sold technology—including centrifuges for producing highly enriched uranium and blueprints for a nuclear warhead—to Libya (Hilsum 2012, 129–130). In 2003, shortly after the United States invaded Iraq to destroy Saddam Hussein's alleged WMD program, Gaddafi decided to come clean by dismantling his own program and allowing international inspections.[22] With that move, Gaddafi's international rehabilitation was complete. Tony Blair shook hands with Gaddafi and declared that Gaddafi had made "common cause with us against Al Qaeda, extremists, and terrorism."[23] Similarly, George W. Bush was ready to work with Gaddafi and noted that "old hostilities do not need to go on forever."[24]

21. On Gaddafi's international rehabilitation, see Vandewalle 2012, 173–94.

22. For an analysis of the factors that led Gaddafi to give up his WMD program, see Jentleson and Whytock 2005.

23. "Blair Hails New Libyan Relations," *BBC News*, March 25, 2004.

24. "Bush's Remarks on Arms Agreement with Libya," *New York Times*, December 19, 2003.

With a new group of international friends, the future looked bright for the Gaddafi regime. Moreover, a younger generation of technocratic reformers had attained positions of moderate influence in Libya, which at least offered the hope that the regime might start to reform from within.[25] Most important in this group was Gaddafi's son Saif, who held a doctorate in political philosophy from the London School of Economics and was openly critical of the regime's previous human rights violations.[26] The regional tumult associated with the Arab Spring, however, would soon upend this period of relative calm in Libya.

THE 2011 LIBYAN UPRISING

The Revolution's Origins and Gaddafi's Response. On December 17, 2010, a young man named Mohamed Bouazizi set himself on fire in the middle of a crowded street in Sidi Bouzid, Tunisia. Local police had just confiscated his fruit stand, and Bouazizi self-immolated in an act of protest against government corruption and the lack of economic opportunity for Tunisian youth. This unlikely event sparked mass uprisings against the regime of the Tunisian leader Ben Ali, eventually forcing him to flee into exile in Saudi Arabia on January 14, 2011.[27] Inspired by events in Tunisia, activists in Egypt launched a campaign of civil resistance on January 25 that forced the longtime Egyptian leader Hosni Mubarak to resign on February 11. The upheaval soon spread to Libya, where grievances against the Gaddafi regime had simmered for decades. Emboldened by the successes of their regional counterparts, Libyan activists planned a "Day of Rage" for February 17. The Day of Rage actually started a day earlier than planned when

25. Some question whether Gaddafi truly initiated any meaningful reforms during this period. For instance, Romesh Ratnesar (2011) argues that, "far from initiating domestic reforms or improving human rights, the Libyan leader used the legitimacy conferred on him by the West as cover to crush dissent and steal more of his country's wealth."

26. After the Libyan revolution started, the relationship between Saif Gaddafi and the London School of Economics (LSE) was closely scrutinized. Evidence emerged that Saif Gaddafi's dissertation was plagiarized and that the LSE had accepted a large donation from his charity. Many criticized the LSE, but some defended it by noting, "It was only after bullets started flying in Libya that Saif Gaddafi was found to have cheated. Nor had anyone until then objected that the LSE had received a donation from Saif Gaddafi's Foundation." See Meghnad Desai, "LSE is Paying a Heavy Price for Saif Gaddafi's PhD," *Guardian*, March 4, 2011.

27. Unlike Gaddafi, Ben Ali refrained from engaging in mass killing during the street protests in Tunis. While there were some deaths in the chaos just before and after Ben Ali's flight to Saudi Arabia, the violence was not part of a coordinated government-led attack. Indeed, new evidence from Tunisia suggests that Ben Ali never ordered the military to fire on protestors (Gallopin 2019). As my theory would expect, Ben Ali—a nonculpable leader in the accountability era—was confident that he could safely flee abroad when key figures from his regime defected to the opposition.

the Gaddafi regime arrested Fathi Terbil, a protest organizer and well-known human rights lawyer, in Benghazi. With Terbil's arrest, "the accumulation of grievances had toppled over, like a huge pile of documents. Fathi Terbil's arrest was the last file thrown on top, causing the whole lot to collapse" (Hilsum 2012, 13). Anti-Gaddafi demonstrations erupted throughout Benghazi as protestors waved the flag of pre-Gaddafi Libya, which quickly became a symbol of the revolution.

Gaddafi's security forces responded with a heavy hand by shooting into crowds of unarmed protestors in Benghazi. The next day, the government opened fire on mourners leaving the funeral of those killed during the Day of Rage, which further inflamed grievances against the Gaddafi regime and altered the goals of the protestors. As Ronald St. John (2011, 283) explains, "the thrust of the protests shifted from complaints about a lack of housing, social services, and jobs to a call for regime change." In Benghazi and the surrounding environs, Human Rights Watch documented the killings of hundreds of civilians during the first four days of anti-Gaddafi demonstrations (Human Rights Watch 2012, 16). The protests, which later morphed into an armed rebellion, were not confined to Benghazi for long. Other towns in eastern Libya rose up against Gaddafi in solidarity with the people of Benghazi. By the end of February, a number of key cities in eastern Libya—including Benghazi, Tobruk, and Misrata—were liberated from the Gaddafi regime.

As the revolution gained momentum, Gaddafi's forces made it standard practice to fire on unarmed civilians and indiscriminately shell cities and neighborhoods deemed unfriendly to the regime. These brutal tactics soon drew the international community into the conflict. Responding to the Gaddafi regime's repression of the largely peaceful protests, the UN Security Council passed Resolution 1970 on February 26, 2011. Resolution 1970 contained a number of punitive measures against the Gaddafi regime, including an arms embargo, travel bans for the Gaddafi family and other high-level officials, and the freezing of the regime's assets.

Even more importantly, the resolution referred the situation in Libya to the ICC, giving it the authority to open an investigation of the "widespread and systematic attacks" on Libyan civilians. As the ICC prosecutor Luis Moreno-Ocampo's application for an arrest warrant for Gaddafi summarized, "The evidence demonstrates that Gaddafi conceived a plan to quell the popular demonstrations of February 2011 by all means, including through the use of extreme and lethal violence. Pursuant to this plan, the Security Forces carried out a widespread and systematic policy of attacks against civilians perceived as dissidents with the purpose of maintaining Gaddafi's power."[28] Moreover, the arrest warrant left no doubt about whom

28. See "Prosecutor's Application Pursuant to Article 58 as to Muammar Mohammed Abu Minyar Gaddafi, Saif al-Islam Gaddafi, and Abdullah al-Senussi," in *Situation in the*

the ICC held responsible for the violence: "Muammar Gaddafi, as the recognized and undisputed leader of Libya had . . . absolute, ultimate, and unquestioned control over the Libyan State apparatus of power, including the Security Forces."[29]

The exact number of civilians killed by the Libyan government during the protests remains something of mystery. In a briefing before the UN Security Council, Moreno-Ocampo acknowledged that calculating a precise death toll was difficult because the Libyan government was actively taking steps to cover up the killings.[30] Nonetheless, Moreno-Ocampo's team concluded that "shooting at protesters was systematic" and found highly credible evidence that between five hundred and seven hundred civilians were shot and killed by the Libyan security forces *in February alone*.[31] In other words, at least five hundred documented civilian killings occurred during the initial period of peaceful protests against the regime and *before* the uprising morphed into a civil war.

Not surprisingly, during the civil war period in the spring and summer of 2011, the Gaddafi regime's use of violence against civilians escalated further.[32] Some of the government's most egregious violence occurred during the siege of rebel-held Misrata, Libya's third largest city. Libyan forces—led by Gaddafi's son Khamis and the elite corps of fighters under his command—indiscriminately shelled the city for months using mortar-fired cluster munitions (Human Rights Watch 2012, 18). These weapons pulverized entire neighborhoods, killed thousands, and prevented humanitarian medical teams from entering the city. The journalist Lindsey Hilsum described the siege in vivid terms: "At the height of the conflict, an artillery round

Libyan Arab Jamahiriya (No. ICC-01/11), May 16, 2011, available at https://www.icc-cpi.int/CourtRecords/CR2011_06155.PDF.

29. See "Warrant of Arrest for Muammar Mohammed Abu Minyar Gaddafi," in *Situation in the Libyan Arab Jamahiriya* (No. ICC-01/11), June 27, 2011, available at https://www.icc-cpi.int/CourtRecords/CR2011_08351.PDF.

30. Moreno-Ocampo's application to the ICC judges for an arrest warrant noted: "This cover-up has taken numerous forms: internet services and cell phone networks were disrupted to prevent communication between the demonstrators; military checkpoints and squads have confiscated cameras, memory cards, computers and internet devices to prevent any citizen from spreading images of the protests; access to hospitals, ambulance transport and blood transfusions have been forbidden to injured demonstrators; doctors were not allowed to document the number of dead and injured admitted to hospitals after the violent clashes began; and Security Forces have searched hospitals looking for wounded or killed demonstrators." See "Prosecutor's Application Pursuant to Article 58 as to Muammar Mohammed Abu Minyar Gaddafi, Saif al-Islam Gaddafi, and Abdullah al-Senussi," in *Situation in the Libyan Arab Jamahiriya* (No. ICC-01/11), May 16, 2011, available at https://www.icc-cpi.int/CourtRecords/CR2011_06155.PDF.

31. Marlise Simons and Neil MacFarquhar, "Hague Court Seeks Warrants for Libyan Officials," *New York Times*, May 4, 2011.

32. An update to the Ulfelder and Valentino 2008 dataset codes the onset of a mass killing campaign in 2011.

was coming in every six minutes. Thousands were killed and wounded, and the buildings along Tripoli Street turned into burning shells, pockmarked and holed by tank fire and rockets" (Hilsum 2012, 213). Moreover, "regime snipers targeted civilians and [rebel fighters] indiscriminately and were reported to be killing children. There was evidence of systematic rape by regime militias, sometimes proudly reported by regime troops themselves" (Chivvis 2014, 102). While Misrata may stand out for its level of brutality, similar scenes of government-sponsored mass killing played out across Libya during the conflict.[33]

Why No Deterrence? As I mentioned earlier, this chapter examines the Gaddafi case primarily to explore how the absence of a viable exit option can incentivize culpable leaders to double down on the battlefield. But it is worth taking a small detour to investigate a different aspect of my argument. Recall that the theory makes predictions about three outcomes: exile, conflict duration, and mass killing onset. Indeed, one of my key claims about the justice dilemma is that the threat of an international prosecution will typically cause forward-looking leaders to think twice about resorting to atrocities in the accountability era. Therefore, the Gaddafi regime's brutal response to the 2011 uprising, a clear case of mass atrocities, begs the question: Why was Gaddafi not deterred from targeting civilians?

This section provides an answer by drawing on the theory outlined in chapter 2. While I argued that the justice cascade should lower the overall probability of mass killing in the accountability era, I also noted that there were two conditions under which deterrence would likely fail. First, since leaders typically only have reason to fear international arrest if and when they lose power, I pointed out that deterrence is unlikely if a leader thinks that committing atrocities will increase the odds of political survival by a sufficiently large amount. Second, if a leader is already culpable for past crimes, then there is no marginal cost to committing atrocities again. Both of these conditions applied to Gaddafi at the outset of the 2011 revolution, which explains why deterrence failed.

To begin with, if history is any guide, Gaddafi had compelling reasons to think that turning to violence would increase his chances of remaining in power. Of course, it is impossible to know exactly what went on inside Gaddafi's mind before he decided to initiate the crackdown on protestors in

33. For instance, a Reuters investigation into government violence in the relatively small, provincial town of Khoms found evidence of "an organized system of repression with methods including delivering electric shocks to suspects' genitals, keeping them for weeks in baking heat with only a few sips of water a day, and whipping them with an electrical cable while their hands were bound with plastic ties. The squads allegedly then disposed of their bodies in unmarked graves in a campaign to smash the revolt against his rule." See "Gaddafi Squads Tortured People in Shipping Containers," *Telegraph*, September 6, 2011.

2011. However, we do know that Gaddafi had used strategies of civilian victimization to crush and/or cower opposition to his rule several times in the past. Indeed, Gaddafi faced "at least eight serious coup plots and a number of assassination attempts" during his reign (J. L. Anderson 2011, 52). Each time, Gaddafi had responded with a heavy hand toward anyone suspected of having even the slightest connection to the opposition. This ruthless strategy proved to be effective: it kept Gaddafi in office for over four decades.

Out of Gaddafi's long history of using mass violence to pursue his political goals, the example of the Libyan Islamic Fighting Group (LIFG) stands out. Created in the early 1990s, the LIFG initially consisted of Libyan veterans of the mujahideen campaign in Afghanistan against the Soviet Union. Once established in Libya, the LIFG worked to pull together Libyan Islamists of all stripes with the goal of ousting Gaddafi. By the mid-1990s, the LIFG was regularly initiating attacks against influential members of Libya's security apparatus, including at least one failed assassination attempt on Gaddafi. The group operated clandestinely whenever possible, keeping the Gaddafi regime in the dark about its membership and bases. The LIFG was undoubtedly effective: "at its peak the group represented the strongest challenge the Libyan regime ever faced" prior to the 2011 revolution (Pargeter 2005). However, a botched attempt to rescue one of its members eventually allowed the regime to discover the LIFG's network of cells and its territorial bases of support.

Armed with this information, Gaddafi responded mercilessly. The LIFG fell back to their Green Mountains redoubt, but the regime pursued them with an "iron fist" and "uncompromising repression" (Ronen 2002, 12). After the Libyan air force pounded areas where support for the LIFG was suspected to be high, Gaddafi unleashed his ground forces on the civilian population. Moreover, the regime cut off water supplies to the entire area where LIFG fighters operated or enjoyed civilian support, a devastating tactic in an isolated desert community (Solomon 2012, 142). All told, Gaddafi's response to the LIFG challenge amounted to "a large-scale liquidation campaign" (Pargeter 2005). Notably, Gaddafi's campaign of violence was effective in destroying the opposition to his rule. By the late 1990s, "the LIFG knew it was beaten. The group's leadership called an end to the struggle and ordered its shattered members to leave the country. . . . Gaddafi had triumphed" (Pargeter 2012, 170). Thus, the LIFG example shows that employing massive and largely indiscriminate violence had worked for Gaddafi before. When the revolution broke out in 2011, Gaddafi presumably had reason to think it might work again.

The other reason why the threat of international justice was not likely to deter Gaddafi from killing civilians is that Gaddafi was already widely perceived as a culpable leader prior to the events of 2011. Initiating a crackdown on civilians during the revolution therefore carried little marginal cost. Indeed, Gaddafi had already presided over thousands of civilian deaths stemming from mass killings, repression, and state-sponsored terrorism.[34]

As just described, Gaddafi's forces led a "liquation campaign" against the LIFG and civilians deemed sympathetic to their cause in the mid-1990s. But arguably the worst crime of that campaign—and perhaps even Gaddafi's entire tenure—occurred after the LIFG's destruction. The regime rounded up anyone even loosely connected to the LIFG or other Islamist groups and threw them into Abu Salim, a prison notorious for torture. The details of what happened next are still somewhat blurred, but the broad contours of the Abu Salim massacre have become clearer over time.[35] On June 28, 1996, the prisoners—many of whom were innocent civilians—staged a protest against their harsh treatment. One prison guard was killed, and Gaddafi's intelligence chief and brother-in-law Abdullah al-Senussi was sent to the prison to negotiate with the leaders of the protest. Some kind of agreement apparently was struck, and the prisoners were led into Abu Salim's large courtyard. Instead of learning the details of an agreement on improved treatment, as many prisoners had expected, they were massacred using a combination of grenades and machine-gun fire. An estimated 1,270 political prisoners were killed that day in Abu Salim (Hilsum 2012, 8), making it the single deadliest crime of Gaddafi's time in office.[36] The Gaddafi regime did everything possible to keep the massacre a secret, which worked for several years, but eventually information leaked within Libya and to international audiences. Recognizing this reality, Saif Gaddafi, often considered to be the most moderate member of

34. To be fully transparent, it is worth noting that the Ulfelder and Valentino dataset does not code a mass killing onset in Libya prior to 2011. However, this does not undermine my point that Gaddafi should be understood as a culpable leader before then for two reasons. First, as I explained when introducing the data for the quantitative tests, the one-thousand-death threshold was only a blunt indicator that was useful for making comparisons across the universe of cases. The Gaddafi case study offers an opportunity to take a broader and more nuanced view of culpability. When doing so, I show that there are several reasons to consider Gaddafi to have been a culpable leader before the 2011 revolution began. Second, there is evidence that the Gaddafi regime had in fact already engaged in mass killing that claimed over one thousand victims (e.g., the Abu Salim massacre in 1996, which will be discussed shortly). Ulfelder and Valentino excluded this massacre due to their very high standards of evidence and their preference to err toward false negatives (personal email communication with Ben Valentino, November 30, 2017).

35. This summary of events draws on Hilsum 2012, 99–116.

36. See also "Libya: June 1996 Killings at Abu Salim Prison," *Human Rights Watch*, June 27, 2006. Some have speculated that other atrocities occurred at Abu Salim, but the Gaddafi regime was able to keep them secret. One fact consistent with this view is that a storeroom of documents at Abu Salim was set on fire—"presumably by a Gaddafi loyalist," according to the journalist Jeremy Bowen—just before opposition forces captured Tripoli. This destroyed a potential treasure trove of evidence that might have further established the culpability of Gaddafi and his associates. On this point, see Bowen 2012, 229.

the ruling family, acknowledged in 2008 that the government had used "disproportionate force."[37]

In addition to the civilian massacres, Gaddafi could also be considered a culpable leader for other reasons if we take a broader view of culpability. For instance, Gaddafi's Libya was one of the most repressive countries in the world. As Marieke Wierda (2015, 154) puts it, "By most definitions of international law as well as under Libya's criminal code, [Gaddafi's] crimes against his own people were systematic and severe." The numbers back up this claim. For example, consider the quantitative data on torture, one of the most explicit human rights violations. The Cingranelli-Richards Human Rights Dataset uses reports from Amnesty International and the US State Department to track the extent to which governments have employed torture in every country around the world from 1981 to the present.[38] Gaddafi's regime received the worst possible score for torture in every single year except for 2000 (this was during Gaddafi's international rehabilitation period, and Libya received the second-worst score that year). Thus, human rights violations were endemic to the Gaddafi regime.

The quantitative indicators capture the widespread nature of repression in Gaddafi's Libya, but qualitative anecdotes more vividly illustrate the barbarism of the regime. Throughout his tenure, Gaddafi worried about challenges from the country's youth, particularly university students. As a result, students with even the most tenuous connections to anti-Gaddafi causes were frequently singled out for high-profile political executions. The following example illustrates this sad reality:

> Recalcitrant students and political dissidents were picked up, tortured, given show trials, and either imprisoned or hanged. The hangings often took place on the grounds of universities, with fellow-students and parents forced to watch. An especially vivid and exemplary execution came in 1984, when a young man named Sadiq Hamed Shwehdi was tried in Benghazi's basketball stadium on charges of terrorism. Hundreds of schoolchildren were bused in to attend, and the trial was broadcast live on national television. Shwehdi, on his knees, wept as he confessed to joining the "stray dogs"—Qaddafi's term for his exiled opponents—while he was studying in the United States. A panel of revolutionary judges sentenced him to death, and he was led to a waiting gallows. Shwehdi hung from the noose, slowly strangling, until suddenly a young woman in an olive-green uniform, a "volunteer" named Huda Ben Amer, strode up and violently pulled on his legs. Qaddafi rewarded Ben Amer for her show of

37. Ali Shuaib, "Libya Appoints Judge to Probe 1996 Prison Massacre," *Reuters*, September 6, 2009.

38. For a description of this dataset, see Cingranelli and Richards 2009.

> revolutionary zeal, and she later served two terms as the mayor of Benghazi. (J. L. Anderson 2011, 51–52).

Since the international media had virtually no presence in Libya for the long period before Gaddafi's international rehabilitation (and, of course, there was no press freedom in Libya itself), it is difficult to know the full extent of these political executions.

Finally, one could argue that Gaddafi was culpable for his notorious support for international terrorism. To be sure, there is an ongoing debate among legal scholars regarding whether terrorism constitutes a core international crime, with many arguing that terrorism falls short (Cassese 2008, 146). Nonetheless, Gaddafi's financial and logistical support to terrorist organizations proved to be deadly in many cases. As previously discussed, Gaddafi orchestrated the Lockerbie bombing that killed all 259 passengers of a Pan Am flight in 1988. At the time, the Lockerbie bombing represented the world's third deadliest transnational terrorist attack.[39] But Gaddafi did not stop there. Instead, he used his oil wealth to become one of the major funders of terrorism worldwide. In addition to a host of the more radical Palestinian groups, Gaddafi extended his largesse to the Italian Red Brigades, the Irish Republican Army, the Nicaraguan Sandinistas, the Basque Country ETA, the Moro National Liberation Front in the Philippines, and Venezuela's Carlos the Jackal. All together, Gaddafi can be linked to several thousand deaths via the terrorist attacks carried out by Libyan regime agents directly or the funding Gaddafi provided for attacks carried out by other groups.[40]

To conclude, Gaddafi is exactly the sort of leader my theory expects *not* to be deterred. By the time of the 2011 conflict, Gaddafi was already a culpable leader with a long list of crimes, so exile would have been extremely risky for him regardless of how he treated the protestors. In other words, Gaddafi's history of sordid behavior meant that the constraint against civilian killing identified in my theory—exercising restraint now so as to keep one's future exit options open—was largely absent for Gaddafi when he faced the 2011 uprising. Moreover, Gaddafi had effectively used large-scale violence to put down previous challenges to his rule, and he had no reason to think he could not do so again. Indeed, wielding overwhelming violence to retain power had been the modus operandi of Gaddafi's regime for decades.

39. At the time of the Lockerbie bombing in 1988, the only two acts of transnational terrorism to have killed more people were the 1983 marine barracks bombing in Beirut and the 1985 bombing of Air India Flight 182.

40. For an extensive accounting of Gaddafi's support for transnational terrorism, see J. L. Anderson 2011; Davis 1990; Pargeter 2012, 136; and Vandewalle 2012, 130.

GADDAFI'S OPTIONS: NEGOTIATE, FIGHT, OR FLIGHT?

I now return to the main theme of this chapter: the relationship between a leader's exile options and civil war duration. In what follows, I illustrate how the threat of international punishment undermined a safe retirement abroad for Gaddafi, which in turn gave him an incentive to fight it out on the battlefield in Libya.

Gaddafi's violence against the civilian population eventually transformed the antiregime protests into a full-scale civil war. As large swaths of eastern Libya came under their control, opposition forces needed a mechanism to govern the liberated territory and a leadership structure to interact with the international community. Thus, the various localized rebel groups that had sprung up seemingly overnight coalesced loosely under the National Transitional Council (NTC). Much of the NTC's leadership, perhaps surprisingly, consisted of former Gaddafi regime technocrats—such as Mustafa Abdul Jalil and Mahmoud Jibril—who had defected to the opposition early in the uprising. On March 5, the NTC declared itself the sole representative of the people of Libya, and within a few months it gained widespread international recognition as the legitimate government of the Libyan State.[41]

During March, Gaddafi regrouped his forces in Tripoli and launched a counteroffensive against the rebels. As they marched eastward, the regime quickly recaptured most of the territory it had just lost. Gaddafi's forces soon reached the outskirts of Benghazi, the very heart of the uprising. Remembering Gaddafi's televised *zenga zenga* speech of February 22 in which he compared the opposition to "cockroaches" and "rats" and promised to "cleanse Libya house by house," Western leaders began to fear a bloodbath in Benghazi.[42] Then, as his forces encircled Benghazi on the night of March 17, Gaddafi proclaimed on the state radio: "I will finish the battle of Benghazi tonight."[43] Terrified at what might happen, the international community sprang into action. The UN Security Council immediately passed Resolution 1973, which imposed a no-fly zone over Libya and authorized member states to take "all necessary measures" to protect civilians. In less than forty-eight hours—and just after Gaddafi's forces had started to move on Benghazi—French Rafale fighters rained missiles down on Gaddafi's tanks and armored vehicles in Operation Odyssey Dawn.[44]

41. Sebnem Arsu and Steven Erlanger, "Libya Rebels Get Formal Backing, and $30 Billion," *New York Times*, July 15, 2011.

42. "Libya Protests: Defiant Gaddafi Refuses to Quit," *BBC News*, February 22, 2011.

43. David D. Kirkpatrick and Kareem Fahim, "Qaddafi Warns of Assault on Benghazi as U.N. Vote Nears," *New York Times*, March 17, 2011.

44. For a book-length treatment of the military aspects of the Libya intervention, see Chivvis 2014.

The expected massacre in Benghazi was averted, and the tide of the war began to turn as NATO took over responsibility for the UN-mandated no-fly zone.

The mandate to protect civilians was remarkably broad, and over time it was used to justify expanded international assistance to the NTC in the form of weapons, intelligence, and airstrikes. With their newfound international backing, the rebels gained the upper hand in the war and began marching toward the capital city of Tripoli. Yet, by the early summer of 2011, the war seemed to be settling into a stalemate. Fighting continued as the rebels slowly crept toward the capital, but neither side was able to make a military breakthrough. The rebels controlled eastern Libya, while Gaddafi still reigned supreme in the western part of the country, including Tripoli.

With the civil war dragging on longer than many in the international community had anticipated or desired, there were several attempts to craft a negotiated settlement. In theory, a negotiated settlement might have taken one of two forms. On the one hand, Gaddafi could have granted policy concessions in exchange for the opposition laying down their arms. On the other hand, Gaddafi could have given up power in exchange for a promise of protection from the NTC. As one historian of modern Libya explains, a negotiated deal to end the fighting was the preferred option for many outside actors, yet it would also turn out to be "the least attractive scenario for both sides in the conflict" (Vandewalle 2012, 206).

The push for a negotiated settlement began in earnest when representatives of the African Union's High Level Panel on Libya flew to Tripoli on April 10 in the hopes of brokering a peace deal. The star-studded AU panel included the presidents of five African countries: South Africa's Jacob Zuma, Mauritania's Mohamed Ould Abdel Aziz, Uganda's Yoweri Museveni, the Democratic Republic of the Congo's Denis Sassou Nguessou, and Mali's Amadou Toumani Toure. Gaddafi met with his fellow African heads of state and readily agreed to their peace plan.[45] The AU roadmap called for an immediate ceasefire, the delivery of humanitarian aid, and a new dialogue between the warring parties. Even more important, the AU plan made it clear that Gaddafi would remain in power. As Karim Mezran and Alice Alunni (2015, 267) explain, "This was the main reason the regime accepted the roadmap and the opposition forces firmly rejected it." Over the course of the spring and summer, South Africa's Jacob Zuma returned to Libya several times with similar plans, but the NTC consistently rejected them.[46]

45. "Gaddafi Said to Accept 'Truce Road Map,'" *Al Jazeera*, April 10, 2011.

46. John F. Burns, "Qaddafi and Zuma Meet but Reach No Agreement," *New York Times*, May 31, 2011.

To understand the rebel's intransigence, recall the familiar credible commitment problem in civil war termination (e.g., Walter 1997). While the Gaddafi regime was keen to accept a peace deal that kept it in power, the opposition had good reason to be wary of this type of settlement. From the NTC's perspective, it was doubtful that Gaddafi genuinely wanted peace. Instead, Gaddafi's overtures might be an attempt to buy time for regrouping his forces or to stall the rebels' march toward Tripoli. As one commentator acknowledged, "[The rebels] had little reason to trust that Gaddafi would negotiate in good faith once they stopped their attacks" (Chivvis 2014, 150). Such thinking was pervasive among NTC leaders whenever Gaddafi stated that he supported a ceasefire. For instance, when commenting on one of the AU's mediation attempts that Gaddafi claimed to support, the NTC foreign minister Fathi Baja remarked, "We refuse completely. We don't consider it a political initiative, it is only some stuff that Gaddafi wants to announce to stay in power."[47] Even more troubling for the NTC, if they implemented a peace deal that kept Gaddafi in control, the regime would be able to renege on any policy concession or power-sharing agreement once the opposition disarmed and demobilized. This fear was not a mere hypothetical for the rebels: Gaddafi had both a general reputation for breaking promises and a specific history of killing disarmed political opponents (e.g., the Abu Salim massacre).

The NTC therefore insisted that Gaddafi give up power as a precondition for any settlement. In the words of the NTC chairman Mustafa Abdul Jalil, "The African Union initiative does not include the departure of Gaddafi and his sons from the Libyan political scene, therefore it is outdated."[48] An NTC spokesman similarly noted, "If there is any negotiation it will be on one single thing—how Gaddafi is going to leave the country or step down so we can save lives. There is nothing else to negotiate."[49] In short, the NTC wanted Gaddafi to hand over all power before sorting out the details of a negotiated transition.

From Gaddafi's perspective, however, ceding power to the NTC was a nonstarter. Once again, credible commitment problems frustrated the bargaining process. In this scenario, Gaddafi's fate in a new Libya would have been highly uncertain. Gaddafi and his loyalists knew the NTC could cheat on any promise of protection it gave Gaddafi once he stepped down.

47. "Libya: Zuma Says Gaddafi Will Not Quit," *BBC News*, May 31, 2011. Also note that many in the international community were skeptical of Gaddafi's motives regarding a potential ceasefire. For instance, NATO's secretary-general Anders Fogh Rasmussen pointedly noted that the Gaddafi regime "did not keep their promises" when they had previously announced ceasefires. See "Libyan Rebels Reject African Union Peace Plan," *Independent*, April 11, 2011.

48. "Libyan Rebels Reject African Union Peace Plan," *Independent*, April 11, 2011.

49. "Libya Revolt: Rebels Say No Talks Unless Gaddafi Goes," *BBC News*, March 4, 2011.

Indeed, there would be nothing to prevent the rebels—the very individuals risking their lives to overthrow Gaddafi—from settling old scores once Gaddafi was powerless. On top of that, Gaddafi had a particularly compelling reason to anticipate punishment at the hands of the rebels: the statements of NTC officials themselves. As one official, Guma el-Gamaty, put it: "The only negotiation is how to apprehend him, [for him] to tell us where he is and what conditions he wants for his apprehension: whether he wants to be kept in a single cell or shared cell or whether he wants to have his own shower or not, you know. These are the kind of negotiations we are willing to talk about."[50] Thus, the writing was on the wall for Gaddafi should he cede power. Anticipating what lay ahead, why would Gaddafi negotiate himself into prison (or worse)?

Overall, the failed bargaining attempts between the two sides show that any settlement that kept Gaddafi in office was unacceptable to the NTC, and any agreement that brought the NTC into power was unacceptable to Gaddafi. As a Turkish diplomat involved in the mediation attempts described the state of affairs, "Both sides are inflexible. One side, the opposition, is insisting that Qadhafi should go and that the presence of any member of the Qadhafi family in the new administration is not acceptable. The other side is saying that Qadhafi should stay. So there is no breakthrough yet."[51] As we now know, a breakthrough would never emerge. A negotiated settlement to the war was problematic regardless of whether it kept Gaddafi in office or transferred power to the opposition.

Given the intractable negotiating problems at the domestic level, exile in a third-party state may have seemed like the best course of action for Gaddafi. Several different actors advocated for this option. Saif Gaddafi, Muammar's son and former heir apparent, reportedly had tried on multiple occasions to convince his father to go into a "respected retirement" in a foreign country (Chorin 2012, 185).[52] Similarly, the NTC made it clear they thought that exile for Gaddafi would be an acceptable way to resolve the conflict. The NTC foreign minister Ali Al Issawi stated: "He has to choose between three options; he can either join Milosevic at the ICC, or his friend

50. David Smith, "Gaddafi Offers to Negotiate with Libya Rebels over Transition of Power," *Guardian*, August 28, 2011.

51. Thomas Seibert, "Turkey Pursues Its Libya Mediation Efforts Despite Setbacks," *National*, April 7, 2011.

52. A number of Western policymakers expected that Saif would be willing and able to broker a transition deal. As Julian Borger reports, many in the West "hoped the London School of Economics–educated Gaddafi son's contacts to London could be a conduit for talks." These connections, however, never produced a negotiating breakthrough. See Julian Borger, "International Criminal Court to Name Libyan War Crimes Suspects," *Guardian*, May 12, 2011.

Chavez [in Venezuela], or have the same fate as Hitler [death]. . . . His only option to avoid death is to go to a country that has not signed the ICC Agreement [the Rome Statute]. The African [exile] option remains in place, and we are not against this."[53] Hence, within Libya, many viewed exile for Gaddafi as a mechanism to end the war.

Outside of Libya, there was also a push to convince Gaddafi to leave the country. Most notably, the American president Barack Obama, the British prime minister David Cameron, and the French president Nicolas Sarkozy jointly published an op-ed in the *New York Times* outlining their Libya policy. The Western leaders wrote: "It is impossible to imagine a future for Libya with Qaddafi in power. . . . It is unthinkable that someone who has tried to massacre his own people can play a part in their future government. . . . *Qaddafi must go and go for good*."[54] Just in case Gaddafi did not get the message, the United States sent three high-ranking diplomats—Derek Chollet, Gene Cretz, and Jeremy Feltman—to meet with Gaddafi's envoys in Tunisia in July. Their message was stark: "The only way to move forward is for Gaddafi to step down."[55] Furthermore, these sentiments were not limited to the Western democracies. The Russian president Dmitri Medvedev publicly stated, "Gaddafi's regime has lost its legitimacy—he has to go."[56] Thus, the key players in the international community were on the same page. While they refrained from using the word "exile" in their statements, the implication was that they supported Gaddafi leaving Libya.

On top of that, representatives of nearly every powerful state made it clear that they recognized the potential value of giving Gaddafi an exit option and brokering a peace-for-exile deal. Speaking anonymously to the press, British officials acknowledged that letting Gaddafi escape to a comfortable exile could be acceptable if it brought an end to the Libyan conflict.[57] Moreover, in a behind-the-scenes diplomatic maneuver, the British inquired whether Equatorial Guinea would be willing to serve as a

53. "Gaddafi Will Either Share Milosevic's or Hitler's Fate: Libyan Rebel Foreign Minister," *Asharq Al-Awsat*, April 30, 2011, available in English at http://english.aawsat.com/2011/04/article55246671/gaddafi-will-either-share-milosevics-or-hitlers-fate-libyan-rebel-foreign-minister. Note that Ali Al Issawi got the details of the Milosevic case wrong (he was prosecuted at the ICTY, not the ICC).

54. Barack Obama, David Cameron, and Nicolas Sarkozy, "Libya's Pathway to Peace," *New York Times*, April 14, 2011.

55. Evidence of this meeting came to light with the declassification and release of Secretary of State Hillary Clinton's emails. See US Department of State, Case No. F-2014-20439, Document No. C05782140, released September 30, 2015.

56. Ellen Barry, "In Shift, Russia Agrees to Try to Talk Qaddafi Into Leaving," *New York Times*, May 27, 2011.

57. Julian Borger and Richard Norton-Taylor, "Diplomats Discuss Libya's Future as Italy Plots Gaddafi's Escape Route," *Guardian*, March 28, 2011.

retirement home for Gaddafi (d'Ancona 2013, 178).[58] Italy worked closely with the AU to try to find a safe haven in Africa for Gaddafi, and France entered into indirect negotiations with the Gaddafi regime about an exit plan.[59] Russia made it clear that they had no intention of hosting Gaddafi, but President Medvedev also promised, "We will find countries that will."[60] The United States took a more hands-off approach to finding an exile destination, but an unnamed senior American official signaled that the United States would not object to Gaddafi going into exile somewhere in Africa and noted that it would be consistent with Obama's call for Gaddafi to leave.[61] Similarly, the US secretary of state Hillary Clinton hinted that exile was a possibility for Gaddafi when she said, "If the violence could be ended by his leaving . . . that might be a good step."[62]

In line with the international consensus that Gaddafi had to go, multiple states offered to give Gaddafi asylum. Over the course of the war, it was reported that Uganda, Guinea-Bissau, Venezuela, Chad, Burkina Faso, Zimbabwe, and Equatorial Guinea had offered to provide a retirement home for Gaddafi.[63] To be sure, the details on some of these exile offers are murky. As one reporter put it, the "negotiations have been closely guarded," but "the African Union has been quietly sounding out potential hosts."[64] The most public and unambiguous offers of asylum came from Uganda and Guinea-Bissau. For example, Guinea-Bissau's prime minister claimed it would "welcome [Gaddafi] with open arms . . . if he needs exile in our country."[65] Similarly, a spokesman for the Ugandan president Yoweri Museveni said the country would roll out the welcome mat for Gaddafi: "We have soft spots for

58. Some of Hillary Clinton's emails that were released as part of the House Select Committee on Benghazi's investigation confirm the United Kingdom's role in trying to find a suitable exile destination for Gaddafi. See US Department of State, Case No. F-2015-04841, Document No. C05739721, released May 13, 2015.

59. Julian Borger and Richard Norton-Taylor, "Diplomats Discuss Libya's Future as Italy Plots Gaddafi's Escape Route," *Guardian*, March 28, 2011; John Lichfield, "France Confirms Negotiations with Gaddafi Regime," *Independent*, July 11, 2011.

60. Ellen Barry, "In Shift, Russia Agrees to Try to Talk Qaddafi Into Leaving," *New York Times*, May 27, 2011.

61. Julian Borger and Richard Norton-Taylor, "Diplomats Discuss Libya's Future as Italy Plots Gaddafi's Escape Route," *Guardian*, March 28, 2011.

62. Andrew Quinn, "Clinton Says Gaddafi Must Go," *Reuters*, February 28, 2011.

63. See William J. Dobson, "Dictator Seeks Second Home? A Guide to Gaddafi's Exile Options," *Washington Post*, March 29, 2011; David E. Sanger and Eric Schmitt, "U.S. and Allies Seek a Refuge for Qaddafi," *New York Times*, April 16, 2011; David Smith, "Where Could Colonel Muammar Gaddafi Go If He Were Exiled?," *Guardian*, February 21, 2011; and Alex Perry, "Where's a Deposed Dictator to Go? Five Top Tyrant Retirement Homes for Gaddafi," *Time*, June 10, 2011. Note that some of the governments reported as having offered safe haven to Gaddafi vehemently denied doing so (e.g., Burkina Faso).

64. See David E. Sanger and Eric Schmitt, "U.S. and Allies Seek a Refuge for Qaddafi," *New York Times*, April 16, 2011.

65. "Guinea-Bissau Offers Sanctuary to Gaddafi," *Al Jazeera*, September 10, 2011.

asylum seekers. Gaddafi would be allowed to live here if he chooses to do so."[66] Thus, there were at least two exile offers on the table for Gaddafi.

The possibility of facing international justice, however, complicated the creation of a golden parachute. The UN Security Council had unanimously passed Resolution 1970 on February 23, which referred the Libyan situation to the ICC.[67] This was a dramatic move and a clear illustration of the global, systemic change associated with the justice cascade. Writing about the ICC, David Bosco (2014, 55) marveled that "a leader whose country has not signed onto the Rome Statute, and who is committing crimes entirely within his own borders, could still find himself in the court's crosshairs." This is exactly what happened with Gaddafi. Libya had neither signed nor ratified the Rome Statute of the ICC, yet the Security Council referral made it clear that Gaddafi would be held to a set of international legal standards which Gaddafi himself had never agreed to follow.

After the referral, the ICC moved rapidly, with the prosecutor Luis Moreno-Ocampo opening an investigation almost immediately. On May 16, Moreno-Ocampo requested that the ICC issue arrest warrants for three individuals—Muammar Gaddafi, his son Saif, and his intelligence chief Abdullah al-Senussi—and the court's Pre-Trial Chamber responded by quickly issuing the warrants.[68] Furthermore, Moreno-Ocampo went to great lengths to signal that the case against Gaddafi was a "slam dunk," proudly telling the press that the evidence was so overwhelming that his investigation was "almost ready for trial" even before the arrest warrants had been issued.[69]

The mixed messages coming from the international community must have been bewildering for Gaddafi. On the one hand, powerful states such as the United States, the United Kingdom, France, and Russia were demanding that Gaddafi leave Libya. Some were even actively working to find Gaddafi a suitable exile destination. On the other hand, by referring the Libyan situation to the ICC, these very same states were responsible for

66. "Qaddafi Offered Refuge in Uganda," *CBS News*, March 30, 2011. The claim of "soft spots for asylum seekers" was a reference to Uganda's long and complicated history with its own leaders—such as Idi Amin and Milton Obote—going into exile.

67. The Libyan referral was just the second time the UN Security Council had referred a case to the ICC. The first occurred when the Security Council referred the situation in Darfur to the ICC in 2005, eventually leading to the arrest warrant for the Sudanese leader Omar Bashir.

68. Several commentators noted the shocking speed with which the ICC moved against Gaddafi. As Mark Kersten (2016, 117) put it, "It represented a remarkable turnaround time from referral to the issuance of warrants. In Darfur, the only other case of a UN Security Council referral to the ICC, the Court took two years to move from accepting the referral to issuing arrest warrants. In Libya, it took a matter of weeks."

69. Julian Borger, "International Criminal Court to Name Libyan War Crimes Suspects," *Guardian*, May 12, 2011.

Gaddafi's international prosecution. As explained in my theory, the two objectives at hand—easing Gaddafi into an early retirement abroad and pursuing international justice—were incompatible. In fact, insisting that Gaddafi be held accountable for his crimes was quite possibly the single most consequential thing the international community could have done to convince Gaddafi to reject the exile option. This incompatibility was not lost on the International Crisis Group (2011, ii), who noted during the crisis, "To insist that [Gaddafi] both leave the country *and* face trial in the International Criminal Court is virtually to ensure that he will stay in Libya to the bitter end and go down fighting."

To be fair, there was no perfect guarantee that going into exile would ultimately land Gaddafi in the dock in The Hague. As one commentator accurately summarized the situation, "The tough talk of relentless pressure aimed to oust the unpredictable and brutal despot who has ruled Libya for 41 years didn't entirely drown out hints of possible exile and the possibility of avoiding a war crimes trial."[70] While it is clear that the exile situation for Gaddafi was far more complicated than it had been for culpable leaders during the impunity era, Gaddafi nonetheless had options.

As mentioned before, the two explicit, unambiguous offers of asylum for Gaddafi came from Uganda and Guinea-Bissau. Both potential exile destinations, however, were problematic in their own way. Uganda had signed the Rome Statute of the ICC, giving it a legal obligation to arrest Gaddafi and extradite him to The Hague if he set foot on Ugandan soil. Of course, Uganda could have simply ignored its legal obligations. It would not have been the first or the last time that a state disregarded international law for the sake of political expedience, but at a minimum Uganda would have taken a reputational hit for failing to live up to its international commitments. With Guinea-Bissau, the issue was that its president, Malam Bacai Sanha, was in the midst of a widely known struggle with diabetes (which would kill him less than a year later). Given his precarious health at the time of Libya's crisis, Gaddafi would have had to worry about how long Sanha would last in power and whether any successor regime in Guinea-Bissau would be willing to continue providing sanctuary.

Beyond these issues with the specific exile destinations, an even deeper problem lurked in the background. Powerful Western states sent decidedly mixed signals about whether they would tolerate the exile option over the long haul. Though Western powers wanted a quick end to the Libyan conflict and appeared willing to let Gaddafi go into exile in another African state, they also made it clear that Gaddafi should face justice eventually. For

70. Paul Koring, "London Summit Doesn't Rule Out Exile for Gaddafi," *Globe and Mail*, March 29, 2011.

instance, while Secretary of State Clinton seemingly advocated for the exile option, she qualified her statement by adding, "But of course, we believe accountability has to be obtained for what he has done."[71] Similarly, the same British officials who acknowledged that letting Gaddafi go into exile might help resolve the conflict also made it clear they would rather see Gaddafi face trial.[72] Even the short and relatively straightforward op-ed from Obama, Cameron, and Sarkozy featured a healthy dose of ambiguity when it came to Gaddafi's fate: after calling on Gaddafi to leave Libya, the three leaders went on to praise the ICC investigation of Gaddafi.[73]

In more general terms, Gaddafi faced a time inconsistency problem: Western powers might encourage him to give up power now only to try to bring him to trial later. If this happened, the issue was simple for Gaddafi—could he count on a country like Uganda or Guinea-Bissau to withstand international pressure on his behalf?

For Gaddafi, the time inconsistency problem must have loomed large because of the fate of his former protégé, Liberia's Charles Taylor.[74] Recall that Taylor was indicted by the Special Court for Sierra Leone (SCSL) but agreed to give up power in 2003 in return for a supposedly safe exile in Nigeria. The deal initially had the backing of the international community, which desperately wanted to end the conflict in Liberia. Furthermore, Nigeria had put its reputation on the line by pledging that it would never turn Taylor over to an international court. Nigeria, however, soon faced a torrent of pressure from international actors who were interested in bringing Taylor to justice. Notably, the very same powerful states that helped broker Taylor's exile deal—including the United States and the United Kingdom—later strong-armed Nigeria into turning Taylor over to the SCSL. The Nigerians eventually decided sheltering Taylor was too costly, and they extradited him to the SCSL in 2006.

The similarity between Taylor's position in 2003 and Gaddafi's in 2011 was striking. In both cases, the international community could never quite decide whether it wanted to prioritize coaxing a violent leader out of power or holding that leader accountable for his crimes. A slew of commentators correctly highlighted the many parallels. When discussing the dual pursuit of peace and justice in Libya, Eric Stover, Victor Peskin, and Alexa Koenig (2016, 314) asked, "Wasn't this similar to what American diplomats had done with Charles Taylor as rebel groups laid siege to Monrovia in 2003?" The journalist Christina Lamb put it even more bluntly in her discussion of

71. Andrew Quinn, "Clinton Says Gaddafi Must Go," *Reuters*, February 28, 2011.

72. Julian Borger and Richard Norton-Taylor, "Diplomats Discuss Libya's Future as Italy Plots Gaddafi's Escape Route," *Guardian*, March 28, 2011.

73. Barack Obama, David Cameron, and Nicolas Sarkozy, "Libya's Pathway to Peace," *New York Times*, April 14, 2011.

74. The Charles Taylor case was discussed in detail in chapter 3.

Gaddafi's options: "What happened with Taylor means diplomacy is off the table [for Gaddafi] and war becomes the only option."[75] After comparing Gaddafi's options with Taylor's ill-fated exile, one analyst perfectly summed up the time inconsistency issue Gaddafi faced: "This is the problem . . . what seems a good idea today can change tomorrow."[76]

For his part, Gaddafi was clearly aware of the implications Taylor's arrest had for other leaders, including him. After Taylor was pulled from his comfortable exile in Nigeria and sent to the SCSL, Gaddafi lamented, "This means that every head of state could meet a similar fate. It sets a serious precedent."[77] In other words, Gaddafi updated his beliefs about the possibility of international punishment in a manner consistent with my theory's expectations. By the summer of 2011, this "serious precedent" had caught up with Gaddafi when he found himself caught in a position similar to the one Charles Taylor had previously occupied. It is therefore not surprising that Gaddafi spurned offers of sanctuary from relatively weak states such as Uganda and Guinea-Bissau. Just as Nigeria had failed to shelter Taylor, Uganda and Guinea-Bissau could not credibly offer to protect Gaddafi over the long haul. As the Libya expert Dirk Vandewalle put it, the anticipation of an international prosecution "further complicated the issue [of Gaddafi's post-tenure fate] for it meant that the possibility of exile for the Libyan leader had become more problematic" (Vandewalle 2012, 207).

Finally, interviews with Gaddafi loyalists who survived the war provide unique insight into Gaddafi's mindset regarding the threat that international justice posed. Most notably, Gaddafi's security chief and close confidant, Mansour Dhao Ibrahim—who was with Gaddafi during his final days—gave a series of revealing interviews at the Misrata detention center shortly after the conflict ended.[78] According to Dhao, Gaddafi justified his decision to fight until the end by telling his loyalists, "I am wanted by the International Criminal Court. No country will accept me. I prefer to die by Libyan hands."[79] Further, Dhao's theory of why Gaddafi decided to risk it all on the battlefield follows the logic of a calculated gamble: "Gaddafi believed he was rolling the dice for the final time" (Bowen 2012, 252). Priscilla Hayner of the Centre for Humanitarian Dialogue, who had the opportunity to interview Dhao, reached a similar

75. Christina Lamb, "Trapped in the Palace," *Spectator*, May 28, 2011.

76. David Smith, "Where Could Colonel Muammar Gaddafi Go If He Were Exiled?," *Guardian*, February 21, 2011.

77. "How the Mighty Are Falling," *Economist*, July 5, 2007.

78. Specifically, Dhao gave interviews to Human Rights Watch, the *New York Times*, the *BBC*, the Associated Press, and Britain's Channel 4.

79. Katya Adler, "Gaddafi: He Died an Angry and Disappointed Man," *BBC News*, October 30, 2011.

conclusion. When summarizing what she learned about Gaddafi's state of mind, Hayner notes, "Gaddafi was extremely aware of, and clearly felt trapped by, the ICC warrants, and did not seem to understand what his options might be other than to continue to fight" (Hayner 2013, 4). Of course, unraveling Gaddafi's decision-making process is a complicated task and no single piece of evidence is definitive. Nonetheless, Dhao's account is exceptionally valuable because it offers a rare glimpse inside Gaddafi's last stand.[80]

Given all of this, the "least bad" option from Gaddafi's perspective was to keep fighting. While continuing to fight is inherently risky, my argument suggests that culpable leaders have an incentive to gamble on the battlefield when they believe there is no other way out. Giving up power—for a retirement either at home or abroad—was a recipe for arrest and punishment. By contrast, fighting it out at least gave Gaddafi the chance (however small) to turn the tide of the war, reestablish control, and avoid punishment entirely. One American diplomat succinctly captured the intuition behind my argument, noting, "If Gaddafi's [other] option is to go from 'king of kings' to handcuffs in The Hague, you know which choice he's going to pursue."[81] Hence, Gaddafi's decision to risk it all on the battlefield conforms to my theory's predictions.

The rebels captured Tripoli in late August. However, Gaddafi and a small band of loyalists had secretly retreated to Sirte, Gaddafi's ancestral homeland, a couple of days earlier. To keep his whereabouts a mystery, Gaddafi spent much of his time shuttling between abandoned homes, reading the Koran, and searching for food in the bombed-out city. According to Dhao, Gaddafi was "angry and disappointed" by the end.[82] The rebels eventually surrounded Sirte on the suspicion that Gaddafi might be there. In response, Gaddafi and his men gathered into a small convoy of vehicles and burst though the rebel line. Once outside of Sirte, however, Gaddafi's convoy was hit by a NATO airstrike, which damaged several vehicles. The rebels, in hot pursuit of the

80. It is important to avoid putting too much faith in a single source, but there is no obvious reason to doubt Dhao's testimony either. As Human Rights Watch points out, Dhao's interviews took place in a private setting. Moreover, Dhao's general testimony fits with the accounts of other survivors not aligned with the Gaddafi regime: "While Human Rights Watch cannot independently confirm the details of events offered by Dhao, they are consistent with the accounts of other survivors who lived through the same experience in District Two [of Sirte]." See Human Rights Watch 2012, 20.

81. Christina Lamb, "Trapped in the Palace," *Spectator*, May 28, 2011.

82. This description of Gaddafi's last days draws heavily on interviews with Dhao. Among others, see Katya Adler, "Gaddafi: He Died an Angry and Disappointed Man," *BBC News*, October 30, 2011; Kareem Fahim, "In His Last Days, Gaddafi Wearied of Fugitive's Life," *New York Times*, October 22, 2011; "Revealed: The Last Days of Col. Gaddafi's Life on the Run," *London Evening Post*, October 23, 2011; "Gadhafi's Final Weeks, as Told by a Top Security Official," *NPR News*, October 25, 2011; and Human Rights Watch 2012.

convoy, soon found an injured Gaddafi hiding in a drainage pipe alongside the road. A shaky, grainy cell-phone video captured Gaddafi's final minutes: a group of rebels began by kicking and beating him, then one stabbed him with a bayonet, and finally another shot him in the head. Once Gaddafi was dead, the rebels publicly displayed his body as a trophy in the freezer of a local meat market.[83] It was an ignominious end for the Brother Leader.

ALTERNATIVE EXPLANATIONS FOR GADDAFI'S FIGHT TO THE DEATH

Gaddafi's gamble on the battlefield obviously failed. With the benefit of perfect hindsight, his decision to fight to the death may appear puzzling, even illogical. My argument, of course, is that Gaddafi made a calculated gamble given the severe constraints he faced at the time. The decision to risk it all on the battlefield *might* have paid off for Gaddafi—as it did for Syria's Bashar Assad, a case discussed in chapter 2—even though it ultimately did not. However, given Gaddafi's seemingly strange decision-making, there are two alternative arguments that should be addressed.

The first counterargument is that Gaddafi was an irrational leader. In its simplest form, this viewpoint contends that Gaddafi fought to the death because he was crazy. Other embattled leaders have historically gone into exile, this argument would posit, because they were rational and chose to save themselves. This idea has some appeal at first glance. To be sure, Gaddafi was endlessly eccentric. When describing Gaddafi near the end of his tenure, Lindsey Hilsum (2012, 4) notes, "To the outside world Gaddafi had become a clown, a Botox-enhanced oddball in bizarre headgear who wanted to pitch his Bedouin tent in New Jersey while attending the UN." A leaked cable written by Gene Cretz, the US ambassador to Libya, described in detail several of Gaddafi's eccentricities such as his reliance on an all-female security force dubbed the "Amazonian Guard."[84]

Despite the strange behavior, the "Gaddafi was crazy" argument is an unconvincing explanation for his decision-making during the 2011 Libyan revolution. First off, there is no evidence that Gaddafi was in fact an incompetent leader. To the contrary, Gaddafi stayed in power for forty-two years, which made him the longest serving nonroyal national leader at the time of his death in October 2011.[85] Simply put, there is no way an irrational leader

83. Andrew Netto, Ian Black, and Luke Harding, "Muammar Gaddafi's 'Trophy' Body on Show in Misrata Meat Store," *Guardian*, October 22, 2011.

84. "US Embassy Cables: The Eccentricities of Gaddafi Revealed," *Guardian*, December 7, 2010.

85. Cuba's Fidel Castro stayed in power even longer than Gaddafi (fifty-two years), but Castro ceded power to his brother, Raul, in April 2011. Thus, Gaddafi was the world's longest serving nonroyal political leader at the time of his death in October 2011.

could have survived in power for so long. Jon Lee Anderson (2011, 44) aptly captures this dynamic:

> To the outside world, he was the Michael Jackson of global politics, an unhinged figure whose vast wealth bought him repeated indulgences for unseemly behavior. Inside Libya, his image was defined by the mechanisms and the depth of his control. Although Qaddafi was widely despised, he was held in awe for his cunning—so much so that even after he abandoned Tripoli to the rebels many Libyans feared he was still capable of outwitting his enemies and returning to power. A former senior government official told me, "I feel like a man who was in a dark hole, who has come into the sunlight, and it's hazy. . . . What will happen now?" He fretted about Qaddafi. "He's a genius," the former official said. "He's like a fox. He's a very dangerous man, and he still has tricks up his sleeve. I cannot be convinced he is gone until I see him dead."

As the preceding quote demonstrates, Gaddafi is better understood as a cruel and calculating leader than as an incompetent and irrational one.

Furthermore, while Gaddafi certainly was eccentric, there is no clear connection between individual eccentricities and irrational behavior. Consider Gaddafi in relation to another famously eccentric leader, Uganda's Idi Amin. In fact, Amin is a perfect foil to Gaddafi because they displayed many of the same unusual antics during their tenures. For instance, both developed a penchant for adopting seemingly absurd honorific titles (e.g., Amin's "Lord of All the Beasts of the Earth and Fishes of the Sea" versus Gaddafi's "King of Kings of Africa" and "Universal Theorist"). Moreover, as with Gaddafi, many Westerners took a dim view of Amin during his time in power. Writing in 1973, the American ambassador to Uganda described Amin as "erratic and unpredictable, brutal, inept, bellicose, irrational, ridiculous, and militaristic."[86] Yet, when rebels marched on the Ugandan capital of Kampala in 1979, Amin was anything but irrational: he saved himself by fleeing into exile. Thus, the comparison to Amin shows that eccentricity is an insufficient explanation for Gaddafi's behavior.

The second counterargument is slightly different. In this case, the alternative explanation for Gaddafi's behavior is not that he was irrational per se, but rather that he was firmly committed to staying in Libya no matter what happened. The threat of an international prosecution, in this view, was irrelevant because Gaddafi never would have considered exile in the first place. Such arguments typically put a strong (and arguably paternalistic) emphasis on Gaddafi's tribal background. For instance,

86. See "Telegram 1 from the Embassy in Uganda to the Department of State, January 2, 1973," in *Foreign Relations of the United States, 1969–1976*, vol. E-6, *Documents on Africa 1973–1976*, document 240.

Pargeter (2012, 226) writes, "With his unstinting Bedouin pride and uncompromising self-belief, there was no way the Colonel was going to step aside and walk away from power gracefully—let alone flee the country. He was not simply a head of state. . . . He *was* Libya." Similarly, the popular pundit Robert Kaplan argued that as a "tribal warrior," Gaddafi could not consider fleeing into exile—even though it likely would have been better for his physical safety—because he was fighting for his honor. Kaplan went on to conclude that with leaders such as Gaddafi, "We are not talking about [normal] politicians so much as about warriors" (Kaplan 2011). The best evidence in favor of this interpretation is one of Gaddafi's own statements. In a speech broadcast on Libyan state television in late April, Gaddafi defiantly proclaimed to the Libyan people, "I will not leave my country and will fight to the death."[87]

We can discriminate between this explanation and mine by considering where their predictions differ. The alternative explanation implies that Gaddafi should never even consider the possibility of going into exile, whereas my argument suggests that Gaddafi might have explored the exile option before ultimately rejecting it due to the threat of international prosecution. The available evidence is consistent with my theory. Shortly after NATO began supporting the Libyan rebels and the war turned against Gaddafi, Secretary of State Hillary Clinton told the journalist Diane Sawyer that "people close to" Gaddafi began "making overtures" about potential retirement destinations around the globe.[88] Another report on Gaddafi's options during the crisis that drew on discussions with European officials concluded that "[Gaddafi] is understood to be willing, in spite of the bluster, to consider retirement in exile."[89] This evidence from Western diplomatic sources is suggestive, but actions speak louder than words. That is why the most important evidence demonstrating that Gaddafi considered exile comes from a plan hatched by Saif Gaddafi. In March 2011, Saif dispatched his top aide to London to see if British authorities might accept a plan in which Saif would oversee Libya's transition to democracy, while his father would leave Libya in exchange for immunity from international prosecution (Pargeter 2012, 238). While this plan never came into fruition, it is noteworthy because it shows that Gaddafi entertained the possibility of exile. Given the close relationship between father and son, it is highly unlikely that Saif would have initiated such a bold proposal without Muammar's

87. "Libya Accuses NATO of Trying to 'Assassinate' Col. Gaddafi," *Telegraph*, May 1, 2011.

88. William J. Dobson, "Dictator Seeks Second Home? A Guide to Gaddafi's Exile Options," *Washington Post*, March 29, 2011.

89. Matthew Campbell, "A Brutal Home from Home for Gaddafi," *Sunday Times*, July 17, 2011. According to one diplomat interviewed for the preceding article, "It's a question of Equatorial Guinea making him a serious offer. We think that he might accept it."

approval. Thus, a variety of different sources all point to the conclusion that Gaddafi at least considered going into exile if the circumstances were right.[90]

On top of that, there are compelling reasons to doubt that Gaddafi's promise to stay in Libya and fight to the death was an accurate revelation of his plans or preferences. Most likely, this was a case of a leader "talking tough" to try to dissuade civilians from joining the rebellion. In other words, Gaddafi's statement may have been intended as a deterrent signal for internal audiences. The fact that Gaddafi chose to broadcast his speech on the national television station certainly supports this interpretation. Moreover, there is another reason to be skeptical that Gaddafi's quote was anything more than cheap talk: exiled leaders have a long history of saying virtually the same thing shortly before heading into retirement abroad. For instance, in a televised address only three days before fleeing the Philippines, Ferdinand Marcos proclaimed that he had "no intention of going abroad" and vowed to "fight to the last drop of blood."[91] One week before his flight from Haiti, Jean-Claude Duvalier took to national television and radio to promise, "I'm not going anywhere."[92] Just before fleeing Uganda, Idi Amin declared on the national radio station that he was "prepared to die in the defense of the motherland" (Avirgan and Honey 1982, 121). Thus, history suggests that it would be a mistake to put much stock in the bombastic claims of an embattled ruler.

Overall, both alternative explanations fail to hold up under the weight of the evidence. In the end, my argument that Gaddafi's fight to the end was a rational but risky response to the threat of international justice remains the most persuasive explanation for his behavior.

This chapter provided an evaluation of my theory's hypothesis on how the justice cascade influences civil war duration. I argued that if culpable leaders in the accountability era are reluctant to go into exile because they worry about post-tenure international punishment, they should also be more willing to risk a fight to the bitter end during civil conflicts. Without an attractive exit option, culpable leaders have an incentive to keep fighting—even when the prospects for victory are slim—and hope to turn the tide of the war. The results presented in this chapter, both quantitative and qualitative, are consistent with these expectations.

The statistical tests showed that the effect of leader culpability on civil war duration is statistically indistinguishable from zero during the

90. Additionally, we already know from Dhao's account that the possibility of an ICC prosecution was one of the specific reasons Gaddafi thought that the circumstances for a foreign retirement were *not* right.

91. "Reagan Calls on Marcos to Quit," *Los Angeles Times*, February 14, 1986.

92. "Haiti Declares State of Siege as Violence Flares," *Los Angeles Times*, February 2, 1986.

impunity era. In the accountability era, however, civil wars last significantly longer when culpable leaders are in office. The results are also meaningful in a substantive sense: if a culpable leader is in power during the accountability era, the likelihood of war termination is cut in half. When we consider the staggering death tolls associated with many civil wars, it is easy to see how the recent push for global accountability may come with a steep price.

The Muammar Gaddafi case study illustrated how the justice cascade has altered the incentives culpable leaders now face when making fight or flight decisions. The very real threat of international justice undermined the exile option for Gaddafi, creating incentives for him to risk it all on the battlefield. To be sure, exile was still a *possibility* for Gaddafi. But the evidence shows that exile was a far riskier and more complicated option for Gaddafi than it had been for past culpable leaders. The near-ironclad guarantee of a safe retirement abroad that virtually all ousted dictators had once enjoyed was no longer on the table. In fact, exile looked risky enough from Gaddafi's perspective to convince him that he was better off continuing to fight. Therefore, both Gaddafi's general behavior (doubling down on the battlefield) and the specific reason for that behavior (the lack of a good exit option) are consistent with my theory's expectations.

This finding represents a novel contribution to the academic literature. While pundits have speculated that international justice might exacerbate conflict, such as when the *Washington Post*'s Jackson Diehl mused that Libyans were "stuck in a civil war in large part because of Gaddafi's international prosecution," much of the scholarly literature has denied such claims.[93] For instance, when discussing academic research on how international justice might block peace processes, Hyeran Jo and Beth Simmons (2016, 445) conclude that "practically no systematic evidence has been produced to date to support such concerns." While that may have previously been correct, the results presented here contradict such claims by providing some of the strongest evidence to date that international justice can in fact encourage brutal leaders to fight longer.

93. Jackson Diehl, "After the Dictators Fall," *Washington Post*, June 5, 2011.

CHAPTER 5

The Positive Effect

Deterring Mass Atrocities

This chapter tests the third observable implication of my theory. It builds explicitly on the results already reported. In previous chapters, I provided evidence of two main findings. First, a leader's decision to flee into exile is conditional on the threat international justice poses. It is only after the justice cascade that leaders culpable for atrocity crimes are less likely to go into exile (chapter 3). Second, international justice produces a perverse effect. By undermining the possibility of a safe retirement for culpable leaders, the justice cascade can incentivize such leaders to keep fighting during civil wars when they would otherwise flee abroad (chapter 4). This chapter examines an interrelated—and positive—effect of the pursuit of international justice. Precisely because leaders now know that committing atrocity crimes will foreclose exile possibilities, the justice cascade should increase the perceived cost of brutality and create a deterrent effect.

Understanding mass atrocities is a disheartening but necessary task. State-sponsored mass killing is one of the gravest threats to human life in modern history. To give an example, during an approximately one-hundred-day killing spree in 1994, Rwanda's Hutu-led government and state-sponsored militias killed an estimated eight hundred thousand Tutsis and moderate Hutus. Despite the horrific nature and scale of the violence, the death toll in Rwanda was small compared to other campaigns of mass killing such as the Holocaust, the Armenian Genocide, and China's Cultural Revolution. By some estimates, more civilians were murdered by their own governments during the twentieth century than the number of soldiers killed on the battlefield in all wars over the same time period (Rummel 1995).

At first glance, my claim that international justice deters mass killing may seem intuitive, even obvious. After all, of the many possible justifications for international criminal accountability, deterrence is often considered to be "the most important justification and the most important goal"

(Wippman 1999, 474).[1] Policymakers and international lawyers commonly justify international tribunals on the grounds of their supposed deterrent effect. For instance, the ICC's first president, Philippe Kirsch, asserted, "By putting potential perpetrators on notice that they may be tried before the Court, the ICC is intended to contribute to the deterrence of these crimes."[2] Within the academy, many scholars agree that international justice mechanisms can, at least under certain circumstances, deter atrocity crimes (e.g., Akhavan 2001; Appel 2018; Gilligan 2006; Jo and Simmons 2016; Kim and Sikkink 2010; Olsen, Payne, and Reiter 2010; Orentlicher 1991; Sikkink 2011).[3]

At the same time, the assertion that international justice deters has plenty of critics. After reviewing the scholarly work on the topic, Julian Ku and Jide Nzelibe (2006, 780) conclude that in most studies "the deterrence claim is simply asserted or rejected without much empirical or theoretical analysis." Mark Drumbl (2005, 548) notes that much of the scholarship on deterrence is "driven more by ideology than by empiricism." The absence of strong evidence in favor of deterrence led David Wippman (1999, 474) to assert that "the connection between international prosecutions and the actual deterrence of future atrocities is at best a plausible but largely untested assumption." At least some in the policy realm agree with this assessment. John Bolton asserts that it is a "basic error" to assume international tribunals will prevent heinous abuses and concludes that "rarely, if ever . . . has so sweeping a proposal had so little empirical evidence to support it" (Bolton 2001, 175).

The impasse on the subject of whether international justice deters atrocities is largely due to three points of confusion in the current literature. The first issue involves identifying which types of trials are relevant. Most existing work does not distinguish between different types of prosecutions. Instead, it is common to lump all human rights trials together to create independent variables that attempt to measure each country's "experience" with prosecutions.[4] This can be problematic across several dimensions. For starters, it treats domestic, foreign, and international trials as equivalent. As

1. For discussions of international justice's goals beyond deterrence, see Bass 2000; Damaska 2008; Drumbl 2007; and Shklar 1964.

2. Quoted in Hillebrecht 2016, 616.

3. Surprisingly, however, the academic literatures on mass killing and international criminal justice rarely engage with one another. For instance, a review article of the political science literature on mass atrocities (Valentino 2014) contains only a single reference to work explicitly addressing the potential deterrent effect of international law.

4. Relatively common empirical measures include the cumulative number of human rights prosecutions in each country or the number of trial years in a country's history. For examples, see Kim and Sikkink 2010; Olsen, Payne, and Reiter 2010; Sikkink 2011; and Sikkink and Walling 2007.

my theory makes clear, however, domestic trials should not produce effects similar to foreign or international trials because domestic prosecutions do not raise implications for the exile option. Hence, there are fundamental differences across the various types of trials that current research often fails to acknowledge. Moreover, it ignores the identity of the prosecuted individual. The existing approach would, for example, treat the prosecution of a common foot solider or paramilitary as comparable to the prosecution of a head of state. In addition to glossing over important legal distinctions such as head-of-state immunity, this approach is troublesome because it ignores one of the main conclusions of the political violence literature: campaigns of mass killing are typically initiated by leaders and small groups of loyalists, not the population writ large (e.g., Valentino 2004, 2014). When it comes to deterrence, it therefore may be appropriate to view prosecutions of heads of state as qualitatively different than prosecutions of low-level perpetrators.

A second issue is endogeneity. When searching for evidence of deterrence, one strategy is to examine differences between states that held trials and those that did not. While this may seem like a reasonable empirical approach, endogeneity is a notable threat to causal inference because states may strategically decide to hold or forego human rights trials. If states are more likely to hold trials when human rights abusers are already weak, the estimated effect of prosecutions will be biased.[5]

The third shortcoming concerns measurement validity. There is a notable mismatch between how deterrence is often theorized to work and how scholars typically attempt to measure it. Existing work primarily examines the effect of prosecutions on subsequent behavior *in the same state*. But if, as many policymakers argue, high-profile arrests and trials are effective because they send "shockwaves into the homes of other leaders" (Goldstone 2000, 136), then deterrence should operate *across borders*.[6] If this is correct, a leader could be deterred from initiating a campaign of atrocities even though his country has not yet experienced a single human rights

5. This endogeneity concern is especially acute for scholars who examine domestic prosecutions. However, international tribunals such as the ICC have some autonomy to choose the cases they become involved in, so selection effects can threaten our ability to draw reliable inferences when comparing states that experienced international prosecutions and those that did not. My empirical strategy of examining systemic, over-time variation associated with the justice cascade helps mitigate this problem.

6. These different notions of how deterrence might work are sometimes called "specific" and "general" deterrence. Specific deterrence refers to the actions of the particular individual or country targeted with legal sanctions, whereas general deterrence concerns the signal sent to the broader community that atrocity crimes will be punished (e.g., Akhavan 1998; Drumbl 2007). Thus, another way to state my critique of the existing literature is to say that it focuses too much on specific deterrence at the expense of general deterrence.

prosecution. The intuition behind this view in the policy community is nearly identical to the empirical strategy used in this book: leaders update their beliefs about the likelihood of punishment based on the fates of their peers.[7]

In this chapter, I build on the empirical strategy used throughout the book to minimize the aforementioned problems in the deterrence literature. As before, I view the events of 1998—the Pinochet arrest and the Rome Conference—as the watershed moment in a transition from an era of impunity to one of accountability. The rapid change in the likelihood of punishment for political leaders provides a unique opportunity to estimate the potential deterrent effect of international justice. Controlling for a host of factors believed to influence mass killing, I estimate regression models that show leaders are less likely to commit mass atrocities after 1998 than they were previously. However, a word of caution is necessary: successful deterrence is famously hard to prove. This book is no exception, as I detail later in this chapter. Therefore, it would be wise to interpret the evidence in this chapter as *consistent with* my argument rather than as *proof of* deterrence.

In the second part of this chapter, I probe my theory's causal mechanism with a case study of Blaise Compaoré during the 2014 revolution in Burkina Faso. This is important because the quantitative tests do not address *why* mass killing is less common in today's accountability era—qualitative evidence is needed to show that leaders think and act in a manner consistent with my theory.[8] The Compaoré case effectively illustrates the interrelated nature of exile and mass killing in today's accountability era. As I document, Compaoré opted not to use mass violence against the civilian population in part because doing so would have undermined his ability to retire to a foreign safe haven later in the crisis. By exercising restraint in Burkina Faso, Compaoré faced a very low risk of international arrest and therefore had no trouble finding a secure retirement destination in the Ivory Coast.

7. To their credit, Hunjoon Kim and Kathryn Sikkink (2010) consider the possibility of deterrence across borders and find some evidence consistent with such an effect. Specifically, they present evidence of regional deterrence: prosecutions in a country's neighbors decrease repression in that particular country. However, they do not explore the possibility of global deterrence nor do they examine over-time variation in the threat international justice poses to leaders.

8. It is also important to show that my causal mechanism is doing some of the work since there are other plausible arguments that may help explain the decline in mass killings (e.g., Pinker 2011). To be clear, my argument is meant to complement rather than contradict other accounts. It would be a mistake to argue that any one factor is entirely responsible for the decline of violence over time.

Mass Killing Onset Statistical Tests

DATA

To investigate patterns of mass killing onset, I start with a dataset of all countries included in Kristian Gleditsch and Michael Ward's (1999) state membership list for the 1960–2010 period. Specifically, the unit of analysis is the country year. The dependent variable is the onset of a state-sponsored mass killing event. I focus on onset rather than incidence for theoretical reasons. The question is whether the threat of international justice can deter leaders from initiating a campaign of mass killing. After atrocities begin, however, there is no marginal cost to continuing them since the leader is already culpable.[9] I measure state-sponsored mass killing using data from Ulfelder and Valentino 2008, the same dataset used to create the leader culpability variable in the previous two chapters. Recall that mass killing is defined as "any event in which the actions of state agents result in the intentional death of at least 1,000 noncombatants from a discrete group in a period of sustained violence" (Ulfelder and Valentino 2008, 2). The onset of a mass killing episode is coded as the first year in which at least one hundred intentional noncombatant fatalities occur.[10]

The independent variable of interest is *Post-1998*, a dummy variable that takes a value of 1 for all country years beginning in 1998 and 0 otherwise. This variable captures the more credible threat of international punishment reflected in the shift from the impunity era to the accountability era. My research design here follows the logic of an interrupted time-series (ITS) model. The ITS approach, which is sometimes considered to be a quasi-experimental design (D. T. Campbell 1969), is ideal for data with an intervention at a specific point that interrupts the time-series. ITS analysis is commonly used in the social sciences to estimate the impact of a new law, policy, or high-profile event. For example, scholars have previously examined the effects of new traffic laws on car accidents (D. T. Campbell 1969), US Supreme Court decisions on public opinion (Johnson and Martin 1998), and oil booms on regime survival (B. Smith 2004).

9. Future researchers might consider drawing a distinction between the frequency and the magnitude of mass killings. Even though the justice cascade appears to have reduced the number of mass killings, today's culpable leaders might have a reason to go all the way when committing abuses, thereby increasing the magnitude of the mass killings that still do occur. The horrific scale of the violence witnessed in cases such as Syria and Yemen appears consistent with this concern.

10. There are eighty-seven mass killing onsets in the 1960–2010 period.

I also control for several factors that are believed to influence mass killing. One prominent explanation for patterns of mass killing is regime type. Many argue that the structural characteristics and normative values of democracies make them less likely to resort to mass atrocities. This hypothesis is most closely associated with the work of Rudolph Rummel (e.g., Rummel 1995). Though Rummel discusses several reasons why democracies might be less likely to use mass violence against civilians, his central point addresses the distribution of power across regime types. Since power is diffuse in democratic states, there are several possible checks against mass killing. By contrast, in nondemocratic states, power is often highly concentrated in one individual or group. This leaves rulers unchecked when considering the use of mass killing to eliminate opponents or carry out a revisionist agenda. In addition to the evidence presented in Rummel's body of work, several other studies find that democracies are less likely to engage in state-sponsored mass killing (e.g., Harff 2003; Valentino, Huth, and Balch-Lindsay 2004).[11] Therefore, I include a dichotomous measure of *Democracy* from Geddes, Wright, and Frantz 2014.

A second factor thought to influence mass killing is the extent to which a country is integrated into the international system. In a widely cited study, Barbara Harff (2003) shows that higher levels of trade openness decrease the likelihood of genocide. The logic used to explain this relationship is that the leaders of highly isolated states are more likely to believe they can kill their own citizens without international repercussions. Consequently, I control for *Trade Openness*, which measures the value of each state's international trade relative to the size of its economy, using data from the World Bank (2013).

Another potential explanation is that highly polarized societies are more likely to witness mass killing. In this view, discrimination and deep social cleavages between ethnic groups are a permissive condition encouraging mass killing. The ethnic character of violence in several high-profile cases, such as Rwanda and Yugoslavia, appears consistent with this view.[12] To account for this possibility, I include an *Ethnic Polarization* variable using data from Montalvo and Reynal-Querol 2008.[13]

11. For a counterpoint to the claim that democracy necessarily inhibits civilian victimization, see Downes 2008.

12. While the fighting in these conflicts—along with several others—has certainly taken place along ethnic lines, some have questioned whether ethnic hatreds were in fact the cause of the violence (Mueller 2000).

13. Polarization is conceptually distinct from fractionalization, another commonly used measure of ethnic diversity. Fractionalization measures the probability that two randomly selected individuals from a country are not part of the same ethnic group. The polarization variable used here measures how far the distribution of ethnic groups strays from a perfectly bipolar distribution (which is the highest possible level of polarization). Jose Montalvo and

Others see a role for elite ideology in civilian victimization. Leaders who propagate an exclusionary ideology, a "belief system that identifies some overriding purpose or principle that justifies efforts to restrict, persecute, or eliminate certain categories of people," may be more likely to engage in mass killing (Harff 2003, 63). Regimes that adhere to strict variants of communism and sharia law, in particular, are sometimes linked to violence against civilians. Regarding communism, Valentino (2004) shows that mass killings in the Soviet Union, China, and Cambodia were largely a result of efforts to impose radical, ideologically motivated agricultural policies on resistant peasant populations. Hence, I add a dummy variable from the Center for Systemic Peace 2015 for regimes with an *Exclusionary Ideology*.

Yet another factor thought to influence mass killing is economic development. Indeed, most studies of political violence—including but not limited to mass killing—find that wealthier states generally are more peaceful. To address this fact, I include *Development*, which measures the natural log of each country's GDP per capita using data from K. Gleditsch 2002.

While the factors described thus far explain which types of states are likely to experience mass killing, they tell us little about when mass killing occurs. To understand the *timing* of mass killing onsets, Matthew Krain (1997, 335) argues for a focus on situations that "create 'windows of political opportunity' during which elites may and must more freely act to consolidate power and eliminate the opposition." Consistent with this view, perhaps the most robust finding in the existing literature is that mass killing usually occurs during times of instability such as civil war or political upheaval. I capture this dynamic in two ways. First, I control for *Conflict Intensity* using civil war battle deaths data from the UCDP/PRIO armed conflict dataset.[14] Second, to account for the degree of *Political Stability* in each country, I include data on regime age (i.e., the number of years the ruling regime has been in power) from Geddes, Wright, and Frantz 2014.

Finally, since the data have a Binary Time-Series Cross-Sectional (BTSCS) structure, the dependent variable may exhibit temporal dependence. For example, countries that have recently experienced mass killing may be more likely to relapse into it compared to countries that have never experienced mass killing. Following Nathaniel Beck, Jonathan Katz, and Richard

Marta Reynal-Querol (2008) find that increased levels of ethnic polarization are linked to a higher likelihood of political mass murder.

14. Importantly, one-sided state violence against civilians is excluded from this measure. The *Conflict Intensity* variable equals 2 if there are over 1,000 battle deaths in a given year; 1 if there are between 25 and 999 battle deaths; and 0 otherwise. While some datasets attempt to code the exact number of battle deaths, I use the ordinal variable provided in the UCDP/PRIO dataset because it has less missing data and covers a longer time period.

Tucker's (1998) advice on BTSCS data, I control for the number of years since the last mass killing onset and the associated cubic splines.

MAIN RESULTS

Mass killing onset is a binary outcome, so I estimate logit models to test my hypothesis about the deterrent effect of the justice cascade. Since observations of the same country over time are not independent, I cluster standard errors on the country. The coefficient of interest is *Post-1998*, which estimates the difference in the likelihood of mass killing onset in the impunity and accountability eras conditional on the covariates.

Before proceeding to the results, however, it is important to note the assumptions underlying this empirical strategy. Providing evidence of deterrence is a notoriously difficult task. For instance, there is a substantial literature in international relations on the challenges of empirically testing theories of deterrence pertaining to military aggression.[15] Richard Lebow and Janice Stein (1990) even call deterrence "the elusive variable" in international relations. Two main challenges stand out, both of which are neatly summarized in former secretary of state Henry Kissinger's magnum opus, *Diplomacy*. The first is that "deterrence can only be tested negatively, by events that do *not* take place" (Kissinger 1994, 608). Since deterrence is the absence of an outcome, systematic examination is difficult. At times, it is hard even to identify the relevant population of cases where deterrence might have occurred. The second issue is that there may be a discrepancy between observed behavior and intentions. In studies of military aggression, the absence of an attack is often interpreted as evidence of deterrence. But as Kissinger (1994, 608) points out, it is "impossible to prove whether the adversary ever intended to attack in the first place." Hence, deterrence rests on a counterfactual that is not easy to assess.

A study of whether international justice deters atrocity crimes faces a similar set of issues. How can we be certain that the threat of a prosecution deterred a leader from committing atrocities when there rarely is definitive evidence that the ruler would have turned to civilian targeting in the first place? While there is no perfect solution, transparency about assumptions is an important first step toward minimizing the aforementioned challenges. In this chapter, I do not make claims about the intentions of individual leaders beyond the simple assertion that it is at least possible for each leader to preside over a campaign of mass killing. I acknowledge that some leaders may be more likely than others to perpetrate violence against

15. Among many others, see Fearon 1994; Huth and Russett 1990; Jervis 1989; and Lebow and Stein 1990.

Table 4. Logit models of mass killing onset

	(1)	(2)	(3)
Post-1998	–1.784**	–1.811**	–1.629**
	(0.511)	(0.522)	(0.519)
Conflict Intensity	1.572**	1.475**	1.026**
	(0.208)	(0.209)	(0.423)
Political Stability	–0.013	–0.012	–0.010
	(0.010)	(0.010)	(0.010)
Democracy	0.039	0.127	0.125
	(0.335)	(0.325)	(0.411)
Ethnic Polarization	–0.200	–0.639	–1.856**
	(0.634)	(0.645)	(0.891)
Exclusionary Ideology	0.015	0.016	0.356
	(0.281)	(0.281)	(0.373)
Trade Openness	–0.001	0.000	0.002
	(0.003)	(0.002)	(0.004)
Development	–0.442**	–0.385**	–0.617**
	(0.170)	(0.176)	(0.256)
Years w/o Mass Killing	–0.058	–0.049	–0.033
	(0.114)	(0.113)	(0.115)
Constant	–4.470**	–4.163**	–3.062**
	(0.545)	(0.547)	(0.716)
N	4970	3450	941
Country Years Included	All	History of conflict	Ongoing conflict
AIC	548.46	525.35	340.50
BIC	633.11	605.25	403.51

Notes: Standard errors clustered by country in parentheses. Cubic splines included but not reported.
* $p < 0.10$, ** $p < 0.05$ (two-tailed)

civilians based on individual personality quirks, private preferences, risk tolerances, and so forth. In an ideal study, one would be able to account for these factors, but that of course is not feasible. However, the next best option is to control for the country-level factors that are thought to encourage rulers to engage in violence or exercise restraint. If, conditional on all these factors, I find that mass killing is on average less likely in the accountability era, then there is evidence consistent with a deterrent effect for the justice cascade. To put it another way, it is easy to identify who is not deterred, but it is hard to identify who is. The purpose of the statistical tests is simply to show that the number of leaders who fall into the "not deterred" category is lower in the accountability era.[16]

16. The case study of Blaise Compaoré presented later in the chapter returns to this issue and offers qualitative evidence that mass killing could plausibly have occurred in Burkina Faso if not for the incentives international justice created.

The main statistical results are reported in table 4. Given my argument that the cost of mass killing in the accountability era is higher since launching a campaign of civilian victimization restricts a leader's future exile options, my expectation is that *Post-1998* will be negative and significant. Using the data described in the previous section, I estimate the same regression model with three different samples of cases. I employ these different samples because, as outlined earlier, one of the challenges of studying deterrence is identifying the relevant sample of cases where atrocities might conceivably have occurred (even when they ultimately did not). This is not an easy task, but using three separate samples of cases mitigates concerns of bias. If all three samples produce similar results, our confidence in the purported deterrent effect should increase.

The sample of cases used in model 1 is the broadest. I include all country years since it is possible that mass killing could occur in any state at any time. Indeed, ruling regimes have resorted to atrocities in times of war as well as peace, in autocracies as well as democracies, and so forth. Thus, model 1 usefully captures the full universe of cases. However, one could argue that not all states have a comparable risk of mass killing onset. A state with a long tradition of political stability such as, say, Switzerland may not be comparable to a state like Sudan. Including the Switzerlands of the world in the sample might distort the results since mass atrocities presumably are extraordinarily unlikely in such countries regardless of the changing landscape for international justice. To address this issue, I limit the sample in model 2 to states with at least one episode of civil war in the post–World War II era. Finally, in model 3, I further limit the sample to country years that feature an ongoing civil war. One could reasonably point out that this sample is overly restrictive because atrocity crimes can and do occur outside the context of civil war. Nonetheless, this model serves an important function: it allows me to address the potential critique that the decline of mass killing after 1998 might be due to a decreased stock of civil conflicts rather than an increased likelihood of punishment for atrocity crimes.

I find support for my hypothesis across all three samples. The statistically significant and negative coefficient on *Post-1998* in model 1 indicates that leaders are less likely to initiate a campaign of mass killing after 1998 even when accounting for other factors typically linked to mass killing such as the intensity of battlefield combat, political instability, regime type, ethnic polarization, exclusionary elite ideology, trade openness, and economic development. Additionally, the results are consistent when we turn to the more restrictive samples. Model 2 shows that *Post-1998* remains significant and negative when the analysis is limited to countries with a history of civil war, and model 3 confirms the result when the sample only includes states with ongoing conflicts. Thus, all three samples of cases suggest the same thing: the justice cascade serves as a powerful inhibition against civilian targeting.

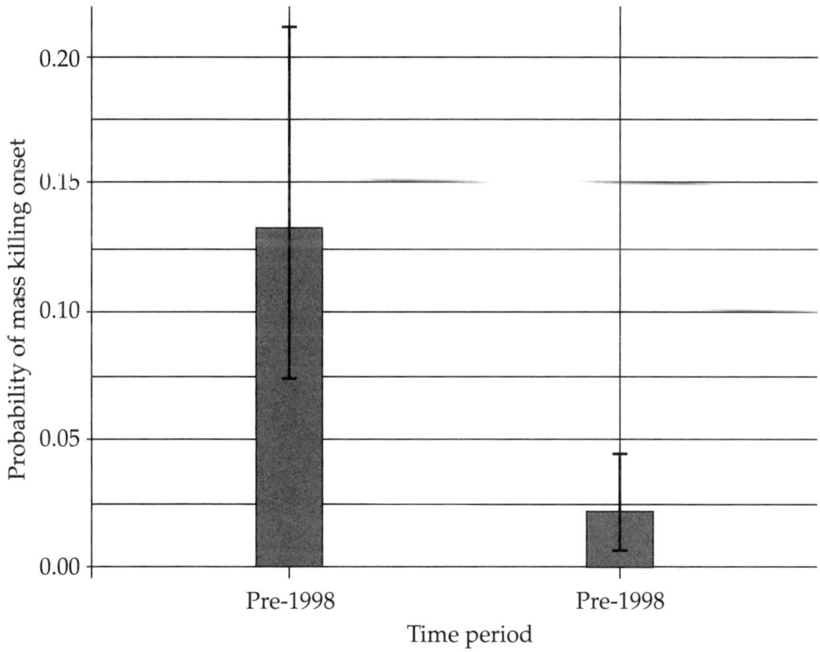

Figure 5. International justice and the probability of mass killing

The models reported in table 4 show that leaders today are significantly less likely to initiate campaigns of mass killing than they were previously. Since the models are nonlinear, however, it is difficult to interpret the magnitude of the effect through regression estimates alone. To remedy this, I calculate substantive effects using the estimates obtained in model 1.[17] These simulations compare the predicted probability of a leader initiating a mass killing event in the impunity and accountability eras during otherwise identical country years. In the specific simulation reported here, all the control variables are held at their median values except for the conflict intensity variable, which is held at the value of a full-scale civil war. The results, which are shown in figure 5, are compelling. The predicted probably of mass killing during a civil war year in the impunity era is .13, but it falls to only .02 during the accountability era. In other words, leaders are about six times less likely to commit atrocities after 1998.

I also conduct several robustness checks to ensure that my findings are durable.[18] Since mass killing occurs infrequently, I employ a regression technique that corrects for rare events bias. To parse out the effect of the end

17. The simulations are conducted using Clarify (King, Tomz, and Wittenberg 2000).
18. The results are reported in the appendix.

of the Cold War from the justice cascade, I limit my analysis to the post–Cold War period only.[19] I also investigate whether the results hold when using a different measure of state-sponsored mass atrocities. Specifically, I code the onset of a genocide or politicide identified by the Political Instability Task Force (Marshall, Gurr, and Harff 2014) as an alternative dependent variable. Finally, I test whether the time polynomials approach (Carter and Signorino 2010) to modeling temporal dependence produces the same results as the cubic splines approach (Beck, Katz, and Tucker 1998) used in table 4. In every robustness check, my conclusions are consistent.

DOES TREATY RATIFICATION MATTER?

My approach to estimating deterrence exploited over-time variation in the threat international justice poses to leaders. Many other scholars, however, are more interested in cross-case variation between countries. In fact, there is a closely related (and considerably larger) literature on the relationship between the ratification of international treaties and human rights violations. These international human rights treaties are typically designed to take declared human rights and codify them into legal responsibilities. For instance, countries that ratify the Genocide Convention pledge not to commit genocide and accept a duty to prosecute those guilty of the crime. Scholars typically ask a pair of related questions: Are countries that ratify treaties less likely to violate human rights? And if so, why?

Though these questions are straightforward, answering them presents a thorny set of theoretical and empirical challenges. Consider the "why" question: Why would treaty ratification actually decrease human rights violations? At a glance, the connection between treaty ratification and deterrence may appear tenuous because international treaties (like international courts) do not have independent enforcement mechanisms. There is no international police force to track down and punish the leaders of states who fail to live up to their international commitments. Acknowledging this enforcement gap, scholars have proposed other mechanisms that might plausibly link treaty ratification to better behavior. Some focus on socialization, arguing that states are susceptible to peer pressure to ratify and comply with international human rights treaties (e.g., Goodman and Jinks 2013; Risse-Kappen, Ropp, and Sikkink 1999). Others focus on how domestic politics

19. The most direct link between the end of the Cold War and mass killing involves the relationship between system polarity and the nature of warfare. Stathis Kalyvas and Laia Balcells (2010) find that insurgencies were common during the Cold War, but they are relatively rare in the post–Cold War period. This change in the nature of warfare could influence patterns of mass killing since different types of warfare are thought to produce different incentives for civilian victimization (Krcmaric 2018b; Valentino, Huth, and Balch-Lindsay 2004).

drives compliance with international treaties (Keck and Sikkink 1998; Lupu 2013a; E. J. Powell and Staton 2009; Simmons 2009; Slaughter 1995; von Stein 2016). Civil society groups, for example, are thought to mobilize support for treaty compliance by naming and shaming governments that do not keep their international promises.[20] Similarly, independent domestic judiciaries, which theoretically issue rulings based on legal principles rather than the government's preferences, provide a venue for citizens to challenge their own government for failing to comply with its international commitments. If these arguments are correct, then states that ratify international human rights treaties should in fact be more likely to respect human rights.

Yet testing this proposition is no easy task. When examining cross-country variation in treaty ratification, endogeneity is a notable threat to causal inference because states strategically select into international agreements. This makes it difficult to determine whether international treaties induce changes in behavior or states only sign agreements they intend to keep anyway (Chapman and Chaudoin 2013; G. W. Downs, Rocke, and Barsoom 1996; von Stein 2005). In a sweeping review of the literature on treaty compliance, Beth Simmons (2010, 292) goes so far as to say that selection effects "mar many, if not most," studies of treaty ratification and human rights behavior.[21] Given these empirical and theoretical complexities, it may not be surprising that the results in the existing literature are ambiguous.

On the one hand, several studies present evidence consistent with a deterrent effect, at least under certain conditions. Eric Neumayer (2005) shows that ratification of the Convention against Torture (CAT) and the International Covenant on Civil and Political Rights (ICCPR) is associated with greater respect for human rights, but only in consolidated democracies and states with a strong civil society. Courtenay Conrad and Emily Ritter (2013) show that commitment to the CAT has no effect on repression in states with insecure leaders, but it has a positive effect on rights protection in states with secure leaders. Beth Simmons (2009) tests whether ratification of several different UN-sponsored human rights treaties influences states' subsequent human rights practices. She presents evidence that treaty ratification is linked to improved outcomes across issue areas ranging from torture to civil rights, but only in "middle-ground" states transitioning to democracy. Finally, Beth Simmons and Allison Danner (2010) and Hyeran Jo and Beth Simmons (2016) find that ratification of the Rome Statute of the ICC can help to ratchet down levels of violence.

20. For a less optimistic take on the ability of naming and shaming campaigns to influence government behavior, see Hafner-Burton 2008.

21. To their credit, some studies have taken steps to lessen—but not eliminate—endogeneity concerns using techniques such as Heckman selection models (Neumayer 2005), instrumental variables (Simmons 2009; von Stein 2016), propensity-score matching (Hill 2010), and spatial models of treaty preferences (Lupu 2013b).

On the other hand, there is a good deal of evidence suggesting that commitment to international legal agreements does not reduce human rights violations. Indeed, it seems that for every work presenting evidence of a deterrent effect, there is a counterpart that fails to find such evidence. In one of the earliest works on the topic, Linda Keith (1999) found that ratification of the ICCPR has no effect on commonly used indicators of civil and political rights. Similarly, Oona Hathaway (2002) found that ratification of the Genocide Convention, the CAT, and the ICCPR is not linked to improved practices. If anything, ratification is actually linked to more violent and repressive behavior.[22] Using more sophisticated quantitative methods, Daniel Hill (2010) and Yonatan Lupu (2013b) confirm these results: the CAT and the ICCPR both fail to deter human rights violations. Finally, Emilie Hafner-Burton and Kiyoteru Tsutsui (2005) show that the total number of human rights treaties a country has ratified is not associated with any reduction in state repression.

I contribute to this unresolved debate on deterrence by adding variables for the ratification of four major international treaties closely linked to international crimes and human rights violations—the Genocide Convention, the Geneva Convention, the ICCPR, and the CAT—to my main model of mass killing onset.[23] This research design allows for a head-to-head test between my justice dilemma argument and treaty ratification arguments. I expect that the effect of the justice cascade is systemic. All leaders should update their beliefs about the likelihood of punishment after observing some of their peers face arrest starting in the late 1990s. The treaty ratification school, by contrast, maintains that any deterrent effect should be limited to the countries that ratify. By including both my post-1998 accountability era variable and the treaty ratification variables in the same empirical specification, I can gauge the relative importance of each when it comes to deterrence.[24]

22. To explain this puzzling result, James Hollyer and Peter Rosendorff (2011) propose that a leader might sign and then purposefully violate a human rights treaty to signal to domestic opposition groups that the leader is willing to do anything to remain in power.

23. There are several different Geneva Conventions. I focus here on the Fourth Geneva Convention, which addresses the protection of the civilian population during times of war (the first three Geneva Conventions covered the treatment of combatants).

24. Note that I do not include a variable for ratification of the ICC's Rome Statute in the models. Since the Rome Statute opened for signature and ratification in 1998, an investigation into whether ratification matters would be limited to 1998 onward. This time period, of course, perfectly coincides with the accountability era. Hence, I cannot directly compare the effects of ICC ratification to the effects of the justice cascade writ large in the same model, which is the goal of this section. Moreover, there are so few cases of mass killing onset after 1998 (which is consistent with my claims about the justice cascade's deterrent effect) that it is not possible to estimate the effect of ICC ratification with any degree of accuracy.

Table 5. Does treaty ratification matter?

	(1)	*(2)*	*(3)*	*(4)*	*(5)*
Genocide Convention	0.216				
	(0.333)				
Geneva Convention		–0.929			
		(0.691)			
ICCPR			–0.094		
			(0.307)		
CAT				–0.363	
				(0.462)	
Treaty Index					0.033
					(0.271)
Post-1998	–1.820**	–1.779**	–1.700**	–1.761**	–1.880**
	(0.486)	(0.513)	(0.530)	(0.610)	(0.596)
Conflict Intensity	1.552**	1.625**	1.514**	2.080**	2.077**
	(0.209)	(0.224)	(0.257)	(0.439)	(0.439)
Political Stability	–0.014	–0.013	–0.008	–0.018	–0.017
	(0.010)	(0.009)	(0.009)	(0.019)	(0.019)
Democracy	0.021	0.045	0.179	0.279	0.252
	(0.333)	(0.337)	(0.362)	(0.464)	(0.480)
Ethnic Polarization	–0.252	–0.223	–0.299	–1.424	–1.504
	(0.634)	(0.653)	(0.687)	(1.036)	(1.067)
Elite Ideology	–0.006	0.013	0.148	–0.017	0.051
	(0.286)	(0.287)	(0.283)	(0.460)	(0.448)
Trade Openness	–0.001	–0.001	0.000	0.001	0.002
	(0.003)	(0.003)	(0.002)	(0.002)	(0.002)
Development	–0.475**	–0.444**	–0.525**	–0.875**	–0.910**
	(0.183)	(0.172)	(0.190)	(0.340)	(0.374)
Years w/o Mass Killing	–0.057	–0.054	0.009	–0.014	–0.006
	(0.113)	(0.115)	(0.115)	(0.131)	(0.126)
Constant	–4.504**	–3.688**	–4.816**	–5.301**	–5.518**
	(0.549)	(0.884)	(0.550)	(0.929)	(1.154)
N	4970	4970	4544	2829	2829
AIC	549.96	548.78	498.86	246.16	246.71
BIC	641.11	639.93	588.76	329.43	329.97

Notes: Standard errors clustered by country in parentheses. Cubic splines included but not reported
* $p < 0.10$, ** $p < 0.05$ (two-tailed)

The results, reported in table 5, cast doubt on claims about the effectiveness of treaty ratification for limiting state-sponsored violence against civilians. Models 1–4 control for ratification of the Genocide Convention, the Geneva Convention, the ICCPR, and the CAT, respectively.[25] Model 5

For an analysis of how ratification of the Rome Statute influences lower levels of violence against civilians, see Jo and Simmons 2016.

25. The number of observations in each model varies because I only examine the time period after which each treaty opened for signature (1948 onward for the Genocide

follows the empirical strategy of Hafner-Burton and Tsutsui (2005) by including a treaty index variable that counts how many of the aforementioned treaties each state has ratified. In all five models, treaty ratification is not associated with a statistically significant reduction in the likelihood of mass killing onset. By contrast, the post-1998 variable capturing the shift from the impunity era to the accountability era remains significant and negative in every specification. Hence, the results are more consistent with my claims about a systemic justice cascade.

Instead of simply declaring victory for my argument over treaty ratification arguments, it is more productive to consider why there consistently is a null result for treaty ratification. One possibility is that treaty ratification simply is not the right place to look for evidence of deterrence. Recall that a key insight from research in both criminology (Kleiman 2009; Nagin 1998) and the economics of crime (Becker 1968) is that individuals are deterred from committing crimes when their expectations about the likelihood of punishment increase. Why, exactly, should ratification of a human rights treaty increase a leader's punishment expectations? A leader does not need to sign and ratify, for example, the Genocide Convention to be punished for genocide or the Geneva Conventions to be punished for war crimes. Such acts are widely recognized as core international crimes, which means that international tribunals and foreign courts can prosecute leaders for these crimes regardless of whether they ratified the relevant treaties.[26] In this way, international criminal law is unique because it violates the notion that "states cannot be legally bound except with their own consent," often considered to be "the most basic principle of international law" (Chayes and Chayes 1993, 179). On top of that, since international tribunals and foreign courts can exercise extraterritorial (and in some cases truly universal) jurisdiction, leaders do not even need to select into the jurisdiction of any international court to be held accountable. In fact, of all the heads of state who have been arrested for alleged international crimes to date, only one—Laurent Gbagbo—selected into the jurisdiction of the international court that indicted him.[27] Hence, treaty ratification has only a weak connection to punishment

Convention; 1949 onward for the Fourth Geneva Convention; 1966 onward for the ICCPR; 1984 onward for the CAT; and 1984 onward for the treaty index).

26. The idea that an individual who commits an international crime is liable under international criminal law regardless of the national law or treaty commitments of that person's state goes back at least to the Nuremberg Trials.

27. Even the Gbagbo example is not a classic case of treaty ratification. At the time of his arrest, the Ivory Coast was not a state party to the Rome Statute of the ICC, although it technically accepted the ICC's jurisdiction under an Article 12(3) declaration.

expectations, suggesting that scholars may be looking for evidence of deterrence in the wrong place.

These findings are bound to be controversial, especially for those in the policy realm. As Hafner-Burton (2013, 4) puts it, "Much of today's policy efforts focus on creating more international treaties . . . as well as expanding the number of countries that sign and ratify those agreements." By contrast, my results suggest that deterring human rights violations requires hard-nosed political action from the international community (i.e., actually making arrests) rather than purely legal solutions. This conclusion, however, does dovetail with the experiences of at least one seasoned policymaker. For instance, when looking back on his time as the first American ambassador-at-large for war crimes, David Scheffer acknowledged: "I learned that international justice has as much to do with the vagaries of global politics . . . as it does with treaties, courtrooms, prosecutors, judges, and defendants" (Scheffer 2012, 8). Going forward, this research suggests that policymakers in powerful countries such as the United States could be more effective at deterring atrocity crimes by devoting additional resources to the apprehension of war criminals rather than pressuring other states to ratify yet another treaty.

Blaise Compaoré's Surprising Restraint

The quantitative results reported in the previous section showed that the general patterns of mass killing onset fit with my argument's expectations. This section zooms in on the behavior of one specific ruler, Blaise Compaoré during Burkina Faso's 2014 uprising, to illuminate the connection between leaders exercising restraint and retiring abroad during the accountability era. After witnessing other leaders either face international justice or die trying to avoid it, Compaoré knew a massive crackdown on civilian protestors would likely have foreclosed a secure post-tenure exile. The possibility of facing international justice therefore increased the perceived costs of mass killing and produced a deterrent effect. As a result, the Burkinabe revolution was far less violent than it otherwise might have been.

BACKGROUND

Blaise Compaoré was born in 1951 in Ouagadougou, the capital of Burkina Faso (then known as Upper Volta). Compaoré joined the military as a young man, which eventually put him in contact with another junior officer, Thomas Sankara. The two became friends and allies, and their relationship would transform Burkina Faso's political landscape for the coming decades.

Compaoré, Sankara, and a group of like-minded officers launched a bloodless coup in 1983 against the incumbent regime of Jean-Baptiste Ouedraogo, who had taken power in a military coup just a year earlier. The charismatic Sankara, sometimes considered to be "Africa's Che Guevara," became the new president, while Compaoré served as his top deputy. The Sankara regime adopted the language of revolutionary Marxism and pursued a more pro-Soviet foreign policy by joining the radical wing of the Non-Aligned Movement. Relations with France, the old colonial power that still enjoyed a great deal of influence in Burkina Faso, soon deteriorated. Moreover, Sankara made plenty of enemies at home as he attempted to institute widespread social and political change throughout the country. Sankara was "unforgiving towards those he considered to be counter-revolutionaries . . . [and] unpopular with those whose privileges he attacked" (Reza 2016, 98). A split eventually emerged within the regime between Sankara's revolutionary followers and a more pragmatic faction associated with Compaoré.

In 1987, a group of commandos ousted Sankara and installed Compaoré as president in yet another coup. The coup was mostly nonviolent with one glaring exception: Sankara was shot and killed during the coup's chaotic climax. Decades later, the precise circumstances of Sankara's death—and Compaoré's role in the putsch—still remain something of a mystery (e.g., Engels 2015, 2).[28] Once in power, Compaoré pursued a policy of "rectification" that reversed or at least moderated many of Sankara's policies. Instead of embracing the inflammatory rhetoric of Marxist revolution, Compaoré "adopted a deliberately lackluster, technocratic discourse" that focused on economic liberalization (Harsch 2017, 108). Domestically, Compaoré's approach appealed to Burkina Faso's urban middle class and business community. Internationally, his rectification policies were popular with the same audiences Sankara had previously alienated, including France and the Ivory Coast, then the key regional player in West Africa under its influential president Félix Houphouët-Boigny.[29] Compaoré's

28. A few points of consensus, however, have emerged. While Compaoré played no active role in the coup, the gunmen who stormed the presidential palace and shot Sankara almost certainly were commandos under the direction of another military commander who was allied with Compaoré (Harsch 2017, 106). Compaoré has always denied ordering the killing of his old friend, and there is some evidence suggesting that Compaoré wanted Sankara to be placed under house arrest rather than killed (Rake 2001, 25).

29. Compaoré's marriage to Houphouët-Boigny's adopted daughter further solidified the relationship between the two leaders.

quick reversal from a Sankara-allied revolutionary to a supposedly pro-business technocrat was widely noted. To his supporters, this move showcased Compaoré's political savvy and adaptability; to his detractors, it signified Compaoré's ideological bankruptcy and overwhelming obsession with power.

The end of the Cold War closely followed Compaoré's ascension to Burkina Faso's presidency, and this geopolitical shift played a crucial role in his governing strategy. In 1990, President François Mitterand of France gave his famous La Boule speech proclaiming that France would no longer automatically give aid to its former colonies but would instead condition its largesse on each state's commitment to democracy. Compaoré responded to this new external pressure to democratize by instituting a number of reforms. He presided over the adoption of a new constitution that had the support of Burkina Faso's opposition parties and was approved in a referendum with 93 percent of the vote (Harsch 2017, 118). In 1991, Compaoré resigned his military position and was elected as the first president of Burkina Faso's Fourth Republic. These moves early in his tenure allowed Compaoré to present himself as a champion of democracy, especially when dealing with Burkina Faso's international donors.

The reality of the Compaoré regime, however, was more complicated. The move toward democracy was a "tightly managed transition" in which Compaoré "[made] concessions only when necessary to preserve his hold" on power (Harsch 2017, 116). More generally, Burkina Faso under Compaoré was a classic case of a post–Cold War hybrid regime that mixed elements of democracy and autocracy. Often dubbed "competitive authoritarian regimes" (Levitsky and Way 2010) or "illiberal democracies" (Zakaria 1997), these regimes hold meaningful elections that give the appearance of democracy while simultaneously undermining democratic institutions and depriving citizens of basic freedoms. Compaoré's regime certainly fits the bill: one NGO report accurately concluded that Burkina Faso "oscillates between democratic aspirations and authoritarian temptations" (International Crisis Group 2013, 43).

This authoritarian underside of the ostensibly democratic Compaoré regime can be seen most vividly with regard to term limits. After his initial election in 1991, Compaoré was elected to another seven-year term in 1998. By 2000, however, the regime's creeping authoritarianism had triggered protests throughout the country. As a concession to the opposition, Compaoré agreed to amend the constitution such that the president was limited to two terms (and the terms themselves were shortened from seven to five years). The opposition believed this would oblige Compaoré to step down in 2005 after his second term ended, and the protests faded away. But Compaoré had no intention of stepping down, and his supporters soon advanced the argument that the new rules should not be applied retroactively to Compaoré's previous terms. Burkina Faso's Constitutional Court, packed with Compaoré's cronies, not surprisingly sided with the president. Thus, Compaoré ran for election again in 2005 and 2010, winning both times in part by using state resources to aid his campaign (Harsch 2017, 131).

The issue of term limits, however, would not go away. Under the amended constitution's rules, Compaoré was unambiguously barred from staying in power beyond 2015. But once again, Compaoré would attempt to extend his time in power, which triggered the 2014 Burkinabe revolution that eventually forced him into exile. Yet, before we turn to Compaoré's ouster, it is worth discussing how he fits into my theoretical framework.

COMPAORÉ: CORRUPT BUT NOT CULPABLE

Blaise Compaoré should be considered a nonculpable leader. To be sure, Compaoré was a deeply flawed ruler. As already mentioned, he rigged Burkina Faso's ostensibly democratic system in his favor and had no respect for term limits. Moreover, Compaoré and his family were extremely corrupt. Inequality surged in Burkina Faso as economic winners and losers were determined by their proximity to Compaoré. While much of the country, particularly disenchanted youths, struggled to make ends meet, "Compaoré and his family built an empire that dominated the Burkinabe economy" (Reza 2016, 103). Lavish lifestyles and conspicuous consumption for the Compaoré clan soon followed. In addition to setting his family up in opulent villas around Ouagadougou, the president himself built a pair of new palaces and purchased the private jet previously owned by the pop star Michael Jackson (Harsch 2017, 111). Compaoré's corruption and mismanagement took a toll on the country: Burkina Faso consistently ranked near the bottom of the UN's Human Development Index.

Despite these shortcomings, Compaoré was not a culpable leader according to the notion of culpability used throughout this book. This is not meant to imply that he ought to be considered a good leader in any sense, but it is clear that Compaoré ruled primarily by dividing and co-opting opponents rather than using violence. Of course, providing "evidence of absence" of culpability for atrocity crimes is a tricky endeavor, but there are several reasons we can be confident that Compaoré was not a culpable mass killer.

To begin, the Ulfelder and Valentino 2008 dataset, which was used to construct the leader culpability variable in the quantitative tests, does not code a mass killing event at any point during Compaoré's tenure. As discussed in previous chapters, however, this variable only provides a rough proxy for leader culpability. Indeed, one potential critique of my culpability variable is that the Ulfelder and Valentino 2008 dataset uses an arbitrary (though reasonable) threshold of one thousand civilian deaths to identify mass killings. Hence, it is worth delving deeper than the measure used in the statistical tests. Did Compaoré preside over (1) civilian massacres that came close to the threshold or (2) other large-scale human rights abuses that could plausibly make him a culpable leader if we take a broader definition of culpability?

Even in these cases, the available evidence suggests that Compaoré is best understood as a nonculpable leader. For instance, one NGO report that was generally critical of Compaoré (especially his antidemocratic tendencies) nonetheless concluded that "brutal practices are certainly rare in Burkina Faso" (International Crisis Group 2013, 27). At worst, Compaoré could be considered a "benign dictator."[30] Even analysts who condemned many aspects of Compaoré's tenure acknowledged that "compared to contemporaries like Zimbabwe's Robert Mugabe, the late Libyan ruler Muammar Al Ghaddafi, and Liberia's Charles Taylor, Compaoré has . . . managed to prevent becoming associated with the worst expressions of African political life."[31] In fact, Compaoré was even dubbed "the region's peacemaker-in-chief" due to his willingness and ability to mediate conflicts throughout the continent.[32]

To be clear, Compaoré's record with regard to human rights was not perfect. There were several isolated incidents of violence, with the most high-profile example being the killing of Nobert Zongo. As a crusading journalist, Zongo was arguably the most outspoken regime critic in Burkina Faso's press. In December 1998, while pursuing an investigative report on the dubious activities of the president's brother, Zongo was found dead in his bullet-riddled car. Though there was no definitive evidence linking Compaoré or other members of his regime to the murder, Zongo's assassination was widely understood to be politically motivated (Frère and Englebert 2015, 299; Harsch 2017, 179). Some twenty thousand Burkinabe took to the streets to demonstrate against the regime during Zongo's funeral procession, and a wave of strikes erupted throughout the country (Reza 2016, 105). As the Zongo murder exemplifies, Compaoré's regime occasionally engaged in targeted repression, but what separates Compaoré from culpable mass killers is his muted response to the protests following Zongo's death. Rather than initiate a violent crackdown, "Compaoré survived the

30. Michael Keating and Coulibaly Nadoun, "Compaoré's Continuing Will to Power," *African Arguments*, August 9, 2012.

31. Peter Dorrie, "Blaise Compaoré and the Politics of Personal Enrichment," *African Arguments*, August 15, 2012.

32. Colin Freeman, "President Blaise Compaoré of Burkina Faso: The Man Who Could Help Solve Africa's al-Qaeda Crisis," *Telegraph*, November 17, 2012.

crisis with a mix of mild concessions . . . and successful efforts at dividing the opposition, many of whom let themselves be co-opted for political, material, or financial benefits" (Frère and Englebert 2015, 299). Thus, despite not having perfectly clean hands, Compaoré fits within my theory's framework as a nonculpable leader since he never committed the sort of mass atrocity crimes—such as crimes against humanity, war crimes, or genocide—that would be likely to trigger an international prosecution or preclude a safe exile.[33]

Why was Compaoré able to hold on to power for so long, even during periods when his popularity was low, without resorting to brutality? In short, he was a master at co-opting his political opponents. Indeed, Compaoré's response to the Zongo crisis was part of a larger trend in how he responded to challenges to his rule. The political opposition in Burkina Faso was remarkably fragmented—there were over seventy different opposition parties—and this provided ample opportunities for the cagey leader to exploit. Compaoré "mastered the art of the electoral tightrope act, conceding just as much power as was necessary to survive, without relinquishing his grip altogether" (Reza 2016, 106). One of Compaoré's favorite tactics was offering the leaders of relatively successful opposition parties a position in his regime. The opposition figures usually accepted since they would personally gain access to patronage networks, but doing so undermined their long-term political prospects since they could no longer credibly claim to oppose the regime (Harsch 2017, 135). This shrewd co-option solidified Compaoré's hold on power and generally made large-scale violence unnecessary.

Overall, then, Compaoré was not responsible for mass atrocity crimes on the eve of Burkina Faso's 2014 uprising. As I will show in the following sections, Compaoré's status as a nonculpable leader shaped the incentives he faced during the crisis.

THE 2014 BURKINABE UPRISING

Origins of the Revolution. Terms limits, a long-standing source of controversy in Burkina Faso, inspired the revolution that eventually ousted Blaise Compaoré. To understand the 2014 Burkinabe revolution, it is useful to return to 2011, a year of protest around much of the globe. While the Arab Spring in the Middle East and North Africa justifiably received the most attention, feelings of discontent with long-entrenched autocrats also spread to many countries south of the Sahara. Burkina Faso was no exception, and

33. As discussed in chapter 2, international tribunals like the ICC and foreign courts exercising universal jurisdiction are generally understood to have jurisdiction over only this limited set of particularly horrendous crimes.

Compaoré faced the largest antiregime demonstrations to date in early 2011. Yet, by the summer of 2011, organized opposition to the regime had largely faded away as the wily Compaoré "solved the crisis once again with token concessions" (Frère and Englebert 2015, 299). These concessions, which included the dismissal of his cabinet and the promise of economic reforms, did little to address the underlying causes of Burkinabe grievances, but they were just enough to get protestors off the streets of Ouagadougou. Part of the reason the opposition did not push particularly hard to oust Compaoré in 2011 was the "perception that Compaoré's exit was just a matter of time" (Harsch 2017, 189). After all, given the constitutional changes that Compaoré agreed to in 2000, he was clearly barred from running again. When his final term expired in 2015, Compaoré would have to step down.

As 2015 approached, however, Compaoré and his allies dismantled the expectation that retirement was imminent.[34] When it came to extending his mandate, Compaoré had several options—all technically legal—for disposing of Article 37, the part of the constitution that imposed the two-term presidential limit. One option was to introduce changes to the constitution via a public referendum, but the regime initially considered this too risky given that public opinion was against extending Compaoré's tenure yet again (2015 would have marked twenty-eight years in power for Compaoré). A parliamentary vote provided another option for modifying Article 37, but Compaoré's political party (the Congress for Democracy and Progress, or CDP) was just shy of the required 75 percent majority in the National Assembly required to make such a strategy viable. Compaoré therefore turned to a third option: he created a Senate. Burkina Faso's Senate, formally created in May 2013, was little more than a mechanism to serve Compaoré's political interests. Since he and other CDP elites would wield a good deal of influence over the selection of the new senators, Compaoré hoped he would be able to achieve the 75 percent majority in the combined parliament.

The transparent attempt to create a Senate solely for the purpose of modifying the constitution produced considerable backlash throughout Burkina Faso. Opposition parties predictably protested, but the real change was that the plans for the Senate brought Burkinabe civil society into the protests in a more extensive manner than ever before. For instance, one new group, dubbed "Citizens' Broom" because they wanted to sweep Compaoré and his cronies out of office, used the star power of some of Burkina Faso's most popular musicians to mobilize huge crowds for antiregime protests (Engels

34. The opening salvo in the battle over term limits occurred when Compaoré supporters began advancing the argument that term limits were "anti-democratic in principle" (Harsch 2017, 191).

2015, 3). Confronted with a surprisingly well-organized and ever-growing opposition, Compaoré agreed to a review of the Senate in August that effectively ended the second parliamentary body before it ever got off the ground.

But the collapse of Compaoré's new Senate did not diminish his desire to amend the constitution. In December 2013, he changed tactics and announced plans to hold a public referendum on Article 37. While public support for prolonging Compaoré's tenure indefinitely was low, there nevertheless was widespread concern that the regime would find a way to pass the referendum using the dubious electoral machinations that had kept it in power for so long. Compaoré's plan for the referendum electrified Burkina Faso's political scene and led to accusations from opposition parties that Compaoré was organizing a "constitutional coup."[35] Civil society groups, so important to undermining the Senate months before, remobilized and planned campaigns of civil obedience. But arguably the most crucial response to the referendum plan came from within the regime itself. In January 2014, about one hundred of the four hundred members of the CDP's national political bureau—including party stalwarts such as the former president of the National Assembly, the former mayor of Ouagadougou, and the former vice president of the CDP—resigned collectively and defected to the opposition (Engels 2015, 3; Frère and Englebert 2015, 300). With blowback to his referendum mounting over the course of 2014, Compaoré changed tactics yet again. He had one last trick up his sleeve: After secret talks on October 21, Compaoré cut a deal with one of the smaller opposition parties that induced it to back the president's plan to abolish term limits (Harsch 2017, 203). With these new allies in the National Assembly, Compaoré no longer needed the public referendum since he now had enough votes in parliament to modify Article 37 directly.

A National Assembly vote was quickly scheduled for October 30, but it never took place. As I will describe later on, historically unprecedented numbers of Burkinabe took to the streets of Ouagadougou (by some accounts, over one million people in a city of just over two million) to disrupt the parliamentary vote. By the end of October, Compaoré was in exile in the Ivory Coast—and Burkina Faso had experienced a leadership transition without the large-scale civilian victimization that so often accompanies the end of unpopular regimes.

Was Mass Killing Possible? This case study attempts to show that Compaoré did not engage in mass killing against the civilian population in part

35. "Burkina Faso: Rassemblement en faveur d'une nouvelle candidature de Compaoré," *Jeune Afrique*, June 22, 2014.

because doing so would have undermined his ability to retire abroad later in the crisis. But before discussing *why* Compaoré did not initiate a violent crackdown, it is necessary to discuss *whether* mass killing was a realistic possibility in the first place. If mass killing was never going to occur anyway, it would be a mistake to attribute its absence to any deterrent effect of international justice. This begs the question: Was mass killing actually possible in Burkina Faso in 2014?

This question touches on a larger methodological debate about case selection. According to James Mahoney and Gary Goertz (2004), selecting appropriate negative cases where the outcome of interest does *not* occur is one of the central challenges of qualitative research. Regardless of the topic of study, typically there are large numbers of cases in which the outcome of interest is virtually impossible, making such observations irrelevant. To address this issue, Mahoney and Goertz propose that scholars employ a "possibility principle" to select negative cases that maximizes leverage for making causal inferences. In short, the possibility principle places the burden of proof on the researcher to show that the outcome of interest had a real possibility of occurring.

I follow this advice by offering two types of evidence that mass killing was a realistic possibility in Burkina Faso near the end of Compaoré's tenure.[36] First, consider an informative anecdotal comparison to a pair of other cases mentioned in this book: the early stages of the conflicts in Libya and Syria. While each case is undoubtedly unique, Burkina Faso in 2014 shares a number of important similarities to those two countries in 2011. In all three cases, (1) people took to the streets in hopes of ousting an unpopular and long-tenured ruler, (2) the regime suffered notable defections to the opposition even though its core remained intact, and (3) holding on to power through nonviolent means was not a viable option, forcing the ruler to choose between initiating a violent crackdown or stepping aside. Libya and Syria suffered mass killings, whereas Burkina Faso did not. The fact that comparable conditions produced mass atrocities in Libya and Syria suggests that a similar outcome was also possible in Burkina Faso.

A second type of evidence comes from the Early Warning Project (EWP), a statistical risk assessment project affiliated with the US Holocaust Museum. The EWP aims to identify the countries most at risk of suffering a state-led mass killing and focuses on many of the same variables included in the logit models of mass killing reported earlier in this

36. Note that in the statistical analysis of mass killing onset presented earlier in the chapter, I followed a logic similar to the one Mahoney and Goertz (2004) propose. Specifically, I estimated models where the sample of cases only included countries with ongoing civil wars. Given that mass killings typically occur in the midst of political upheaval, this sample only includes observations where the possibility principle is unambiguously met.

chapter.[37] However, instead of relying on a single model, the EWP combines several different types of statistical models into a forecast average. By looking at the EWP risk assessment, we can get a sense of how likely mass killing was in Burkina Faso relative to other states in 2014.[38] The results once again confirm that mass killing was certainly possible. Of the 162 countries included in the assessment, Burkina Faso ranked sixteenth, placing it in the top decile of at-risk countries that year. In more tangible terms, this put Burkina Faso just below violence-prone countries such as Somalia, Ethiopia, Mali, and Iraq. Therefore, the EWP forecast suggests that the conditions present in Burkina Faso made mass killing a realistic possibility.

To be clear, the aforementioned evidence is not meant to imply that mass killing definitely would have occurred if Compaoré's decision-making had not taken place in the shadow of the international legal regime. It does, however, compellingly show that the Burkina Faso case meets the possibility principle criteria. In what follows, I return to this chapter's main theme: the relationship between exercising restraint toward the civilian population and the availability of a safe exile option in the accountability era. I illustrate how Compaoré, a nonculpable leader, had an extra incentive to refrain from mass killing that did not exist for leaders during the impunity era.

Compaoré and the Restraint-Exile Connection

Throughout virtually the entire crisis, the Compaoré regime displayed a noteworthy level of restraint in its treatment of the civilian population. For instance, the spring and summer of 2014—the period after Compaoré announced plans for a referendum and before he moved to amend the constitution via a parliamentary vote—witnessed a series of back-and-forth rallies between pro- and antireferendum camps. This process culminated in a so-called battle of the stadiums, with each side holding ever-larger shows of political strength in Burkina Faso's soccer stadiums.[39] During this period of contentious mobilization, there were no reports of political killings. One commentator even marveled at how there "[was not] a single scuffle with security forces" (Harsch 2017,

37. I examined the 2015 EWP risk assessment, which uses 2014 data that is most relevant to the Compaoré case. The EWP forecast uses the same definition of state-led mass killing as Ulfelder and Valentino (2008), making our results comparable.

38. In theory, I could have used my logit model of mass killing to generate a predicted probability of mass killing for Burkina Faso and the other countries in my sample. However, the time series in my model ends in 2010, making the EWP forecast preferable.

39. "Burkina Faso: Rassemblement en faveur d'une nouvelle candidature de Compaoré," *Jeune Afrique*, June 22, 2014.

202) when an opposition protest of some one hundred thousand people marched through the streets of Ouagadougou.[40]

Burkina Faso's crisis reached its apex in late October 2014 as the National Assembly prepared to vote on extending term limits for Compaoré. After October 21, the day the regime announced that parliament would vote on modifying the constitution, Ouagadougou was in a state of perpetual protest. Opposition groups called for a mass campaign of civil disobedience to last until October 30, the day of the scheduled vote. By October 28, Ouagadougou's central square, the Place de la Nation, was teeming with unprecedented crowds. The opposition claimed they had over one million people participating in the protest, whereas the international media put the number at several hundred thousand. Regardless of the exact number, it was "certainly the biggest single action ever held in Burkina Faso" (Harsch 2017, 250).

Despite the extensive antiregime mobilization, many opposition leaders were convinced that peaceful civil disobedience tactics had little chance of pressuring Compaoré into canceling the parliamentary vote.[41] Herve Ouattara, the head of a prominent antireferendum group, acknowledged to his network that "peaceful demonstrations would not be enough" to force Compaoré out.[42] Early in the morning on October 30, before members of parliament had gathered for the controversial vote, crowds marched on the National Assembly intending to prevent the vote using any means necessary. The Compaoré regime, not surprisingly, had anticipated that the protestors might try to disrupt the vote. The regime's security forces, including local police and Compaoré's elite presidential security unit (widely known by its French acronym, RSP), were tasked with standing guard outside the National Assembly. Both were reportedly ordered to follow relatively strict rules of engagement: police were told not to use their firearms at all (although they could use tear gas or water hoses), and the RSP was authorized to fire warning shots only.[43] When the opposition turned violent, attacking the police and the RSP stationed outside the parliament building with stones, the response from the security forces was muted and consistent with their instructions. The police first attempted to use tear gas to disperse the crowd and prevent them from storming the National Assembly. After they had exhausted their supply of tear gas, the RSP fired warning shots into the air. When the marchers saw that the security forces did *not*

40. The restraint shown by both sides is also consistent with Jessica Stanton's (2016) prediction that governments and rebels relying on international constituencies for support have strong incentives to minimize violence.

41. For an analysis suggesting that civil resistance generally is an effective tactic, see Chenoweth and Stephan 2011.

42. "Transition politique au Burkina Faso," *L'Observateur Paalga*, November 7, 2014.

43. "Le récit de la chute de Compaoré, heure par heure," *Jeune Afrique*, November 18, 2014.

intend to fire live ammunition into the crowd, protestors surged toward the National Assembly, prompting the regime's security forces to retreat. Within hours, crowds had ransacked the National Assembly building and set it ablaze.

Burning down the parliament building ensured that a vote on the constitutional amendment could not take place, but Compaoré was still in power. Most of the crowd now marched on the presidential palace to, in the words of one opposition leader, "finish off President Compaoré" (Harsch 2017, 208). Others headed for the homes of Compaoré's relatives and CDP leaders, which the crowds promptly looted and set on fire.[44] In this context, Compaoré might have been expected to initiate a brutal crackdown on the protestors, who—despite their substantial numbers—were poorly armed relative to the regime's forces. Instead, he met with opposition leaders and tried to negotiate an end to the crisis. Compaoré offered to withdraw his constitutional amendment and step down at the end of his term in November 2015, but the opposition leaders insisted that he resign immediately. Compaoré also went on the radio and promised "to open talks with all the actors to end the crisis," but this was not sufficient to calm the crowds in Ouagadougou agitating for his ouster.[45]

On October 31, Compaoré surprised many people by resigning as president. In a final statement, Compaoré stressed the importance of preserving "social peace" and concluded, "I declare a vacancy of power with a view to allowing a transition that should finish with free and transparent elections in a maximum period of 90 days."[46] As news of his resignation was still spreading throughout Ouagadougou, Compaoré fled the capital city in a convoy of vehicles headed toward a military base at Po, in the south of the country. Along the way, he met with French forces, who provided a helicopter to fly Compaoré and his family to the safety of the Ivory Coast.[47] After twenty-seven years in office, Compaoré was finally out of power—and it had happened *without* a bloody fight to the finish.

To be clear, there was some state-sponsored violence against civilians during the Burkinabe revolution. For example, when protestors stormed the mansion of the president's brother, François, security forces shot and killed one person and injured a few others. Furthermore, the RSP, the part of the military specifically tasked with Compaoré's security, killed at least a

44. "Le récit de la chute de Compaoré, heure par heure," *Jeune Afrique*, November 18, 2014.

45. Hervé Taoko, Alan Cowell, and Rukmini Callimachi, "Violent Protests Topple Government in Burkina Faso," *New York Times*, October 30, 2014.

46. David Smith, "Power Struggle in Burkina Faso after Blaise Compaoré Resigns as President," *Guardian*, November 1, 2014

47. "Le récit de la chute de Compaoré, heure par heure," *Jeune Afrique*, November 18, 2014.

couple of protestors while trying to stop the crowds from breaching the presidential palace. Depending on the source one chooses to believe, a total of somewhere between four and thirty-three people died throughout Burkina Faso in the turmoil of October 2014.[48]

While certainly tragic, this violence is more accurately described as a handful of isolated incidents than as a systematic campaign of state-sponsored killing. For one thing, the scale of the violence—with many sources unable to confirm more than four deaths—is substantively different from the cases of mass killing described throughout this book. Indeed, from a comparative perspective, very few long-entrenched rulers have ever been ousted with so little bloodshed. For another, the regime's security forces only shot at protestors after the opposition turned to violent tactics itself (including attacks on the homes of Compaoré's family members). Finally, one of the most relevant details of the Burkinabe crisis is that Compaoré did not at any point urge his supporters to use violence. In sharp contrast to other beleaguered leaders who went on television or radio to incite violence (e.g., Gaddafi's "cockroaches" speech or Assad's "burying sedition" speech), Compaoré's public address urged a negotiated solution to the crisis.[49] Overall, this discussion is not meant to justify the handful of deaths that did occur, but it does highlight how there were far fewer political killings in Burkina Faso than one might have expected given the circumstances.

Compaoré's restraint during the crisis may be especially surprising because, in many ways, he was playing politics through established legal channels whereas the opposition was not. As Pierre Englebert, a leading scholar of Burkina Faso's politics points out, Compaoré "was corrupt, exclusionary, and increasingly autocratic before his abrupt fall from power. . . . But he did have the law on his side in his showdown with the street demonstrators who ultimately pushed him from office."[50] After all, Compaoré's attempt to change the constitution to grant himself another term was done in accordance with the letter of the law (though probably not its spirit). By contrast, Englebert points out that it was "the protestors who did not have much to stand on" since they sought to remove an

48. Agence France-Presse was able to confirm only four deaths. See D. Smith, "Power Struggle in Burkina Faso." Amnesty International concluded that at least ten people died in the days surrounding Compaoré's ouster, the post-Compaoré interim government put the number at nineteen, and a coalition of Burkinabe human rights groups said there were thirty-three deaths (Amnesty International 2015, 5).

49. See "Libya Protests: Defiant Gaddafi Refuses to Quit," *BBC News*, February 22, 2011; and Mike Giglio, "The Speech That Changed Syria," *Buzzfeed News*, January 20, 20014.

50. Pierre Englebert, "Burkina Faso's Reverberating Crisis," *New York Times*, November 14, 2014.

incumbent president using extraconstitutional means.[51] While this assessment is likely more an indictment of illiberal democracy in Compaoré's Burkina Faso than of the Burkinabe opposition, it is worth noting that Compaoré ruled primarily through political deal-making rather than brute force.[52] Once it became clear that he could not amend the constitution or negotiate his way out of trouble, Compaoré gave up power and fled the country.

Why was Compaoré restrained in his use of violence during the crisis? While it is difficult to get inside his head, the available evidence strongly suggests that Compaoré was aware that engaging in mass killing would have foreclosed the exile option for him. The international community—including powerful steward states, regional organizations, and NGOs—sent a number of poignant signals and stern warnings to Compaoré during the crisis. The essence of the message was clear: We are watching you, and it is time for you to leave peacefully. While the international community was willing to allow—and even help facilitate—a safe haven for the nonculpable Compaoré, the welcome mat would have been withdrawn if he crossed the line by carrying out mass atrocities.

More than any other actor, France, the old colonial power in Burkina Faso, took the lead in easing Compaoré out of office without bloodshed. Working in conjunction with other African heads of state, France exerted pressure on Compaoré to step down before the situation in Burkina Faso became too violent. Just after Compaoré left for the Ivory Coast, the French president François Hollande acknowledged, "We told him very clearly he needed to make the right decision, which is to say stepping down from power."[53] This message must have resonated deeply with Compaoré. Just three years earlier, France had sent a similar message to another embattled leader in Francophone Africa, the Ivory Coast's Laurent Gbagbo. After a disputed Ivorian election turned violent, France and other states in the region called on Gbagbo to step aside and leave the country peacefully. When Gbagbo instead tried to hold on to power through brute force, France supported the rebels associated with Alassane Ouattara (the Ivory Coast's future president who would go on to host Compaoré three years later). These French-backed Ivorian rebels eventually captured Gbagbo and transferred him to the ICC, which put Gbagbo on trial for alleged crimes against humanity. Thus, France's insistence that Compaoré "make the right

51. Pierre Englebert, "Burkina Faso's Reverberating Crisis," *New York Times*, November 14, 2014.

52. Indeed, many have rightly pointed out the heroic actions of the Burkinabe opposition (e.g., Harsch 2017).

53. "France Helped Compaoré Flee Burkina Faso Unrest, Hollande Says," *France 24*, November 4, 2014.

decision" carried an implicit threat.[54] If Compaoré clung to power too long and killed too many civilians in the process, he had every reason to expect that his fate might be similar to Gbagbo's.

The French approach was not just about veiled threats. Hollande also dangled an enticing possibility before Compaoré: a coveted job. In a leaked message that was never meant for public consumption (which therefore offers a unique behind-the-scenes look at French diplomacy), Hollande sent Compaoré a warm "Dear Blaise" letter. In the October 7, 2014 note, Hollande played to Compaoré's ego by telling him that he could make Burkina Faso "an example for the region" if he would only step down peacefully. More remarkably, Hollande's letter promised French support in getting Compaoré a prestigious post in international diplomacy "if you want to put your experience and talents at the disposal of the international community."[55] The suggestion running throughout Hollande's letter was that the French offer would not be on the table indefinitely. After all, Compaoré could hardly be a model for the region if he crushed the opposition and entrenched in power. Compaoré therefore had good reason to expect to forfeit this attractive post-tenure option if he used his security forces to crack down on the protestors.

Overall, then, the French strategy used a combination of carrots and sticks to manipulate the incentives Compaoré faced. These moves bolstered deterrence by giving Compaoré a compelling motive to retire before he risked crossing the threshold of tolerable behavior. Initiating a massacre in Burkina Faso would have put Compaoré in a position where neither a domestic nor a foreign retirement would have guaranteed his personal safety. Thus, the evidence is consistent with the theory: the availability of a secure exile option for Compaoré was conditional on how he behaved during the crisis. The French were willing, even eager, to get Compaoré out of office so as to avoid a bloody conflict in Francophone Africa, but their support for a golden parachute was only on the table as long as Compaoré's status as a nonculpable leader continued.

While France may have led the effort to ease Compaoré into retirement, it was hardly the only member of the international community involved in Burkina Faso's crisis. A number of other international actors sent signals to Compaoré that were broadly consistent with the messages coming from Paris. The US Department of State issued a statement saying, "We urge all involved, including Burkina Faso's security forces, to adhere to

54. Hollande certainly viewed France's role in this way. Speaking shortly after Compaoré fled abroad, Hollande acknowledged, "From the start of the crisis, France played its part in warning [Compaoré]." See "Burkina: La France a aidé au départ 'sans drame' de Blaise Compaoré," *RFI Afrique*, November 4, 2014.

55. "La lettre de François Hollande qui mettait en garde Blaise Compaoré," *Jeune Afrique*, October 30, 2014.

non-violence."[56] Similarly, the American Embassy in Ouagadougou communicated that the United States was "deeply concerned" about the unfolding crisis in Burkina Faso and urged a peaceful solution.[57] The UN secretary-general Ban Ki Moon issued a statement that he was "following with great concern the deteriorating security situation in Burkina Faso" and called on all parties to "exercise calm and restraint."[58] The African Union published a press release emphasizing that it was following the situation "very closely" and called for Compaoré to navigate the crisis with the "utmost restraint."[59] Amnesty International publicly reminded the Compaoré regime that it "must comply with international law" and warned that the "excessive use of force will not be tolerated."[60]

Invoking international law would have struck a chord with Compaoré. He was intimately aware of developments in the international justice landscape since he presided over Burkina Faso's ratification of the Rome Statute and had long been one of the ICC's staunchest defenders in Africa. For instance, Compaoré was one of the few African leaders who were willing to defend the court after it issued an arrest warrant for Sudan's Omar Bashir. Compaoré even traveled to The Hague in 2011 to deliver remarks at a symposium on "international justice, peace, and crisis management," a topic that would become strikingly relevant to him just three years later.[61] Furthermore, Compaoré had a firsthand view of how committing atrocities can foreclose exile possibilities during Muammar Gaddafi's fight to the death in 2011. Due to his role as "the region's peacemaker-in-chief," Compaoré was involved in mediation attempts to resolve the Libyan civil war.[62] As described in chapter 4, there were lengthy discussions in diplomatic circles about finding an exile destination for Gaddafi, but a retirement home

56. Press statement from Jen Psaki, US State Department spokesperson, "Proposed Changes to Burkina Faso Term Limits," October 28, 2014, available at https://2009-2017.state.gov/r/pa/prs/ps/2014/10/233469.htm.

57. Hervé Taoko, Alan Cowell, and Rukmini Callimachi, "Violent Protests Topple Government in Burkina Faso," *New York Times*, October 30, 2014.

58. United Nations Secretary-General's office, "Statement attributable to the Spokesman for the Secretary-General on the situation in Burkina Faso," October 30, 2014, available at https://www.un.org/sg/en/content/sg/statement/2014-10-30/statement-attributable-spokesman-secretary-general-situation-burkina.

59. African Union Press Release, "AU Deeply Concerned by the Unfolding Situation in Burkina Faso," October 30, 2014, available at http://www.peaceau.org/uploads/auc-com-burkina-faso-30-10-2014.pdf.

60. Amnesty International News, "Burkina Faso Must End Excessive Use of Force against Protesters," October 31, 2014, available at https://www.amnesty.org/en/latest/news/2014/10/burkina-faso-must-end-excessive-use-force-against-protesters/.

61. "Top Officials in Burkina Faso Defend ICC's Work in Africa," *Sudan Tribune*, November 10, 2011.

62. Colin Freeman, "President Blaise Compaoré of Burkina Faso: The Man Who Could Help Solve Africa's al-Qaeda Crisis," *Telegraph*, November 17, 2012.

that could provide credible long-term protection for the Libyan dictator never materialized. Shortly after the Libyan crisis ended, Compaoré's foreign minister Dijibril Bassole summed up the position that his country—along with many others—took when he stated, "If a perpetrator of crimes is indicted [by] the ICC, we can't protect this person."[63] Hence, Compaoré had personally witnessed how difficult it can be to negotiate a secure exit for an embattled ruler who presides over atrocity crimes.

Compaoré and those around him understood the situation in similar terms. Initiating a massive crackdown might help keep him in office (i.e., the Assad precedent), but if this strategy failed, Compaoré would have crossed a line that left no option other than fighting it out to the bitter end (i.e., the Gaddafi precedent). Luc Adolphe Tiao, Compaoré's prime minister, pointedly described his boss's two options during the regime's final days as "all or nothing."[64] Compaoré needed either to step down quickly or commit to doing anything and everything to stay in power. In Tiao's words, Compaoré "did not want a bloodbath," so he fled abroad before the situation spiraled out of control.[65] Compaoré himself offered a similar assessment. In an interview a few days after heading into exile, he described his mindset: "I felt that the regiment was going to shoot, we were on the verge of disaster. I said to myself, 'OK, stop.'"[66] Moreover, Compaoré took to Twitter and thanked his supporters for "showing restraint" during the crisis.[67] Of course, one might argue that Compaoré's statements after fleeing abroad should be discounted since he had an incentive to represent his actions in the best possible light. While this is a reasonable assessment, it misses a larger point: Compaoré felt the need to advertise his restraint to international audiences in a way that exiled rulers in the impunity era never could have imagined.

AFTERMATH

After fleeing to the Ivory Coast, Compaoré settled into the Villa des Hotes, a state-owned mansion previously reserved for visiting dignitaries in Yamoussoukro, the Ivorian capital. Since then, arguably the most notable part of Compaoré's exile is what is *missing*. In sharp contrast to the experience of countries that hosted culpable leaders during the accountability era—recall Nigeria's ordeal while hosting Charles Taylor or Senegal's troubles while sheltering Hissène Habré—there has been

63. "Top Officials in Burkina Faso Defend ICC's Work in Africa," *Sudan Tribune*, November 10, 2011.
64. "Blaise Compaoré, sa Version des Faits," *Jeune Afrique*, November 17, 2014.
65. "Blaise Compaoré, sa Version des Faits," *Jeune Afrique*, November 17, 2014.
66. "Blaise Compaoré, sa Version des Faits," *Jeune Afrique*, November 17, 2014.
67. See Blaise Compaoré's Twitter profile at https://twitter.com/PF_Compaoré.

virtually no international pressure on the Ivory Coast to extradite the nonculpable Compaoré.

In fact, the international community appears to be remarkably pleased with the outcome of Compaoré quietly retiring abroad. France viewed Compaoré's exile as a case of successful conflict management that enabled a relatively peaceful transition. President Hollande noted with satisfaction that France helped "to avoid a bloodbath" in Burkina Faso and that Compaoré's departure for the Ivory Coast occurred "without drama."[68] Moreover, Hollande saw Compaoré's actions during the last days of the crisis as consistent with the messages coming from Paris. "I made a statement asking Blaise Compaoré to make the right decision, that is, to leave," Hollande noted, before adding, "He did in the hours that followed."[69] The United States, which had previously warned Compaoré and urged a peaceful solution to the crisis, issued a statement "welcoming" his "commitment to a democratic transition."[70] The African Union praised Compaoré's resignation as an "important step in the search for a consensual and lasting solution to the crisis in that country."[71] For their part, international tribunals and foreign courts have expressed no interest in pursuing Compaoré. The ICC, for example, which has jurisdiction since Compaoré signed and ratified the Rome Statute while in office, has remained silent since Compaoré never committed crimes that reached the level of gravity required for an international prosecution. To sum up, the international actors who could conceivably complicate Compaoré's exile have not only refrained from doing so but have also actively endorsed Compaoré's Ivorian retirement plans.

The only actor seemingly unhappy with Compaoré's secure exile is the successor regime in Burkina Faso. Not long after Compaoré fled the country, talk of initiating a domestic prosecution in Burkina Faso's courts gained momentum. Some of the former opposition wanted to prosecute Compaoré for the alleged murder of Thomas Sankara in 1987, others wanted to focus on the violence that occurred in October 2014, and still others preferred the

68. "France's Hollande Spells Out Foreign Policy Goals," *France 24*, November 28, 2014; "France Helped Compaoré Flee Burkina Faso Unrest, Hollande Says," *France 24*, November 4, 2014.

69. "Comment la France a-t-elle aidé Blaise Compaoré à fuir en Côte d'Ivoire?," *Huffington Post France*, November 4, 2014.

70. Press statement from Jen Psaki, US State Department spokesperson, "Welcoming President Compaoré's Commitment to a Democratic Transition," October 30, 2014, available at https://2009-2017.state.gov/r/pa/prs/ps/2014/10/233567.htm.

71. African Union press release, "Communiqué of the Peace and Security Council of the African Union at Its 465th Meeting," November 4, 2014, available at http://www.peaceau.org/en/article/communique-of-the-peace-and-security-council-of-the-african-union-au-at-its-465th-meeting-held-in-addis-ababa-on-03-november-2014-on-the-situation-in-burkina-faso.

more general charge of treason. Regardless of the legal niceties, there was one major problem: the new regime in Burkina Faso had no way to get its hands on Compaoré. With the international community refusing to put any pressure on the Ivory Coast, Burkina Faso had to settle for a largely symbolic in absentia trial (which Burkina Faso's High Court suspended in 2017 without a conviction). But even if that trial were to produce a conviction, the practical impact on Compaoré's status would likely be negligible. The Ivorian president Alassane Ouattara signed a decree making Compaoré a citizen of the Ivory Coast, signaling to the new Burkinabe leadership that Compaoré was under Ouattara's protection and that any hopes for his extradition back to Burkina Faso were fanciful.[72] Unless some drastic change takes place that alters the Ivory Coast's willingness or ability to host Compaoré, the former Burkinabe leader will likely continue to live out his days in the safety of exile.

To conclude, the Blaise Compaoré case played out exactly as we might hope international justice would work with regards to deterrence: a controversial ruler gave up power *before* mass atrocities occurred. An international prosecution was therefore not necessary after the fact. In the end, Burkina Faso's transition was less violent than it otherwise likely would have been in part because the availability of a secure retirement option for Compaoré was conditional on how he behaved during the crisis.

In this chapter, I asked whether the justice cascade deters leaders from launching campaigns of mass killing. Building on the previously reported results on patterns of exile and civil war duration, I examined deterrence as an interrelated and positive effect of the justice cascade. I argued that because leaders now know that committing mass atrocities will limit their future exit options—something leaders would like to avoid since they might need to flee abroad at a later date—international justice effectively increases the costs of brutality.

Estimating deterrence is a notoriously challenging endeavor. No research design is perfect, but I developed an empirical strategy that mitigates some of the problems faced in the existing literature. Instead of focusing on cross-case variation in human rights trials or the ratification of international treaties, I leveraged over-time variation in the threat international justice poses to leaders afforded by the justice cascade. After estimating interrupted time-series models of mass killing, I found quantitative results that are consistent with my argument: leaders are significantly less likely to initiate campaigns of mass killing after 1998 than they were previously. Furthermore, the deterrent effect of international justice is substantively large, with

72. "Burkina Faso Ex-Leader Blaise Compaoré Becomes Ivorian," *BBC News*, February 24, 2016.

leaders today being about six times less likely to engage in mass killing than they were in the past.

The case study of Burkina Faso's Blaise Compaoré complemented the statistical analysis by illustrating the theory's causal mechanism. As I documented, mass killing was a real possibility in Burkina Faso around the time Compaoré's regime fell apart. Yet mass killing never occurred. Rather than try to hold on to political power using brute force, Compaoré—a nonculpable leader—was confident he could safely flee into exile in the Ivory Coast. The possibility of an international prosecution was always an important factor in the background of the case. The international community unambiguously signaled that a safe retirement abroad, and perhaps even a prestigious elder statesman–type international post, was on the table for Compaoré *if* he refrained from using mass violence against civilians. While there may not be a smoking-gun piece of evidence, Compaoré could clearly see that trying to cling to power using any means necessary—as leaders like Muammar Gaddafi and Laurent Gbagbo had done only a few years prior—would have foreclosed the possibility of a secure exile. Compaoré ultimately decided that a gilded retirement in a friendly regime with the backing of the international community was a better option than assuming the risks of fighting it out in Burkina Faso. Thus, the Compaoré case vividly highlighted the interrelated nature of exile and mass killing in the accountability era that my theory described.

Stepping back, it is worth emphasizing the significance of this finding given the devastating history of state-sponsored mass killing. Indeed, in the past century, the number of civilians killed by their own governments may exceed the number of combat deaths in all international and civil wars combined (Rummel 1995). What might prevent such brutality? Human rights advocates have long hoped that international justice would deter atrocities, but the existing scholarly work has yielded mixed results. The results in this chapter, however, suggest that a credible threat of post-tenure international arrest can sometimes stay the hand of would-be mass killers.

CHAPTER 6

Grasping the Dilemma

This book started with a simple premise: something new is happening in the world of international justice. Gone are the days when a brutal leader could terrorize his own people and then disappear to a safe exile when he was no longer welcome at home. Rulers who commit massive human rights abuses—including several who once seemed untouchable—are now held accountable in a way that was unthinkable just a few decades ago.

How is this justice cascade reshaping world politics? When attempting to answer this question, most scholars offer unabashedly optimistic or pessimistic predictions. This book, by contrast, suggests a more nuanced answer. The pursuit of international justice has been helpful in some ways and harmful in others.

The theory outlined in chapter 2 explained that exile traditionally offered an attractive golden parachute for all embattled rulers. However, the recent trend toward holding leaders accountable for atrocity crimes irrespective of national borders complicates the exile option. In this new era of accountability, the attractiveness of a foreign retirement is conditional on a leader's culpability for mass atrocities. Nonculpable leaders can still safely go into exile because they do not need to fear international arrest, but today's culpable leaders have incentives to cling to power in hopes of avoiding punishment.

By influencing the viability of exile as a retirement option, the justice cascade also shapes the behavior of leaders while they are still in power. In fact, the pursuit of international justice produces two opposing effects. On the one hand, the justice cascade prolongs conflict since it incentivizes culpable leaders to keep fighting during civil wars when they would otherwise retire abroad. On the other hand, the justice cascade deters atrocities because leaders now know that committing abuses will decrease their exit options if they ever need to flee abroad. These predictions, taken together, constitute the justice dilemma: deterring atrocities and prolonging conflicts are two sides of the same coin.

To develop testable hypotheses, I exploited stark over-time variation in the threat international justice poses to leaders. The push for global accountability reached a tipping point in the late 1990s. Specifically, two groundbreaking events in 1998—the arrest of Augusto Pinochet on foreign soil and the creation of the ICC—marked a watershed moment in the quest to bring culpable leaders to justice. Before 1998, leaders lived in an impunity era where the expected probability of international punishment for atrocities was virtually zero. Starting in 1998, the world shifted toward an accountability era in which a slew of culpable leaders have been arrested and transferred to international courts, causing other leaders to update their beliefs about the likelihood of facing international justice.

After outlining the theoretical approach, the rest of the book was devoted to evaluating my predictions regarding patterns of exile, civil war duration, and mass killing onset. Chapter 3 examined exile. The statistical tests indicated that leader culpability had essentially no effect on the likelihood of exile in the impunity era, but culpable leaders have been less likely to retire abroad in the accountability era. A case study of Charles Taylor's exile in Nigeria showed that culpable leaders do in fact get punished on the rare occasions when they go into exile in the accountability era. Indeed, this case illustrated how the pursuit of international justice undermined Nigeria's promise of safe haven and ultimately led to Taylor's prosecution at the SCSL. Chapter 4 turned to civil war duration. Quantitative analyses confirmed my hypothesis that culpable leaders fight longer civil wars in the accountability era only, and a case study of Muammar Gaddafi during Libya's 2011 conflict highlighted the close link between the lack of good exit options abroad and the decision to fight it out at home. Chapter 5 investigated mass killing onset and the prospects for deterrence. Conditional on the other factors thought to cause mass atrocities, today's leaders appear less likely to initiate mass killings than their peers were previously. Moreover, a case study of Blaise Compaoré's behavior during Burkina Faso's 2014 revolution was consistent with the theory's causal mechanism: Compaoré could see that using mass violence against civilians would have undermined his ability to retire abroad later in the crisis, creating an extra incentive to exercise restraint.

Questions for Future Research

The findings presented in this book open several intriguing avenues for future research. Three potential areas stand out.

WORKING AROUND ACCOUNTABILITY

The bulk of this book was devoted to showing how leaders have responded to the new international legal environment by making different strategic calculations regarding exile, civil war duration, and mass atrocity onset. But rather than necessarily viewing the legal environment as a constraint on their behavior, leaders might instead search for ways to work around new standards of accountability. This would hardly be surprising since, in other contexts, we know that actors strategically strive to limit their legal liability. For instance, Tanisha Fazal (2018) shows that the codification of international humanitarian law made states reluctant to issue formal declarations of war since doing so would place restraints on the way states fight.

In the context of the justice cascade, leaders might pursue at least three different strategies to evade accountability for human rights violations. First, leaders may outsource shameful violence to militias loosely allied with the state to attempt to conceal their personal culpability.[1] Creating blurred lines of responsibility and plausible deniability could be just enough for brutal rulers to get off scot-free even when they are ultimately responsible for the crimes. Second, leaders might initiate "fake" domestic judicial processes to mitigate international pressure for accountability but then let the perpetrators off the hook in the end. These sorts of human rights half measures may accurately describe what happened to the pursuit of justice in Sri Lanka (Cronin-Furman 2020). Third, leaders may think they can avoid international justice by substituting one type of repression for another. Given the focus of international tribunals on major atrocities (i.e., war crimes, crimes against humanity, and genocide), leaders may commit fewer large-scale massacres but increase their use of more velvet-glove repression techniques that are less likely to attract unwanted international attention.[2] Looking ahead, it is important for scholars to be mindful of the ways in which oppressive rulers may try to sidestep the constraints that international justice is meant to impose.

BEYOND NATIONAL LEADERS

Another area for future research involves investigating whether the argument developed here helps explain the behavior not only of heads of state but also of other individuals who might need to worry about accountability for past misdeeds. A remarkably diverse set of actors—military officers, rank-and-file soldiers, rebel group leaders, heads of major corporations, and so forth—have been accused of playing a role in human

1. In 2015, the *Journal of Conflict Resolution* published a special issue on militias in civil wars that explores similar issues. See especially Carey, Colaresi, and Mitchell 2015; and Cohen and Nordås 2015.

2. This potential substitution effect relates to broader debates on (1) whether human rights practices are improving over time and (2) the relationship between mass killings and other forms of state repression (e.g., Cingranelli and Filippov 2018; Fariss 2014).

rights abuses.[3] Does the justice cascade affect them too? In particular, extending the argument to rebel groups would be valuable since it fits with a growing trend of modifying theories about leaders in international politics to rebel leaders in the civil war context (e.g., Prorok 2016).

While a systematic test is beyond the scope of this book, anecdotal evidence suggests that my argument may be germane to rebel leaders. To give one example, the Ugandan government entered into the Juba peace talks with a rebel group, the Lord's Resistance Army (LRA), in 2006. The talks appear to have failed partly because the ICC issued arrest warrants for several LRA leaders, including the infamous Joseph Kony, shortly before the negotiations began. The LRA leaders therefore had good reason to fear that if they made peace, they would ultimately end up in a jail cell in The Hague. Indeed, LRA leaders clearly saw things that way. One LRA member who defected from the group later described Kony's thinking: "In the bush, the ICC is always the main discussion. Sometimes they talk about it five times a day. . . . Joseph Kony is afraid of [the] ICC."[4] These words are consistent with Kony's actions; on at least one occasion, he met with private attorneys in the bush to discuss the rules of the ICC (Bosco 2014, 129). Similarly, Vincent Otti, the LRA's second-in-command, vowed that he would "not sign any peace agreement in Juba which sends me to prison. I can only sign an agreement that brings peace, not one that leads me to the International Criminal Court."[5] Thus, the LRA case suggests that my argument might apply to rebel group leaders as well as heads of state. Exploring this issue further would be a valuable contribution to the literature on civil war and rebellion.[6]

COERCIVE DIPLOMACY

A final avenue for future research moves beyond the justice dilemma itself and considers the implications of my theory for coercive diplomacy. A large literature in international relations examines why some coercive threats succeed and others fail, with most scholars highlighting variables

3. Concerning the rank and file, it is worth exploring whether the actual perpetrators of mass atrocities (the individuals wielding the guns or guarding the death camps) can flee abroad with impunity more easily than the well-known leaders who order the violence. As the investigative journalist Eric Lichtblau has shown, legions of ex-Nazis lived freely in America (sometimes not even bothering to change their names) for several decades after World War II (Lichtblau 2014). Future work could explore the extent to which this is still possible.

4. See the interview with the former LRA member Patrick Makasi in the documentary film *The Reckoning* (Skylight Pictures, 2008).

5. Dennis Ojwee, "LRA Will Not Sign Incriminating Peace Deal," *All Africa*, September 9, 2007.

6. On rebel groups and international law, see Jo 2015.

like regime type or relative power (e.g., Art and Cronin 2003; Downes and Sechser 2012; Schultz 2001; Sechser 2010). My theory implies an important role for leaders since coercive threats often take the basic form of "step down or face the consequences."[7] The argument presented in this book implies that culpable leaders in the accountability era should be especially likely to resist this sort of international coercion. Such leaders will be wary of both a domestic retirement among the people they once oppressed and an exile abroad where international justice poses a threat. In other words, since today's culpable leaders do not have a good mechanism for giving up power, they may refuse to concede in international crises.

By way of example, consider two culpable leaders who faced similar predicaments. Let us start with the impunity era. In 1991, Raoul Cedras led a coup in Haiti that ousted the democratically elected leader Jean-Bertrand Aristide. Cedras and his military junta ruled with an iron fist and committed a host of human rights violations. By 1994, the United States was fed up with Cedras's antics. Bill Clinton delivered an ultimatum to Cedras: "Your time is up. Leave now or we will force you from power."[8] The United States geared up for an invasion of Haiti, but it was canceled when Cedras decided he was better off retiring to Panama. Now fast-forward to the accountability era. On the eve of the 2003 American invasion of Iraq, George W. Bush promised to call off the entire attack if Saddam Hussein would give up power and head into exile.[9] Yet, as my argument would expect, a foreign retirement was not an attractive option for Saddam. The Iraqi leader rejected Bush's proposal, and the United States was forced to go to war to oust him. Thus, coercive diplomacy failed. It is a tempting thought experiment to imagine how the extensive costs of the Iraq War—human, financial, political, cultural, and so forth—might have been spared if Saddam had taken Bush's offer.

Implications for Policy

For policymakers, this book raises some tough questions.[10] Over a decade ago, the journalist-turned-diplomat Samantha Power famously wrote that

7. On this particular type of coercive threat, see Downes 2018.

8. Carl M. Cannon, "Clinton Gives Ultimatum, 'Your Time Is Up,' President Tells Haiti's Leaders," *Baltimore Sun*, September 16, 1994.

9. See Julian Borger, "Bush Gives Saddam and His Sons 48 Hours to Leave Iraq," *Guardian*, March 17, 2003.

10. When it comes to answering these questions, the stakes are high. Roy Licklider (2008, 385) got it right when he noted: "As human rights and conflict management have become more prominent in foreign policy, the research in those fields takes on a new importance. We are not just engaged in academic debates now; we are talking about other people's countries and other people's lives."

genocide and mass killing presented policymakers with "a problem from hell" (Power 2003). The international community still struggles when attempting to confront foreign leaders who launch campaigns of violence against civilians.[11] International prosecutions, however, are increasingly popular. In addition to fighting impunity for atrocity crimes, prosecuting heads of state can be especially attractive because it offers powerful countries a way to do something to address humanitarian disasters without having to resort to riskier endeavors such as military interventions. But are international prosecutions the answer?

This book implies that human rights prosecutions, while certainly useful in some ways, are not the panacea that many in the international community desire. In fact, the policy implications of my justice dilemma theory are stark: an inherent tension exists between atrocity prevention and conflict resolution, two of the international community's signature goals. There is no easy solution when managing these trade-offs. As unappealing as it may be, the injustice of letting a bad leader escape to a safe exile is sometimes the price required for peace, and the sad reality of exacerbating conflict by demanding justice now is sometimes the price required for creating future deterrence. The justice cascade therefore is a more complex and multifaceted phenomenon than previously acknowledged. Going forward, three key issues will likely guide policy debates on international justice.

IS INTERNATIONAL JUSTICE HERE TO STAY?

The fact that prosecuting heads of state for atrocity crimes went from a seemingly impossible idea to a widely accepted practice in a relatively short period of time begs the question: Is a reversal possible? In other words, is international justice here to stay?

Those who work in what Jelena Subotic (2009) aptly labels "the international justice industry" generally assume so. In an op-ed lauding the momentum of the global justice movement after Charles Taylor was sentenced at the SCSL, one of the court's judges, Geoffrey Robertson, concluded that "international justice is here to stay."[12] The UN secretary-general Ban Ki-Moon similarly asserts that "the old era of impunity is over" and that "there is no going back" (Ki-Moon 2010). Louise Arbour, chief prosecutor at both the ICTY and the ICTR, likewise believes that international justice has moved past "a point of no return" (Stover, Peskin, and Koenig 2016, 8). Several scholars, particularly international justice optimists, share

11. For an excellent overview of the international community's different options for dealing with tyrannical leaders, see Escribà-Folch and Wright 2015a.

12. Geoffrey Robertson, "War Crimes: Charles Taylor Now, Bashar al-Assad Next," *Guardian*, May 20, 2012.

this assessment. For instance, after noting the broad extent to which norms of individual legal accountability for atrocity crimes have become embedded in both domestic and international law, Kathryn Sikkink (2011, 262) concludes that it is "unlikely that the trend will be reversed."

At the same time, there has been plenty of backlash against international justice, particularly the ICC. We need look no further than the reactions of states that have been targeted with prosecutions. It appears that some governments were happy to sign up for the ICC when prosecutions in their own countries seemed like a remote possibility, but they later changed their minds once the ICC began investigating. In February 2019, for example, the ICC announced a preliminary investigation into potential crimes against humanity committed during President Rodrigo Duterte's brutal war on drugs in the Philippines. In a clear attempt to stymie the court's investigation, Duterte quickly announced that the Philippines would withdraw from the Rome Statute and ominously warned international investigators: "Do not f**k with me."[13] Perhaps even more troubling for proponents of international justice is the fact that some of the powerful Western democracies that have played key roles in creating and financing international tribunals, not to mention enforcing their arrest warrants, may be losing interest in the issue. In the United States, the Trump administration has shown open hostility toward the ICC, particularly after the court moved to open an investigation of possible US war crimes committed in Afghanistan.[14] The United Kingdom's inward turn during Brexit does not bode well for the international justice project either. If these countries drop their support for pursuing accountability, then the justice cascade might be remembered as just a moment when the interests of several major powers briefly overlapped rather than as an enduring global change.

Hand-wringing over the future of international justice is not new. At least thus far, however, international justice has always managed to survive crises that were deemed to be existential at the time. The ICTY and the ICTR were initially derided as little more than empty prisons that wasted enormous sums of money, but an incredible 252 of the 256 individuals indicted between the two courts were eventually apprehended.[15] In 2011, *Foreign Affairs* published an article titled "Who's Afraid of the International Criminal Court?"

13. "Philippine President Duterte Needs 'Psychiatric Evaluation', Says UN Human Rights Chief," *France 24*, March 9, 2018. Note that, despite Duterte's withdrawal in March 2019, the ICC nonetheless retains jurisdiction over alleged crimes committed in the Philippines before the withdrawal.

14. In April 2019, the ICC dropped the investigation, a move many interpreted as the ICC capitulating to pressure from the Trump administration. But at the same time, one could argue that US concern over a potential ICC investigation in Afghanistan shows just how far international justice has progressed. If international justice was impotent, then the United States would have no reason to fear it. In March 2020, the ICC reversed course and reopened the investigation.

15. For an example of this critique, see Cobban 2006.

(Kaye 2011). The author criticized the ICC prosecutor Luis Moreno-Ocampo's tenure and implied that the court's record of pursuing high-profile suspects was poor enough that war criminals had little to fear. But within a few months of the article's publication, Muammar Gaddafi was dead after attempting to evade international justice, and Laurent Gbagbo was awaiting trial in a jail cell in The Hague. In 2016, the ICC faced the possibility of a coordinated withdrawal of African states from the Rome Statute. Accusations of anti-Africa bias at the court had reached a fever pitch, prompting both the *Washington Post* and the *BBC* to publish headlines asking, "Is This the End of the International Criminal Court?"[16] But it was not the end for the ICC. The crisis quickly subsided after virtually all the African states that had expressed interest in leaving decided against it. Only tiny Burundi went ahead with the plan, and the mass walkout never materialized.

Reports of international justice's imminent death have therefore been exaggerated. But it is also worth emphasizing that the future of international justice remains very much in flux. It is not inevitable that the justice cascade will continue. While a bold answer to the "Is international justice here to stay?" question is unwarranted at this time, it is possible to think about this issue systematically. As Julia Gray (2018) explains, international organizations very rarely die off altogether. More often, they become what she calls "zombies." These zombie institutions continue to exist, but they receive little support from states and make no progress toward their mandates. Looking ahead, this is the risk the ICC and other international tribunals face. If the political will to enforce arrest warrants dries up in powerful Western democracies, the institutions of international justice could conceivably become zombie institutions. The world then might slowly revert to another impunity era. In this hypothetical, the exile option would be back on the table even for culpable leaders, weakening both the deterrence of atrocity crimes and the incentive for brutal leaders to double down on the battlefield during civil wars.

It is conceivable, of course, that the opposite might occur: the enforcement of international criminal law could actually improve. After all, the international justice movement rests on a simple but compelling idea: Some crimes are so heinous that the perpetrator ought to be punished regardless of national borders. The recent backlash against the ICC might reflect frustration with that particular institution more than a problem with the idea of international justice in general. Consider the United States. Around the same time that John Bolton, a policymaker infamous for his antipathy toward the ICC, was elevated to the role of national security adviser, the

16. See Kate Cronin-Furman and Stephanie Schwartz, "Is This the End of the International Criminal Court?," *Washington Post*, October 21, 2016; and Karen Allen, "Is This the End for the International Criminal Court?," *BBC News*, October 24, 2016.

United States also quietly supported European attempts to pursue universal jurisdiction prosecutions of Syrian war criminals. The international justice landscape is larger than any single institution, which ultimately might be a source of staying power.[17] And if international justice really is here to stay, then my book offers a reason for guarded optimism: the positive effect should begin to dominate the perverse effect over time. As more and more leaders are deterred from committing atrocities in the first place, the number of culpable leaders who will have incentives to fight to the bitter end should slowly decrease.[18]

ARE POLICYMAKERS AWARE OF THE DILEMMA?

To what extent are policymakers aware of the justice dilemma? In short, it depends on the type of policymaker. Prosecutors and judges at international tribunals typically ignore the political effects of the indictments they issue. Consider the following statements from the ICC's first two prosecutors. Both argue that there is—and should be—a clear dividing line between political issues such as resolving civil wars and the justice issues that they see as their exclusive mandate. Luis Moreno-Ocampo flatly rejected the notion that international justice ought to accommodate the complex political considerations that are part of reaching settlements to civil wars: "The Prosecutor's duty is to apply the law without bowing to political considerations, and I will not adjust my practices to political considerations. It is time for political actors to adjust to law" (Moreno-Ocampo 2008, 224). His successor, Fatou Bensouda, similarly asserted that political concerns simply have no effect on how she approaches her job: "As the ICC is an independent and judicial institution, it cannot take into consideration the interests of peace, which is the mandate of other institutions, such as the United Nations Security Council."[19] This view is not limited to the ICC. Richard Goldstone, a prosecutor at the Yugoslav and Rwandan tribunals, has argued: "If you have a system of international justice, you've got to follow through. If in some cases that's going to make peace negotiations difficult, that may be the price that has to be paid."[20]

17. As mentioned before, the international justice landscape resembles a case of international regime complexity (Alter and Meunier 2009) featuring several partially overlapping institutions. This diversity of legal venues for prosecuting international crimes suggests that even if the ICC flounders, the international justice movement writ large is not doomed.

18. However, I do not expect the number of culpable leaders ever to fall to zero. As described in the theory, there are certain conditions under which international justice is not likely to deter leaders from initiating campaigns of mass atrocities.

19. Fatou Bensouda, "International Justice and Diplomacy," *New York Times*, March 19, 2013.

20. Chris McGreal, "African Search for Peace Throws Court into Crisis," *Guardian*, January 9, 2007.

Thus, many advocates of global justice, especially those who work at international criminal tribunals, seem to ignore—either willfully or unintentionally—the potentially perverse political effects of international prosecutions. Yet, at other times, these same individuals want to claim the opposite: pursuing international accountability may be conducive to peace. Peace and justice, according to this logic, reinforce one another. Moreno-Ocampo, for example, has argued that "arrest warrants have brought parties to the negotiating table."[21] In a similar vein, Bensouda critiques the belief that the ICC is an obstacle to peace as "narrow and short-sighted," insisting instead that "justice can have a positive impact on peace. . . . The 'shadow of the Court' has helped to . . . kick-start negotiations."[22] This strange juxtaposition of claims that the ICC is both deeply apolitical *and* a force for peace during civil war, as political a process as any, has not been lost on some observers. Mark Kersten (2016, 35), for example, wryly notes that, "whilst maintaining that the ICC does not take the politics of peace into account, the Prosecutor is simultaneously eager to take credit for the court's effects on peace processes—so long as they are positive."

To their credit, at least some in the international justice industry recognize the tension between conflict resolution and atrocity prevention. When taking stock of her time at the ICTY and the ICTR, Louise Arbour noted, "We all repeat the mantra that there can be no lasting peace without justice; and that's true enough. But I don't think that we have yet resolved the inevitable tensions between the two in a workable fashion" (Arbour 2013). The legal scholar Cherif Bassiouni also recognizes this trade-off: "The human rights arena is defined by a constant tension between the attraction of realpolitik and the demand for accountability. Realpolitik involves the pursuit of political settlements unencumbered by moral and ethical limitations. As such, this approach often runs counter to the interests of justice" (Bassiouni 2003, 191). Finally, the architects of the Rome Statute seemed aware of this tension when they wrote Article 16, which gives the UN Security Council the power to delay ICC prosecutions for one-year renewable periods in "the interests of international peace and security." The UN Security Council, however, has not yet used this authority.

21. Luis Moreno-Ocampo, address given at the "Building a Future on Peace and Justice" conference, June 25, 2007, transcript available at https://www.icc-cpi.int/NR/rdonlyres/4E466EDB-2B38-4BAF-AF5F-005461711149/143825/LMO_nuremberg_20070625_English.pdf.

22. Fatou Bensouda, "International Justice and Diplomacy," *New York Times*, March 19, 2013. Interestingly, Moreno-Ocampo and Bensouda both briefly reference Uganda as a case where ICC prosecutions helped bring peace. This, however, contradicts how many view the ICC's role in Uganda. In addition to the statements from Joseph Kony and Vincent Otti mentioned earlier, the following journalist's claim is representative: "The ICC was set up to promote justice. But in Uganda, it is increasingly seen as an obstacle to peace." See Daniel Wallis, "World Court Faces Tough Choices," *Reuters*, September 2, 2006.

National-level policymakers appear the most likely to recognize the trade-offs involved with international justice. This should not be surprising. Unlike international prosecutors, national policymakers do not have the luxury of focusing exclusively on issues of justice. Instead, they must balance several different competing priorities. We saw this in the Muammar Gaddafi and Charles Taylor cases, where specific policymakers were at times highly critical of the effects of international prosecutions on the peace processes in Libya and Liberia, respectively. Andrew Natsios, the US special envoy to Sudan, made a similar point about how the ICC's arrest warrant for Omar Bashir hampered efforts to end Sudan's conflict: "They [the leaders of Sudan's National Congress Party] are prepared to kill anyone, suffer massive civilian casualties, and violate every international norm of human rights to stay in power, no matter the international pressure, because they worry (correctly) that if they are removed from power, they will face both retaliation at home and war crimes trials abroad" (Natsios 2008, 82). Hence, at least some policymakers are aware that threatening to bring leaders to justice can undermine peace processes. However, simply acknowledging the trade-off between peace and justice does not make it any less stark.

IS IT POSSIBLE TO SOLVE THE DILEMMA?

Is there a way out of the justice dilemma? Two main sets of proposals have been put forth to mitigate the tension between peace and justice: one focuses on cutting deals with violent leaders, whereas the other emphasizes the timing of international prosecutions. Both proposals, however, are bound to fail because they do not carefully consider the strategic calculus of leaders.[23]

23. There is, however, a third possibility that may hold some promise: relying on rewards (carrots) rather than punishments (sticks) to shape leader behavior. We saw this in the Blaise Compaoré case, and it is occurring in other venues as well. One example is the Ibrahim Prize for Achievement in African Leadership (the brainchild of Dr. Mo Ibrahim, a Sudanese billionaire philanthropist), which recognizes leaders who strengthen democracy and human rights. What makes the Ibrahim Prize stand out is the huge financial reward: a $5,000,000 windfall plus an additional $200,000 every year thereafter for life. The intuition behind such carrots should be familiar to readers of this book: Leaders only have incentives to step down from power when they have good exit options. When an attractive exit strategy—say, exile on an exotic island or in a sophisticated capital city—is off the table, leaders will likely entrench in power. This, in turn, can be ruinous for democracy, human rights, and conflict resolution. By giving leaders payments and prestige in retirement if they deliver on good governance, carrots like the Ibrahim Prize may incentivize leaders to behave better while still in office. At the same time, however, carrots do not completely solve the justice dilemma. As long as international justice relies on sticks, the trade-off between deterring atrocities and prolonging conflicts identified in this book will still exist regardless of how much leaders might be paid in retirement. Nonetheless, using carrots in addition to sticks might be enough

Timing arguments are premised on the idea that justice should be pursued *after* conflicts end rather than *during* ongoing conflicts. This viewpoint is not meant to imply that justice is any less important than peace. Rather, the logic is that sequencing justice allows the international community to fight impunity, albeit with a delay, in a way that does not produce detrimental effects on peace processes. According to Oskar Thoms, James Ron, and Roland Paris (2008, 3), the appropriate sequence is "first to consolidate peace, and only later to pursue justice." Similarly, after investigating how human rights prosecutions shape peace negotiations, Jack Snyder and Leslie Vinjamuri (2003, 6) conclude, "Justice does not lead; it follows." A slightly different variant of this argument comes from Stephen Macedo (2004), who suggests that all sitting heads of state should be granted immunity no matter how brutal they are, whereas former heads of state should not be granted such protection. This sort of thinking makes its way into policy debates. For example, Human Rights Watch issued an influential report devoted to the issue of whether "justice should wait until after those culpable are no longer in positions of authority" (Human Rights Watch 2009, 2).

Advocates of sequencing justice make an appealing claim: if the international community could just get the timing of prosecutions right, it would be possible to pursue accountability without the perverse effect of leaders violently clinging to power. However, the assertion that international justice can be effectively sequenced fails under closer scrutiny. In practice, it would play out something like this: the belligerents initiate peace negotiations, international tribunals pledge to hold off on pursuing justice, the regime and the opposition reach a peace deal and lay down their arms, and, finally, once the political situation has stabilized, the international community brings the culpable leader to justice. Seen in this way, the shortcoming of trying to sequence justice is clear. Any forward-looking leader will know that he is vulnerable to prosecution after making peace, especially if the peace negotiations involve handing power over to the opposition. Accordingly, the leader will adjust his behavior during the conflict and will still have incentives to dig in his heels to avoid this bait and switch.[24]

to get at least some leaders out of office before they are in a position where it would be tempting to trample democratic norms or commit mass atrocities.

24. It is worth mentioning that there is another version of the "politics first" argument. In this variant, justice is exclusively forward-looking. The basic idea is that past abuses ought to be ignored for the sake of political expediency, but once the political situation has stabilized, any new atrocities should be prosecuted. Executing this strategy effectively could help mitigate the justice dilemma by essentially giving leaders with blood on their hands a clean slate (and therefore a stronger incentive to step down). The challenge with the approach, however, is making the promise not to prosecute old abuses credible. Given the cases examined in this book, there is little reason to have confidence that the international community

The other proposed solution involves cutting deals with brutal dictators. For instance, some have called for a more flexible international legal regime that strikes bargains with culpable leaders to resolve intractable conflicts.[25] In this scenario, a leader who is guilty of committing atrocities could be allowed to bargain away an indictment if he steps down peacefully and leaves the country. Another variant of this argument is found in Alan Kuperman's study of the moral hazard of humanitarian intervention, where he suggests that it would be useful for the international community to "lure entrenched dictators from office by offering 'golden parachutes' [that include] asylum and immunity from subsequent prosecution" (Kuperman 2008, 74). In fact, virtually every time a culpable leader appears to be headed toward a fight to the bitter end, at least some policymakers and pundits take this position.

Advocates of this approach convincingly make the case that striking a deal with a culpable leader could help resolve an ongoing conflict involving *that specific leader*. The problem with this approach is that it ignores the broader context of the justice cascade.[26] If offering peace-for-exile deals becomes the norm again, *other leaders* will know that they too can bargain away arrest warrants and find safe havens abroad. Consequently, the deterrent effect of international justice will be undermined. To put it another way, allowing leaders to negotiate their way out of indictments might help end violence in one state only to encourage it in another.

To illustrate in a more tangible manner why both proposed solutions—sequencing justice and negotiating with culpable leaders—fail to offer a way out of the justice dilemma, let us return to the case of Syria's Bashar Assad. Civil unrest in Syria began in 2011 as part of the broader Arab Spring sweeping through the Middle East and North Africa. Over time, popular protests against the Assad regime morphed into an armed rebellion as Assad's forces brutally repressed the opposition. The conflict has claimed an estimated 500,000 lives, and the Assad regime has violated nearly every law of war—including brutal tactics such as indiscriminate shelling and the use of chemical weapons—to keep its hold on power (e.g., Taub 2016). At various points throughout the conflict, commentators have speculated that Assad was on the verge of giving up power and fleeing abroad.[27] Some

can credibly commit not to dig up the past, but this strategy nonetheless remains an interesting possibility.

25. For a fascinating take on international tribunals and the possibility of pre-arrest plea bargaining, see Ritter and Wolford 2012.

26. Another potential problem with this approach is the issue of whether the international community can credibly commit to upholding its end of the deal over the long term, an important bargaining dynamic described in my theory.

27. For example, when Syrian rebels advanced to the outskirts of Damascus in late 2012, the *New York Times* published an article predicting that the embattled Assad might take the

even argued that Western democracies should encourage such a transition by signaling their willingness to forego an international prosecution. For example, the British leader David Cameron mused about giving Assad a golden parachute option and proclaimed that he was willing to do "anything, anything, to get that man [Assad] out of the country and to have a safe transition in Syria."[28]

So why did attempts to coax Assad out of power fail? Part of the reason is that Assad had to worry about the international community attempting to sequence justice.[29] Though some in the international community no doubt hoped that Assad could be convinced to go into exile rather than continue the war in Syria, statements from American and British officials also made it obvious that they wanted to prosecute Assad for atrocity crimes once he was out of power.[30] On top of that, human rights groups advertised that they had more than enough evidence to prosecute Assad if he ever ended up in the dock.[31] Therefore, Assad had compelling reasons to anticipate a serious push for accountability if and when he gave up power. Given this, why would Assad choose to flee into exile now if he could reasonably expect that doing so would later result in arrest and prosecution? In short, this rather transparent attempt to sequence justice failed.

For the sake of argument, though, consider what would have happened if the international community had somehow convinced Assad to give up power when the Syrian rebels first marched on Damascus in 2012. This hypothetical scenario allows us to see the shortcoming of striking deals

exile option as his regime appeared ready to collapse. See Andrew E. Kramer, "In Russia, Exile in Comfort for Leaders Like Assad," *New York Times*, December 28, 2012.

28. Mohammed Abbas and Khaled Yacoub Oweis, "Bombings Rock Damascus, Brother of Parliament Speaker Killed," *Reuters*, November 6, 2012.

29. In fact, one of the proponents of the "peace first, justice later" camp, Leslie Vinjamuri, argued for a carefully timed referral of the Syrian situation to the ICC: "A Security Council referral of the ICC doesn't need to happen now. There is no evidence to suggest that a referral now is going to help alter the outcome in Syria in a positive and productive way. A referral can come later." See "Leslie Vinjamuri on the ICC and Conflict Zones," *Open Canada*, May 7, 2012.

30. For example, David Cameron qualified his support for the golden parachute option by saying, "Of course I would favor him facing the full force of international law and justice for what he's done." See Mohammed Abbas and Khaled Yacoub Oweis, "Bombings Rock Damascus, Brother of Parliament Speaker Killed," *Reuters*, November 6, 2012. Similarly, the US State Department spokesman Mark Toner asserted that, regardless of where Assad ended up, the United States would insist on accountability for "the horrible abuses he has committed against his own people. No one is getting a free pass here. . . . He has to go, but there are issues of accountability that have to be addressed." See Matthew Lee, "US Aware of Assad Asylum Offers," *Seattle Times*, December 6, 2012. Finally, the US ambassador-at-large for war crimes Stephen Rapp spoke as if it was only an issue of *when*, not *if*, Assad would be prosecuted: "When the day of justice arrives [for Assad], we'll have much better evidence than we've had anywhere since Nuremberg" (Taub 2016, 39).

31. See the work of the Commission for International Justice and Accountability detailed in Taub 2016.

with culpable leaders. If the Western powers had followed Cameron's suggestion and created a secure exile option for Assad, other leaders would realize that the international community is not serious about enforcing international criminal law. As a result, other rulers would not be deterred when contemplating their own campaigns of mass killing. Yet, giving Assad a golden parachute back in 2012 likely could have helped resolve the war in Syria before it became the devastating, intractable conflict that it is today. Of course, there is no easy solution here. As described in my theory, the opposite policy comes with tough trade-offs as well. Insisting that Assad be treated as a war criminal creates incentives for him to fight until the bitter end. Yet, successfully prosecuting Assad would bolster deterrence by sending a message to other brutal dictators that the international community will not tolerate mass atrocities.

In sum, this discussion illustrates the stark policy implications of my argument. When making decisions about whether to pursue or forego global accountability for oppressive leaders, the international community can help resolve today's civil wars *or* help prevent tomorrow's atrocity crimes. It cannot, however, do both at the same time. That is the crux of the justice dilemma.

References

Akhavan, Payam. 1998. "Justice in the Hague, Peace in the Former Yugoslavia? A Commentary on the United Nations War Crimes Tribunal." *Human Rights Quarterly* 20 (4): 737–816.

——. 2001. "Beyond Impunity: Can International Criminal Justice Prevent Future Atrocities?" *American Journal of International Law* 95 (1): 7–31.

——. 2009. "Are International Criminal Tribunals a Disincentive to Peace? Reconciling Judicial Romanticism with Political Realism." *Human Rights Quarterly* 31 (3): 624–54.

Alexander, Robert J. 1979. *Juan Domingo Peron: A History*. Boulder, CO: Westview Press.

Alter, Karen J. 2014. *The New Terrain of International Law: Courts, Politics, Rights*. Princeton, NJ: Princeton University Press.

Alter, Karen J., and Sophie Meunier. 2009. "The Politics of International Regime Complexity." *Perspectives on Politics* 7 (1): 13–24.

Amnesty International. 2011. *Universal Jurisdiction: A Preliminary Survey of Legislation around the World*. London: Amnesty International Publications.

——. 2015. *Just What Were They Thinking When They Shot at People?* London: Amnesty International Publications.

Anderson, Jon Lee. 2011. "King of Kings: The Last Days of Muammar Qaddafi." *New Yorker* 87 (35): 44–57.

Anderson, Kenneth. 2009. "The Rise of International Criminal Law: Intended and Unintended Consequences." *European Journal of International Law* 20 (2): 331–58.

Appel, Benjamin J. 2018. "In the Shadow of the International Criminal Court: Does the ICC Deter Human Rights Violations?" *Journal of Conflict Resolution* 62 (1): 3–28.

Arbour, Louise. 2013. "Doctrines Derailed? Internationalism's Uncertain Future." Presented at the International Crisis Group Annual Briefing, Brussels, October 28, 2013.

Archibugi, Daniele, and Alice Pease. 2018. *Crime and Global Justice*. Cambridge: Polity Press.

Arendt, Hannah. 1992. "Letter to Karl Jaspers, 17 August 1946." In *Hannah Arendt and Karl Jaspers: Correspondence, 1926–1969*, edited by Lotte Kohler and Hans Saner, 51–56. New York: Harcourt Brace.

Arreguin-Toft, Ivan M. 2005. *How the Weak Win Wars: A Theory of Asymmetric Conflict*. New York: Cambridge University Press.

Art, Robert J., and Patrick M. Cronin. 2003. *The United States and Coercive Diplomacy*. Washington, DC: US Institute of Peace Press.

Avirgan, Tony, and Martha Honey. 1982. *War in Uganda: The Legacy of Idi Amin*. Westport, CT.: Lawrence Hill.

Bailey, Michael A., Anton Strezhnev, and Erik Voeten. 2017. "Estimating Dynamic State Preferences from United Nations Voting Data." *Journal of Conflict Resolution* 61 (2): 430–56.

Baker, Bruce. 2004. "Twilight of Impunity for Africa's Presidential Criminals." *Third World Quarterly* 25 (8): 1487–99.

Balcells, Laia. 2010. "Rivalry and Revenge: Violence against Civilians in Conventional Civil Wars." *International Studies Quarterly* 54 (2): 291–313.

Balcells, Laia, and Stathis N. Kalyvas. 2014. "Does Warfare Matter? Severity, Duration, and Outcomes of Civil Wars." *Journal of Conflict Resolution* 58 (8): 1–29.

Banks, Arthur S., and Kenneth A. Wilson. 2013. "Cross-National Time-Series Data Archive." Accessed October 27, 2013. http://www.databanksinternational.com.

Bass, Gary Jonathan. 2000. *Stay the Hand of Vengeance: The Politics of War Crimes Tribunals*. Princeton, NJ: Princeton University Press.

Bassiouni, M. Cherif. 2003. "Justice and Peace: The Importance of Choosing Accountability over Realpolitk." *Case Western Reserve Journal of International Law* 35 (2): 191–204.

Beardsley, Kyle. 2011. *The Mediation Dilemma*. Ithaca, NY: Cornell University Press.

Beck, Nathaniel, Jonathan N. Katz, and Richard Tucker. 1998. "Taking Time Seriously: Time-Series-Cross-Section Analysis with a Binary Dependent Variable." *American Journal of Political Science* 42 (4): 1260–88.

Becker, Gary S. 1968. "Crime and Punishment: An Economic Approach." *Journal of Political Economy* 76 (2): 169–217.

Bennett, Andrew, Ariya Hagh, and Zacchary Ritter. 2020. "The Exit Dilemma: Providing Golden Parachutes to Embattled Dictators." Working paper.

Besley, Timothy, Jose G. Montalvo, and Marta Reynal-Querol. 2011. "Do Educated Leaders Matter?" *Economic Journal* 121 (554): 205–27.

Bolton, John R. 2001. "The Risks and the Weaknesses of the International Criminal Court from America's Perspective." *Law and Contemporary Problems* 64 (1): 167–80.

Bonner, Raymond. 1987. *Waltzing with a Dictator*. New York: Times Books.

Bosco, David. 2014. *Rough Justice: The International Criminal Court in a World of Power Politics*. Oxford: Oxford University Press.

Bowen, Jeremy. 2012. *The Arab Uprisings: The People Want the Fall of the Regime*. London: Simon and Schuster.

Box-Steffensmeier, Janet M., John R. Freeman, Matthew P. Hitt, and Jon C. W. Pevehouse. 2014. *Time Series Analysis for the Social Sciences*. Cambridge: Cambridge University Press.

Box-Steffensmeier, Janet M., and Bradford S. Jones. 1997. "Time Is of the Essence: Event History Models in Political Science." *American Journal of Political Science* 41 (4): 1414–61.

Braumoeller, Bear F. 2019. *Only the Dead: The Persistence of War in the Modern Age*. Oxford: Oxford University Press.

Brody, Reed. 2008. "Interview with Democracy Now." June 12, 2008. https://www.democracynow.org/2008/6/12/the_dictator_hunter_victims_of_us.

——. 2015. "Bringing a Dictator to Justice: The Case of Hissène Habré." *Journal of International Criminal Justice* 13 (2): 209–17.

Brody, Reed, and Michael Ratner. 2000. *The Pinochet Papers*. Cambridge: Kluwer.

Bronner, Michael. 2014. "Our Man in Africa." *Foreign Policy* 204: 34–47.

Brysk, Alison. 2009. *Global Good Samaritans: Human Rights as Foreign Policy*. Oxford: Oxford University Press.

Bueno de Mesquita, Bruce, Alastair Smith, Randolph M. Siverson, and James D. Morrow. 2003. *The Logic of Political Survival*. Cambridge, MA: MIT Press.

Byman, Daniel L., and Kenneth M. Pollack. 2001. "Let Us Now Praise Great Men: Bringing the Statesman Back In." *International Security* 25 (4): 107–46.

Campbell, Donald T. 1969. "Reforms as Experiments." *American Psychologist* 24 (4): 409–29.

Campbell, John. 2013. *Nigeria: Dancing on the Brink*. Lanham, MD: Rowman and Littlefield.

Carey, Sabine C., Michael P. Colaresi, and Neil J. Mitchell. 2015. "Governments, Informal Links to Militias, and Accountability." *Journal of Conflict Resolution* 59 (5): 850–76.

Carson, Austin. 2018. *Secret Wars: Covert Conflict in International Politics*. Princeton, NJ: Princeton University Press.

Carter, David B., and Curtis S. Signorino. 2010. "Back to the Future: Modeling Time Dependence in Binary Data." *Political Analysis* 18 (3): 271–92.

Cassese, Antonio. 1998. "Reflections on International Criminal Justice." *Modern Law Review* 61 (1): 1–10.

——. 2008. *International Criminal Law*. 2nd ed. New York: Oxford University Press.

Center for Systemic Peace. 2015. "Elite Characteristics." Accessed October 6, 2015. http://www.systemicpeace.org/.

Chapman, Terrence L., and Stephen Chaudoin. 2013. "Ratification Patterns and the International Criminal Court." *International Studies Quarterly* 57 (2): 400–409.

Chayes, Abram, and Antonia Handler Chayes. 1993. "On Compliance." *International Organization* 47 (2): 175–205.

Chenoweth, Erica, and Maria J. Stephan. 2011. *Why Civil Resistance Works: The Strategic Logic of Nonviolent Conflict*. New York: Columbia University Press.

Chiozza, Giacomo, and Henk E. Goemans. 2011. *Leaders and International Conflict*. New York: Cambridge University Press.

Chivvis, Christopher S. 2014. *Toppling Qaddafi: Libya and the Limits of Liberal Intervention*. New York: Cambridge University Press.

Chorin, Ethan. 2012. *Exit the Colonel: The Hidden History of the Libyan Revolution*. New York: Public Affairs.

Cingranelli, David, and Mikhail Filippov. 2018. "Are Human Rights Practices Improving?" *American Political Science Review* 112 (4): 1083–89.

Cingranelli, David L., and David L. Richards. 2009. "The Cingranelli-Richards Human Rights Dataset." Accessed May 20, 2014. http://www.humanrightsdata.org.

Cobban, Helena. 2006. "International Courts." *Foreign Policy* 153: 22–28.

Cohen, Dara Kay. 2016. *Rape during Civil War*. Ithaca, NY: Cornell University Press.

Cohen, Dara Kay, and Ragnhild Nordås. 2015. "Do States Delegate Shameful Violence to Militias? Patterns of Sexual Violence in Recent Armed Conflicts." *Journal of Conflict Resolution* 59 (5): 877–98.

Colgan, Jeff D. 2013a. "Domestic Revolutionary Leaders and International Conflict." *World Politics* 65 (4): 656–90.

——. 2013b. *Petro-Aggression: When Oil Causes War*. Cambridge: Cambridge University Press.

Collier, Paul. 2008. *The Bottom Billion: Why the Poorest Countries Are Failing and What Can Be Done about It*. New York: Oxford University Press.

Collier, Paul, and Anke Hoeffler. 2004. "Greed and Grievance in Civil War." *Oxford Economic Papers* 56 (4): 563–95.

Conrad, Courtenay R., and Emily Hencken Ritter. 2013. "Treaties, Tenure, and Torture: The Conflicting Domestic Effects of International Law." *Journal of Politics* 75 (2): 397–409.

Crassweller, Robert D. 1987. *Peron and the Enigmas of Argentina*. New York: Norton.

Croco, Sarah E. 2015. *Peace at What Price? Leaders and the Domestic Politics of War Termination*. New York: Cambridge University Press.

Cronin-Furman, Kate. 2013. "Managing Expectations: International Criminal Trials and the Prospects for Deterrence of Mass Atrocity." *International Journal of Transitional Justice* 7 (3): 434–54.

——. 2020. "Human Rights Half Measures: Avoiding Accountability in Post-War Sri Lanka." *World Politics* 72 (1): 121–63.

Cunningham, David E. 2006. "Veto Players and Civil War Duration." *American Journal of Political Science* 50 (4): 875–92.

Cunningham, David E., Kristian Skrede Gleditsch, and Idean Salehyan. 2009. "It Takes Two: A Dyadic Analysis of Civil War Duration and Outcome." *Journal of Conflict Resolution* 53 (4): 570–97.

Damaska, Mirjan. 2008. "What Is the Point of International Criminal Justice?" *Chicago-Kent Law Review* 83 (1): 329–65.

d'Ancona, Matthew. 2013. *In It Together: The Inside Story of the Coalition Government*. New York: Penguin.

Dancy, Geoff. 2018. "Deals with the Devil? Conflict Amnesties, Civil War, and Sustainable Peace." *International Organization* 72 (2): 387–421.

Dancy, Geoff, and Eric Wiebelhaus-Brahm. 2018. "The Impact of Criminal Prosecutions during Intrastate Conflict." *Journal of Peace Research* 55 (1): 47–61.

Davis, Brian L. 1990. *Qaddafi, Terrorism, and the Origins of the U.S. Attack on Libya*. New York: Praeger.

Debs, Alexandre, and Henk E. Goemans. 2010. "Regime Type, the Fate of Leaders, and War." *American Political Science Review* 104 (3): 430–45.

Del Ponte, Carla. 2009. *Madame Prosecutor: Confrontations with Humanity's Worst Criminals and the Culture of Impunity*. New York: Other Press.

Dix, Robert H. 1982. "The Breakdown of Authoritarian Regimes." *Western Political Quarterly* 35 (4): 554–73.

Donohue, John J., and Justin Wolfers. 2005. "Uses and Abuses of Empirical Evidence in the Death Penalty Debate." *Stanford Law Review* 58: 791–846.

Downes, Alexander B. 2008. *Targeting Civilians in War*. Ithaca, NY: Cornell University Press.

——. 2018. "Step Aside or Face the Consequences: Explaining the Success and Failure of Compellent Threats to Remove Foreign Leaders." In *Coercion: The Power to Hurt in International Politics*, edited by Kelly M. Greenhill and Peter Krause, 93–114. Oxford: Oxford University Press.

Downes, Alexander B., and Todd S. Sechser. 2012. "The Illusion of Democratic Credibility." *International Organization* 66 (3): 457–89.

Downs, Anthony. 1957. *An Economic Theory of Democracy*. New York: Harper.

Downs, George W., and David M. Rocke. 1994. "Conflict, Agency, and Gambling for Resurrection: The Principal-Agent Problem Goes to War." *American Journal of Political Science* 38 (2): 362–80.

Downs, George W., David M. Rocke, and Peter N. Barsoom. 1996. "Is the Good News about Compliance Good News about Cooperation?" *International Organization* 50 (3): 379–406.

Doyle, Michael W., and Nicholas Sambanis. 2011. *Making War and Building Peace: United Nations Peace Operations*. Princeton, NJ: Princeton University Press.

Drumbl, Mark A. 2005. "Collective Violence and Individual Punishment: The Criminality of Mass Atrocity." *Northwestern University Law Review* 99 (2): 539–610.

——. 2007. *Atrocity, Punishment, and International Law*. New York: Cambridge University Press.

Easterly, William. 2006. *The White Man's Burden: Why the West's Efforts to Aid the Rest Have Done So Much Ill and So Little Good*. New York: Penguin.

Ellis, Stephen. 2007. *The Mask of Anarchy: The Destruction of Liberia and the Religious Dimension of an African Civil War*. 2nd ed. New York: New York University Press.

Engels, Bettina. 2015. "Political Transition in Burkina Faso: The Fall of Blaise Compaoré." *Governance in Africa* 2 (1): 1–6.

Enrile, Juan Ponce. 2012. *Juan Ponce Enrile: A Memoir*. Quezon City: ABS-CBN.

Escribà-Folch, Abel. 2013. "Accountable for What? Regime Types, Performance, and the Fate of Outgoing Dictators, 1946–2004." *Democratization* 20 (1): 160–85.

Escribà-Folch, Abel, and Daniel Krcmaric. 2017. "Dictators in Exile: Explaining the Destinations of Ex-Rulers." *Journal of Politics* 79 (2): 560–75.

Escribà-Folch, Abel, and Joseph Wright. 2015a. *Foreign Pressure and the Politics of Autocratic Survival*. Oxford: Oxford University Press.

——. 2015b. "Human Rights Prosecutions and Autocratic Survival." *International Organization* 69 (2): 343–73.

Falk, Richard A. 2004. "Assessing the Pinochet Litigation: Whither Universal Jurisdiction?" In *Universal Jurisdiction: National Courts and the Prosecution of Serious Crimes under International Law*, edited by Stephen Macedo, 97–120. Philadelphia: University of Pennsylvania Press.

Fariss, Christopher J. 2014. "Respect for Human Rights Has Improved over Time: Modeling the Changing Standard of Accountability." *American Political Science Review* 108 (2): 297–318.

Fazal, Tanisha M. 2014. "Dead Wrong? Battle Deaths, Military Medicine, and Exaggerated Reports of War's Demise." *International Security* 39 (1): 95–125.

——. 2018. *Wars of Law: Unintended Consequences in the Regulation of Armed Conflict*. Ithaca, NY: Cornell University Press.

Fearon, James D. 1994. "Signaling versus the Balance of Power and Interests: An Empirical Test of a Crisis Bargaining Model." *Journal of Conflict Resolution* 38 (2): 236–69.

——. 1995. "Rationalist Explanations for War." *International Organization* 49 (3): 379–414.

——. 1997. "Signaling Foreign Policy Interests: Tying Hands versus Sinking Costs." *Journal of Conflict Resolution* 41 (1): 68–90.

——. 2004. "Why Do Some Civil Wars Last So Much Longer Than Others?" *Journal of Peace Research* 41 (3): 275–301.

Fearon, James D., and David D. Laitin. 2003. "Ethnicity, Insurgency, and Civil War." *American Political Science Review* 97 (1): 75–90.

Finnemore, Martha, and Kathryn Sikkink. 1998. "International Norm Dynamics and Political Change." *International Organization* 52 (4): 887–917.

Fortna, Virginia Page. 2008. *Does Peacekeeping Work? Shaping Belligerents' Choices after Civil War*. Princeton, NJ: Princeton University Press.

Frère, Marie-Soleil, and Pierre Englebert. 2015. "Burkina Faso: The Fall of Blaise Compaoré." *African Affairs* 114 (455): 295–307.

Fuhrmann, Matthew, and Michael C. Horowitz. 2015. "When Leaders Matter: Rebel Experience and Nuclear Proliferation." *Journal of Politics* 77 (1): 72–87.

Gallopin, Jean-Baptiste. 2019. "Dilemma and Cascades in the Armed Forces: The Tunisian Revolution." *Democracy and Security* 15 (4): 328–60.

Gberie, Lansana. 2005. *A Dirty War in West Africa: The RUF and the Destruction of Sierra Leone*. Bloomington: Indiana University Press.

Geddes, Barbara, Joseph Wright, and Erica Frantz. 2014. "Autocratic Breakdown and Regime Transitions: A New Data Set." *Perspectives on Politics* 12 (2): 313–31.

Ghobarah, Hazem Adam, Paul Huth, and Bruce Russett. 2003. "Civil Wars Kill and Maim People—Long after the Shooting Stops." *American Political Science Review* 97 (2): 189–202.

Gibler, Douglas M. 2009. *International Military Alliances, 1648–2008*. Washington, DC: CQ Press.

Gift, Thomas, and Daniel Krcmaric. 2017. "Who Democratizes? Western-Educated Leaders and Regime Transitions." *Journal of Conflict Resolution* 61 (3): 671–701.

Gilligan, Michael J. 2006. "Is Enforcement Necessary for Effectiveness? A Model of the International Criminal Regime." *International Organization* 60 (4): 935–67.

Gleditsch, Kristian Skrede. 2002. "Expanded Trade and GDP Data." *Journal of Conflict Resolution* 46 (5): 712–24.

Gleditsch, Kristian Skrede, and Michael D. Ward. 1999. "Interstate System Membership: A Revised List of the Independent States since 1816." *International Interactions* 25: 393–413.

——. 2006. "Diffusion and the International Context of Democratization." *International Organization* 60 (4): 911–33.

Gleditsch, Nils Petter, Peter Wallensteen, Mikael Eriksson, Margareta Sollenberg, and Håvard Strand. 2002. "Armed Conflict 1946–2001: A New Dataset." *Journal of Peace Research* 39 (5): 615–37.

Goemans, Henk E. 2000. *War and Punishment: The Causes of War Termination and the First World War*. Princeton, NJ: Princeton University Press.

Goemans, Henk E., Kristian Skrede Gleditsch, and Giacomo Chiozza. 2009. "Introducing Archigos: A Dataset of Political Leaders." *Journal of Peace Research* 46 (2): 269–83.

Goldsmith, Jack. 2003. "The Self-Defeating International Criminal Court." *University of Chicago Law Review* 70 (1): 89–104.

Goldsmith, Jack, and Stephen D. Krasner. 2003. "The Limits of Idealism." *Daedalus* 132 (1): 47–63.

Goldstein, Joshua S. 2011. *Winning the War on War: The Decline of Armed Conflict Worldwide*. New York: Dutton.

Goldstone, Richard. 2000. *For Humanity: Reflections of a War Crimes Investigator*. New Haven, CT: Yale University Press.

Goodman, Ryan, and Derek Jinks. 2013. *Socializing States: Promoting Human Rights through International Law*. New York: Oxford University Press.

Goodwin, Jeff. 2001. *No Other Way Out: States and Revolutionary Movements, 1945–1991*. New York: Cambridge University Press.

Gourevitch, Peter. 1978. "The Second Image Reversed: The International Sources of Domestic Politics." *International Organization* 32 (4): 881–912.

Gray, Julia. 2018. "Life, Death, or Zombie? The Vitality of International Organizations." *International Studies Quarterly* 62 (1): 1–13.

Hafner-Burton, Emilie M. 2008. "Sticks and Stones: Naming and Shaming the Human Rights Enforcement Problem." *International Organization* 62 (4): 689–716.

——. 2013. *Making Human Rights a Reality*. Princeton, NJ: Princeton University Press.

Hafner-Burton, Emilie M., and Kiyoteru Tsutsui. 2005. "Human Rights in a Globalizing World: The Paradox of Empty Promises." *American Journal of Sociology* 110 (5): 1373–1411.

Hagan, John. 2003. *Justice in the Balkans: Prosecuting War Crimes in the Hague Tribunal*. Chicago: University of Chicago Press.

Harff, Barbara. 2003. "No Lessons Learned from the Holocaust? Assessing Risks of Genocide and Political Mass Murder since 1955." *American Political Science Review* 97 (1): 57–73.

Harsch, Ernest. 2017. *Burkina Faso: A History of Power, Protest, and Revolution*. London: Zed Books.

Hathaway, Oona A. 2002. "Do Human Rights Treaties Make a Difference?" *Yale Law Journal* 111 (8): 1935–2042.

Hathaway, Oona A., Paul K. Stauch, Beatrice A. Walton, and Zoe A. Weinberg. 2019. "What Is a War Crime?" *Yale Journal of International Law* 44 (1): 53–113.

Hayner, Priscilla. 2007. *Negotiating Peace in Liberia: Preserving the Possibility for Justice*. Geneva: Centre for Humanitarian Dialogue.

——. 2013. "Libya: The ICC Enters during War." European Council on Foreign Relations Background Papers. https://www.ecfr.eu/page/-/IJP_Libya.pdf.

Heller, Kevin Jon. 2013. "The Taylor Sentencing Judgment: A Critical Analysis." *Journal of International Criminal Justice* 11 (4): 835–55.

Hicks, Celeste. 2018. *The Trial of Hissène Habré: How the People of Chad Brought a Tyrant to Justice*. London: Zed Books.

Hill, Daniel W. 2010. "Estimating the Effects of Human Rights Treaties on State Behavior." *Journal of Politics* 72 (4): 1161–74.

Hillebrecht, Courtney. 2016. "The Deterrent Effects of the International Criminal Court: Evidence from Libya." *International Interactions* 42 (4): 616–43.

Hillebrecht, Courtney, and Scott Straus. 2017. "Who Prosecutes the Perpetrators? State Cooperation with ICC Indictments." *Human Rights Quarterly* 39 (1): 162–88.

Hilsum, Lindsey. 2012. *Sandstorm: Libya in the Time of Revolution*. London: Faber and Faber.

Hobbes, Thomas. (1651) 1996. *Leviathan*. New York: Oxford University Press.

Hollyer, James R., and B. Peter Rosendorff. 2011. "Why Do Authoritarian Regimes Sign the Convention against Torture? Signaling, Domestic Politics and Non-Compliance." *Quarterly Journal of Political Science* 6 (3–4): 275–327.

Hopgood, Stephen. 2013. *The Endtimes of Human Rights*. Ithaca, NY: Cornell University Press.

Horowitz, Michael C., and Allan C. Stam. 2014. "How Prior Military Experience Influences the Future Militarized Behavior of Leaders." *International Organization* 68 (3): 527–59.

Horowitz, Michael C., Allan C. Stam, and Cali M. Ellis. 2015. *Why Leaders Fight*. New York: Cambridge University Press.

Huband, Mark. 1998. *The Liberian Civil War*. London: Frank Cass.

Human Rights Watch. 1999. *Shocking War Crimes in Sierra Leone*. New York: Human Rights Watch.

——. 2009. *Selling Justice Short: Why Accountability Matters for Peace*. New York: Human Rights Watch.

——. 2012. *Death of a Dictator: Bloody Vengeance in Sirte*. New York: Human Rights Watch.

Huntington, Samuel P. 1991. *The Third Wave: Democratization in the Late Twentieth Century*. Norman: University of Oklahoma Press.

Hurd, Ian. 2017. *How to Do Things with International Law*. Princeton, NJ: Princeton University Press.

Huth, Paul, and Bruce Russett. 1990. "Testing Deterrence Theory: Rigor Makes a Difference." *World Politics* 42 (4): 466–501.

Hyde, Susan D. 2011. *The Pseudo-Democrat's Dilemma: Why Election Observation Became an International Norm*. Ithaca, NY: Cornell University Press.

International Crisis Group. 2002. *Liberia: The Key to Ending Regional Instability*. Brussels: International Crisis Group.

——. 2003. *The Special Court for Sierra Leone: Promises and Pitfalls of a "New Model."* Brussels: International Crisis Group.
——. 2011. *Making Sense of Libya*. Brussels: International Crisis Group.
——. 2013. *Burkina Faso: With or Without Compaoré, Times of Uncertainty*. Brussels: International Crisis Group.
International Justice Monitor. 2010. "Charles Taylor on the Stand." *Charles Taylor at the Special Court for Sierra Leone*. June 4, 2010. http://www.ijmonitor.org/2010/01/charles-taylor-on-the-stand-an-overview-of-his-examination-in-chief-by-u-c-berkeley-monitors/.
Jenke, Libby, and Christopher Gelpi. 2017. "Theme and Variations: Historical Contingencies in the Causal Model of Interstate Conflict." *Journal of Conflict Resolution* 61 (10): 2262–84.
Jentleson, Bruce W., and Christopher A. Whytock. 2005. "Who Won Libya? The Force-Diplomacy Debate and Its Implications for Theory and Policy." *International Security* 30 (3): 47–86.
Jervis, Robert. 1989. "Rational Deterrence: Theory and Evidence." *World Politics* 41 (2): 183–207.
——. 2013. "Do Leaders Matter and How Would We Know?" *Security Studies* 22 (2): 153–79.
Jo, Hyeran. 2015. *Compliant Rebels: Rebel Groups and International Law in World Politics*. New York: Cambridge University Press.
Jo, Hyeran, and Beth Simmons. 2016. "Can the International Criminal Court Deter Atrocity?" *International Organization* 70 (3): 443–75.
Johnson, Timothy R., and Andrew D. Martin. 1998. "The Public's Conditional Response to Supreme Court Decisions." *American Political Science Review* 92 (2): 299–309.
Kahan, Dan M. 1997. "Social Influence, Social Meaning, and Deterrence." *Virginia Law Review* 83 (2): 349–95.
Kaldor, Mary. 1999. *New and Old Wars: Organized Violence in a Global Era*. Stanford, CA: Stanford University Press.
Kalyvas, Stathis N. 1999. "Wanton and Senseless? The Logic of Massacres in Algeria." *Rationality and Society* 11 (3): 243–85.
——. 2006. *The Logic of Violence in Civil War*. New York: Cambridge University Press.
Kalyvas, Stathis N., and Laia Balcells. 2010. "International System and Technologies of Rebellion: How the End of the Cold War Shaped Internal Conflict." *American Political Science Review* 104 (3): 415–29.
Kaplan, Robert D. 2011. "Tribal Warriors." *Foreign Policy*, April 11, 2011. http://www.foreignpolicy.com/articles/2011/04/11/tribal_warriors_why_is_it_so_hard_for_strongmen_to_say_goodbye?page=0,0.
Karnow, Stanley. 1989. *In Our Image: America's Empire in the Philippines*. New York: Ballantine Books.
Kaye, David. 2011. "Who's Afraid of the International Criminal Court? Finding the Prosecutor Who Can Set It Straight." *Foreign Affairs* 90 (3): 118–29.
——. 2013. "America's Honeymoon with the ICC." *Foreign Affairs*, April 17, 2013. http://www.foreignaffairs.com/articles/139170/david-kaye/americas-honeymoon-with-the-icc?page=show.

Keck, Margaret E., and Kathryn Sikkink. 1998. *Activists beyond Borders: Advocacy Networks in International Politics*. Ithaca, NY: Cornell University Press.

Keith, Linda Camp. 1999. "The United Nations International Covenant on Civil and Political Rights: Does It Make a Difference in Human Rights Behavior?" *Journal of Peace Research* 36 (1): 95–118.

Kelley, Judith. 2007. "Who Keeps International Commitments and Why? The International Criminal Court and Bilateral Nonsurrender Agreements." *American Political Science Review* 101 (3): 573–89.

——. 2012. *Monitoring Democracy: When International Election Observation Works, and Why It Often Fails*. Princeton, NJ: Princeton University Press.

Kersten, Mark. 2016. *Justice in Conflict: The Effects of the International Criminal Court's Interventions on Ending Wars and Building Peace*. Oxford: Oxford University Press.

Kim, Hunjoon, and Kathryn Sikkink. 2010. "Explaining the Deterrence Effect of Human Rights Prosecutions for Transitional Countries." *International Studies Quarterly* 54 (4): 939–63.

Ki-Moon, Ban. 2010. "An Age of Accountability." Presented at the International Criminal Court Review Conference, Entebbe, Uganda, May 31, 2010.

King, Gary, Robert O. Keohane, and Sidney Verba. 1994. *Designing Social Inquiry: Scientific Inference in Qualitative Research*. Princeton, NJ: Princeton University Press.

King, Gary, Michael Tomz, and Jason Wittenberg. 2000. "Making the Most of Statistical Analyses: Improving Interpretation and Presentation." *American Journal of Political Science* 44 (2): 347–61.

Kissinger, Henry. 1957. *A World Restored: Metternich, Castlereagh and the Problems of Peace, 1812–1822*. Boston, MA: Houghton Mifflin.

——. 1994. *Diplomacy*. New York: Simon and Schuster.

Kleiman, Mark A. R. 2009. *When Brute Force Fails: How to Have Less Crime and Less Punishment*. Princeton, NJ: Princeton University Press.

Kornbluh, Peter. 2013. *The Pinochet File: A Declassified Dossier on Atrocity and Accountability*. 2nd ed. New York: New Press.

Krain, Matthew. 1997. "State-Sponsored Mass Murder: The Onset and Severity of Genocides and Politicides." *Journal of Conflict Resolution* 41 (3): 331–60.

——. 2012. "J'accuse! Does Naming and Shaming Perpetrators Reduce the Severity of Genocides or Politicides?" *International Studies Quarterly* 56 (3): 574–89.

Krasner, Stephen D. 1999. *Sovereignty: Organized Hypocrisy*. Princeton, NJ: Princeton University Press.

——. 2003. "Interview: Conversations with History." March 31, 2003. http://globetrotter.berkeley.edu/people3/Krasner/krasner-con0.html.

Krcmaric, Daniel. 2014. "Refugee Flows, Ethnic Power Relations, and the Spread of Conflict." *Security Studies* 23 (1): 182–216.

——. 2018a. "Should I Stay or Should I Go? Leaders, Exile, and the Dilemmas of International Justice." *American Journal of Political Science* 62 (2): 486–98.

——. 2018b. "Varieties of Civil War and Mass Killing: Reassessing the Relationship between Guerrilla Warfare and Civilian Victimization." *Journal of Peace Research* 55 (1): 18–31.

——. 2019. "Information, Secrecy, and Civilian Targeting." *International Studies Quarterly* 63 (2): 322–33.

Krcmaric, Daniel, Stephen C. Nelson, and Andrew Roberts. 2020. "Studying Leaders and Elites: The Personal Biography Approach." *Annual Review of Political Science* 23: 133–51.

Ku, Julian, and Jide Nzelibe. 2006. "Do International Criminal Tribunals Deter or Exacerbate Humanitarian Atrocities?" *Washington University Law Review* 84: 777–833.

Kumar, Akshaya. 2017. *When Exposing Abusers Is Not Enough*. New York: Human Rights Watch.

Kuperman, Alan J. 2008. "The Moral Hazard of Humanitarian Intervention: Lessons from the Balkans." *International Studies Quarterly* 52 (1): 49–80.

Kydd, Andrew H., and Scott Straus. 2013. "The Road to Hell? Third-Party Intervention to Prevent Atrocities." *American Journal of Political Science* 57 (3): 673–84.

Lacina, Bethany, and Nils Petter Gleditsch. 2005. "Monitoring Trends in Global Combat: A New Dataset of Battle Deaths." *European Journal of Population* 21 (2–3): 145–66.

Lebovic, James H., and Erik Voeten. 2006. "The Politics of Shame: The Condemnation of Country Human Rights Practices in the UNCHR." *International Studies Quarterly* 50 (4): 861–88.

Lebow, Richard Ned, and Janice Gross Stein. 1990. "Deterrence: The Elusive Dependent Variable." *World Politics* 42 (3): 336–69.

Levitsky, Steven, and Lucan A. Way. 2010. *Competitive Authoritarianism: Hybrid Regimes after the Cold War*. New York: Cambridge University Press.

Lichtblau, Eric. 2014. *The Nazis Next Door: How America Became a Safe Haven for Hitler's Men*. Boston, MA: Mariner Books.

Licklider, Roy. 2008. "Ethical Advice: Conflict Management vs. Human Rights in Ending Civil Wars." *Journal of Human Rights* 7 (4): 376–87.

Lind, Jennifer. 2008. *Sorry States: Apologies in International Politics*. Ithaca, NY: Cornell University Press.

Lischer, Sarah Kenyon. 2005. *Dangerous Sanctuaries: Refugee Camps, Civil War, and the Dilemmas of Humanitarian Aid*. Ithaca, NY: Cornell University Press.

Lizza, Ryan. 2005. "Charles at Large." *New Republic* 232 (15): 10–11.

Lupu, Yonatan. 2013a. "Best Evidence: The Role of Information in Domestic Judicial Enforcement of International Human Rights Agreements." *International Organization* 67 (3): 469–503.

——. 2013b. "The Informative Power of Treaty Commitment: Using the Spatial Model to Address Selection Effects." *American Journal of Political Science* 57 (4): 912–25.

Macedo, Stephen. 2004. *Universal Jurisdiction: National Courts and the Prosecution of Serious Crimes under International Law*. Philadelphia: University of Pennsylvania Press.

Mahoney, James, and Gary Goertz. 2004. "The Possibility Principle: Choosing Negative Cases in Comparative Research." *American Political Science Review* 98 (4): 653–69.

Marinov, Nikolay, and Hein Goemans. 2014. "Coups and Democracy." *British Journal of Political Science* 44 (4): 799–825.

Marshall, Monty G., Ted Robert Gurr, and Barbara Harff. 2014. "State Failure Problem Set: Internal Wars and Failures of Governance, 1955–2013." Accessed October 6, 2015. http://www.systemicpeace.org/inscrdata.html.

McDermott, Rose. 2007. *Presidential Leadership, Illness, and Decision Making*. New York: Cambridge University Press.

McLynn, Frank. 2002. *Napoleon: A Biography*. New York: Arcade.

Mearsheimer, John J. 2001. *The Tragedy of Great Power Politics*. New York: Norton.

——. 2010. "The Gathering Storm: China's Challenge to US Power in Asia." *Chinese Journal of International Politics* 3 (4): 381–96.

Meernik, James. 2005. "Justice and Peace? How the International Criminal Tribunal Affects Societal Peace in Bosnia." *Journal of Peace Research* 42 (3): 271–89.

Meernik, James D., Angela Nichols, and Kimi L. King. 2010. "The Impact of International Tribunals and Domestic Trials on Peace and Human Rights after Civil War." *International Studies Perspectives* 11 (4): 309–34.

Mendeloff, David. 2004. "Truth-Seeking, Truth-Telling, and Postconflict Peacebuilding: Curb the Enthusiasm?" *International Studies Review* 6 (3): 355–80.

Mezran, Karim, and Alice Alunni. 2015. "Libya: Negotiations for Transition." In *Arab Spring: Negotiating in the Shadow of the Intifadat*, edited by I. William Zartman, 249–90. Athens: University of Georgia Press.

Minow, Martha. 1998. *Between Vengeance and Forgiveness: Facing History after Genocide and Mass Violence*. Boston, MA: Beacon Press.

Montalvo, Jose G., and Marta Reynal-Querol. 2008. "Discrete Polarisation with an Application to the Determinants of Genocides." *Economic Journal* 118 (533): 1835–65.

Moreno-Ocampo, Luis. 2008. "The International Criminal Court: Seeking Global Justice." *Case Western Reserve Journal of International Law* 40 (1): 215–25.

——. 2009. "The International Criminal Court." In *Building a Future on Peace and Justice*, edited by Kai Ambos, Judith Large, and Marieke Wierda, 9–13. Berlin: Springer.

——. 2010. "Pursuing International Justice: A Conversation with Luis Moreno-Ocampo." Presented at the Council on Foreign Relations, New York, NY, February 4, 2010. https://www.cfr.org/event/pursuing-international-justice-conversation-luis-moreno-ocampo.

Morgenthau, Hans. 1948. *Politics among Nations: The Struggle for Power and Peace*. New York: Knopf.

Mueller, John. 2000. "The Banality of 'Ethnic War.'" *International Security* 25 (1): 42–70.

Munoz, Heraldo. 2008. *The Dictator's Shadow: Life under Augusto Pinochet*. New York: Basic Books.

Nagin, Daniel S. 1998. "Criminal Deterrence Research at the Outset of the Twenty-First Century." *Crime and Justice* 23: 1–42.

Nalepa, Monika, and Emilia Justyna Powell. 2016. "The Role of Domestic Opposition and International Justice Regimes in Peaceful Transitions of Power." *Journal of Conflict Resolution* 60 (7): 1191–1218.

Natsios, Andrew. 2008. "Beyond Darfur: Sudan's Slide toward Civil War." *Foreign Affairs* 87 (3): 77–93.

Nelson, Stephen C. 2017. *The Currency of Confidence: How Economic Beliefs Shape the IMF's Relationship with Its Borrowers*. Ithaca, NY: Cornell University Press.

Neumayer, Eric. 2005. "Do International Human Rights Treaties Improve Respect for Human Rights?" *Journal of Conflict Resolution* 49 (6): 925–53.

Nili, Shmuel. 2019. *The People's Duty: Collective Agency and the Morality of Public Policy*. New York: Cambridge University Press.
Olsen, Tricia D., Leigh A. Payne, and Andrew G. Reiter. 2010. "The Justice Balance: When Transitional Justice Improves Human Rights and Democracy." *Human Rights Quarterly* 32 (4): 980–1007.
Orentlicher, Diane F. 1991. "Settling Accounts: The Duty to Prosecute Human Rights Violations of a Prior Regime." *Yale Law Journal* 100 (8): 2537–2615.
Page, Joseph A. 1983. *Peron: A Biography*. New York: Random House.
Paine, Jack. 2016. "Rethinking the Conflict 'Resource Curse': How Oil Wealth Prevents Center-Seeking Civil Wars." *International Organization* 70 (4): 727–61.
Paradiso, Dante. 2016. *The Embassy: A Story of War and Diplomacy*. New York: Beaufort Books.
Pargeter, Alison. 2005. "LIFG: An Organization in Eclipse." *Jamestown Foundation Terrorism Monitor*. November 3, 2005. https://jamestown.org/program/lifg-an-organization-in-eclipse/.
——. 2012. *Libya: The Rise and Fall of Qaddafi*. New Haven, CT: Yale University Press.
Petersen, Roger. 2002. *Understanding Ethnic Violence: Fear, Hatred, and Resentment in Twentieth-Century Eastern Europe*. Cambridge: Cambridge University Press.
Pevehouse, Jon C. 2005. *Democracy from Above: Regional Organizations and Democratization*. New York: Cambridge University Press.
Pillinger, Mara, Ian Hurd, and Michael N. Barnett. 2016. "How to Get Away with Cholera: The UN, Haiti, and International Law." *Perspectives on Politics* 14 (1): 70–86.
Pinker, Steven. 2011. *The Better Angels of Our Nature: Why Violence Has Declined*. New York: Viking.
Powell, Emilia Justyna, and Jeffrey K. Staton. 2009. "Domestic Judicial Institutions and Human Rights Treaty Violation." *International Studies Quarterly* 53 (1): 149–74.
Powell, Robert. 2004. "Bargaining and Learning While Fighting." *American Journal of Political Science* 48 (2): 344–61.
Power, Samantha. 2003. *A Problem from Hell: America and the Age of Genocide*. New York: Perennial.
Prorok, Alyssa K. 2016. "Leader Incentives and Civil War Outcomes." *American Journal of Political Science* 60 (1): 70–84.
——. 2017. "The (In)Compatibility of Peace and Justice? The International Criminal Court and Civil Conflict Termination." *International Organization* 71 (2): 213–43.
Przeworski, Adam. 1991. *Democracy and the Market: Political and Economic Reforms in Eastern Europe and Latin America*. Cambridge: Cambridge University Press.
Rabkin, Jeremy. 2007. "No Substitute for Sovereignty: Why International Criminal Justice Has a Bleak Future—And Deserves It." In *Atrocities and International Accountability: Beyond Transitional Justice*, edited by Edel Hughes, William A. Schabas, and Ramesh Thakur, 98–132. Tokyo: United Nations University Press.
Rake, Alan. 2001. *African Leaders: Guiding the New Millennium*. Lanham, MD: Scarecrow Press.

Ratnesar, Romesh. 2011. "Dealing with Dictators: My Meeting with Muammar." *Time*, February 11, 2011. http://content.time.com/time/world/article/0,8599,2055732,00.html.

Reagan, Ronald. 2009. *The Reagan Diaries*. Edited by Douglas Brinkley. New York: Harper Perennial.

Reiter, Dan. 2003. "Exploring the Bargaining Model of War." *Perspectives on Politics* 1 (1): 27–43.

Reno, William. 1998. *Warlord Politics and African States*. Boulder, CO: Lynne Rienner.

Renshon, Jonathan. 2017. *Fighting for Status: Hierarchy and Conflict in World Politics*. Princeton, NJ: Princeton University Press.

Reza, Alexandra. 2016. "New Broom in Burkina Faso?" *New Left Review* 101: 93–119.

Riker, William H. 1982. *Liberalism against Populism: A Confrontation between the Theory of Democracy and the Theory of Social Choice*. Long Grove, IL: Waveland Press.

Risse-Kappen, Thomas, Steve C. Ropp, and Kathryn Sikkink. 1999. *The Power of Human Rights: International Norms and Domestic Change*. Cambridge: Cambridge University Press.

Ritter, Emily Hencken, and Scott Wolford. 2012. "Bargaining and the Effectiveness of International Criminal Regimes." *Journal of Theoretical Politics* 24 (2): 149–71.

Roht-Arriaza, Naomi. 2005. *The Pinochet Effect: Transnational Justice in the Age of Human Rights*. Philadelphia: University of Pennsylvania Press.

Ronen, Yehudit. 2002. "Qadhafi and Militant Islamism: Unprecedented Conflict." *Middle Eastern Studies* 38 (4): 1–16.

Rosato, Sebastian. 2015. "The Inscrutable Intentions of Great Powers." *International Security* 39 (3): 48–88.

Roth, Kenneth. 2001. "The Case for Universal Jurisdiction." *Foreign Affairs* 80 (5): 150–54.

Rummel, R. J. 1995. "Democracy, Power, Genocide, and Mass Murder." *Journal of Conflict Resolution* 39 (1): 3–26.

Salehyan, Idean. 2009. *Rebels without Borders: Transnational Insurgencies in World Politics*. Ithaca, NY: Cornell University Press.

Salehyan, Idean, and Kristian Skrede Gleditsch. 2006. "Refugees and the Spread of Civil War." *International Organization* 60 (2): 335–66.

Saunders, Elizabeth N. 2011. *Leaders at War: How Presidents Shape Military Interventions*. Ithaca, NY: Cornell University Press.

Scharf, Michael P. 2006. "From the eXile Files: An Essay on Trading Justice for Peace." *Washington and Lee Law Review* 63: 339–78.

Scheffer, David. 2012. *All the Missing Souls: A Personal History of the War Crimes Tribunals*. Princeton, NJ: Princeton University Press.

Schelling, Thomas C. 1981. *The Strategy of Conflict*. Cambridge, MA: Harvard University Press.

Schultz, Kenneth A. 2001. *Democracy and Coercive Diplomacy*. New York: Cambridge University Press.

Sechser, Todd S. 2010. "Goliath's Curse: Coercive Threats and Asymmetric Power." *International Organization* 64 (4): 627–60.

Semelin, Jacques. 2007. *Purify and Destroy: The Political Uses of Massacre and Genocide*. New York: Columbia University Press.

Sharman, J. C. 2017. *The Despot's Guide to Wealth Management*. Ithaca, NY: Cornell University Press.

Shklar, Judith N. 1964. *Legalism: Law, Morals, and Political Trials*. Cambridge, MA: Harvard University Press.

Shultz, George P. 1993. *Turmoil and Triumph: My Years as Secretary of State*. New York: Macmillan.

Sikkink, Kathryn. 2011. *The Justice Cascade: How Human Rights Prosecutions Are Changing World Politics*. New York: Norton.

Sikkink, Kathryn, and Carrie Booth Walling. 2007. "The Impact of Human Rights Trials in Latin America." *Journal of Peace Research* 44 (4): 427–45.

Simbeye, Yitiha. 2004. *Immunity and International Criminal Law*. Burlington, VT: Ashgate.

Simmons, Beth A. 2009. *Mobilizing for Human Rights: International Law in Domestic Politics*. New York: Cambridge University Press.

——. 2010. "Treaty Compliance and Violation." *Annual Review of Political Science* 13 (1): 273–96.

Simmons, Beth A., and Allison Danner. 2010. "Credible Commitments and the International Criminal Court." *International Organization* 64 (2): 225–56.

Singer, J. David. 1988. "Reconstructing the Correlates of War Dataset on Material Capabilities of States, 1816–1985." *International Interactions* 14 (2): 115–32.

Sirleaf, Ellen Johnson. 2010. *This Child Will Be Great: Memoir of a Remarkable Life by Africa's First Woman President*. New York: HarperCollins.

Slantchev, Branislav L. 2003. "The Principle of Convergence in Wartime Negotiations." *American Political Science Review* 97 (4): 621–32.

Slaughter, Anne-Marie. 1995. "International Law in a World of Liberal States." *European Journal of International Law* 6: 503–38.

——. 1999. "The Long Arm of the Law." *Foreign Policy* 114: 34–35.

Smith, Alastair, and Allan C. Stam. 2004. "Bargaining and the Nature of War." *Journal of Conflict Resolution* 48 (6): 783–813.

Smith, Benjamin. 2004. "Oil Wealth and Regime Survival in the Developing World, 1960–1999." *American Journal of Political Science* 48 (2): 232–46.

Snyder, Jack, and Leslie Vinjamuri. 2003. "Trials and Errors: Principle and Pragmatism in Strategies of International Justice." *International Security* 28 (3): 5–44.

Solomon, Hussein. 2012. "Political Islam and the State in Africa: The Case of the Libyan Islamic Fighting Group." In *Religious Ideas and Institutions: Transitions to Democracy in Africa*, edited by Edmond J. Keller and Ruth Iyob, 127–48. Pretoria: Unisa Press.

Spagat, Michael, Andrew Mack, Tara Cooper, and Joakim Kreutz. 2009. "Estimating War Deaths: An Arena of Contestation." *Journal of Conflict Resolution* 53 (6): 934–50.

Spruyt, Hendrik. 1996. *The Sovereign State and Its Competitors: An Analysis of Systems Change*. Princeton, NJ: Princeton University Press.

Sriram, Chandra Lekha. 2005. *Globalizing Justice for Mass Atrocities: A Revolution in Accountability*. London: Routledge.

St. John, Ronald Bruce. 2011. *Libya: From Colony to Revolution*. Oxford: Oneworld.

Stanton, Jessica A. 2016. *Violence and Restraint in Civil War: Civilian Targeting in the Shadow of International Law*. New York: Cambridge University Press.

Stedman, Stephen John, Donald S. Rothchild, and Elizabeth M. Cousens. 2002. *Ending Civil Wars: The Implementation of Peace Agreements*. Boulder, CO: Lynne Rienner.

Stover, Eric, Victor Peskin, and Alexa Koenig. 2016. *Hiding in Plain Sight: The Pursuit of War Criminals from Nuremberg to the War on Terror*. Oakland: University of California Press.

Straus, Scott. 2015. *Making and Unmaking Nations: War, Leadership, and Genocide in Modern Africa*. Ithaca, NY: Cornell University Press.

Subotic, Jelena. 2009. *Hijacked Justice: Dealing with the Past in the Balkans*. Ithaca, NY: Cornell University Press.

Sutter, Daniel. 1995. "Settling Old Scores: Potholes along the Transition from Authoritarian Rule." *Journal of Conflict Resolution* 39 (1): 110–28.

Takeyh, Ray. 2001. "The Rogue Who Came in from the Cold." *Foreign Affairs* 80 (3): 62–72.

Taub, Ben. 2016. "The Assad Files." *New Yorker*, April 18, 2016, 36–49.

Tejan-Cole, Abdul. 2009. "A Big Man in a Small Cell: Charles Taylor and the Special Court for Sierra Leone." In *Prosecuting Heads of State*, edited by Ellen L. Lutz and Caitlin Reiger, 205–32. New York: Cambridge University Press.

Thompson, Mark R. 1995. *The Anti-Marcos Struggle: Personalistic Rule and Democratic Transition in the Philippines*. New Haven, CT: Yale University Press.

Thoms, Oskar N. T., James Ron, and Roland Paris. 2008. "Does Transitional Justice Work? Perspectives from Empirical Social Science." Social Science Research Network working paper.

——. 2010. "State-Level Effects of Transitional Justice: What Do We Know?" *International Journal of Transitional Justice* 4 (3): 329–54.

Thyne, Clayton. 2017. "The Impact of Coups d'état on Civil War Duration." *Conflict Management and Peace Science* 34 (3): 287–307.

Tomes, Jason Hunter. 2003. *King Zog of Albania: Europe's Self-Made Muslim Monarch*. New York: New York University Press.

Tomz, Michael. 2012. *Reputation and International Cooperation: Sovereign Debt across Three Centuries*. Princeton, NJ: Princeton University Press.

Truth and Reconciliation Commission of Liberia. 2009. *Final Report*. Monrovia.

Tunks, Michael. 2002. "Diplomats or Defendants? Defining the Future of Head-of-State Immunity." *Duke Law Journal* 52 (3): 651–82.

Ulfelder, Jay, and Benjamin A. Valentino. 2008. "Assessing Risks of State-Sponsored Mass Killing." Working paper.

Valentino, Benjamin A. 2004. *Final Solutions: Mass Killing and Genocide in the Twentieth Century*. Ithaca, NY: Cornell University Press.

——. 2014. "Why We Kill: The Political Science of Political Violence against Civilians." *Annual Review of Political Science* 17 (1): 89–103.

Valentino, Benjamin A., Paul Huth, and Dylan Balch-Lindsay. 2004. "Draining the Sea: Mass Killing and Guerrilla Warfare." *International Organization* 58 (2): 375–407.

Vandewalle, Dirk J. 2012. *A History of Modern Libya*. 2nd ed. New York: Cambridge University Press.

von Stein, Jana. 2005. "Do Treaties Constrain or Screen? Selection Bias and Treaty Compliance." *American Political Science Review* 99 (4): 611–22.

——. 2016. "Making Promises, Keeping Promises: Democracy, Ratification and Compliance in International Human Rights Law." *British Journal of Political Science* 46 (3): 655–79.
Wagner, R. Harrison. 2000. "Bargaining and War." *American Journal of Political Science* 44 (3): 469–84.
Walter, Barbara F. 1997. "The Critical Barrier to Civil War Settlement." *International Organization* 51 (3): 335–64.
——. 2002. *Committing to Peace: The Successful Settlement of Civil Wars*. Princeton, NJ: Princeton University Press.
Waltz, Kenneth N. 1959. *Man, the State, and War: A Theoretical Analysis*. New York: Columbia University Press.
——. 1979. *Theory of International Politics*. Boston, MA: McGraw-Hill.
Ward, Kathy. 2003. "Might v. Right: Charles Taylor and the Sierra Leone Special Court." *Human Rights Brief* 11 (1): 8–11.
Waugh, Colin M. 2011. *Charles Taylor and Liberia: Ambition and Atrocity in Africa's Lone Star State*. New York: Zed Books.
Weeks, Jessica L. P. 2014. *Dictators at War and Peace*. Ithaca, NY: Cornell University Press.
Weiner, Myron. 1996. "Bad Neighbors, Bad Neighborhoods: An Inquiry into the Causes of Refugee Flows." *International Security* 21 (1): 5–42.
Weinstein, Jeremy M. 2006. *Inside Rebellion: The Politics of Insurgent Violence*. New York: Cambridge University Press.
Wickham, Hadley. 2009. *Ggplot2: Elegant Graphics for Data Analysis*. New York: Springer.
Wierda, Marieke. 2015. "Confronting Qadhafi's Legacy: Transitional Justice in Libya." In *The Libyan Revolution and Its Aftermath*, edited by Peter Cole and Brian McQuinn, 153–74. New York: Oxford University Press.
Wippman, David. 1999. "Atrocities, Deterrence, and the Limits of International Justice." *Fordham International Law Journal* 23: 473–88.
Wiseman, John A. 1993. "Leadership and Personal Danger in Africa." *Journal of Modern African Studies* 31 (4): 657–60.
Wood, Elisabeth Jean. 2003. *Insurgent Collective Action and Civil War in El Salvador*. Cambridge: Cambridge University Press.
Wood, Reed M., Jacob D. Kathman, and Stephen E. Gent. 2012. "Armed Intervention and Civilian Victimization in Intrastate Conflicts." *Journal of Peace Research* 49 (5): 647–60.
World Bank. 2013. "World Development Indicators." Accessed May 29, 2014. http://data.worldbank.org/data-catalog/world-development-indicators.
Young, Norwood. 1914. *Napoleon in Exile: Elba*. London: Stanley Paul.
Zakaria, Fareed. 1997. "The Rise of Illiberal Democracy." *Foreign Affairs* 76 (6): 22–43.
Zivot, Eric, and Donald W. K. Andrews. 1992. "Further Evidence on the Great Crash, the Oil-Price Shock, and the Unit-Root Hypothesis." *Journal of Business and Economic Statistics* 10 (3): 25–44.

Index